Ordinary Wisdom

Biographical Aging
and the Journey of Life

William L. Randall and Gary M. Kenyon

PRAEGER

Westport, Connecticut
London

Library of Congress Cataloging-in-Publication Data

Randall, William Lowell, 1950–
    Ordinary wisdom / biographical aging and the journey of life / William L. Randall
and Gary M. Kenyon.
      p.   cm.
    Includes bibliographical references (p.) and index.
    ISBN 0–275–96556–2 (alk. paper)
    1. Aging—Psychological aspects. 2. Aged—Psychology. 3. Wisdom. I. Kenyon,
Gary M. II. Title.
    BF724.55.A35R36   2001
    155.67'18—dc21   00–022889

British Library Cataloguing in Publication Data is available.

Library of Congress Catalog Card Number: 00–022889
ISBN: 0–275–96556–2

First published in 2001

Praeger Publishers, 88 Post Road West, Westport, CT 06881
An imprint of Greenwood Publishing Group, Inc.
www.praeger.com

Printed in the United States of America

The paper used in this book complies with the
Permanent Paper Standard issued by the National
Information Standards Organization (Z39.48–1984).

10 9 8 7 6 5 4 3 2 1

Contents

Prologue   vii

1 Ordinary Wisdom   1

2 Wisdom on Wisdom   17

3 Biographical Aging: Life as Story   33

4 Spiritual Aging: Life as Journey   87

5 Conscious Aging: Life as Adventure   119

Epilogue   165

References   175

Index   191

Prologue

Where is the wisdom we have lost in knowledge?

—Thomas Stearns Eliot (1940)

There's a reason that you can learn from everything. You have basic wisdom, basic intelligence, and basic goodness.

—Pema Chodron (1994)

Like most books, this one has roots in previous projects. For Gary, a philosopher-gerontologist, these include inquiries into the nature of personal existence (Kenyon, 1988), the metaphors that shape gerontological thought (Kenyon, Birren, & Schroots, 1991), and the process of *biographical* (as distinct from biological) aging (Ruth & Kenyon, 1996a, 1996b). For Bill, who came to the study of aging from parish ministry, adult education, and teaching English, the central project has been a meditation on the proverbial "art of living," specifically on the conceptual potential inherent in the notion of *the stories we are* (Randall, 1995). Each of these undertakings has sown the seeds of questions that are central to this volume; questions that, in one form or another, drew us to each other in the first place through the serendipitous and synergistic intersection of our intellectual paths. Some of these questions we developed in an earlier book entitled *Restorying Our Lives* (Praeger, 1997).

Unlike many academic works, *Restorying* had both a *descriptive* and a *prescriptive* dimension. Descriptively, it sketched the stages and contours of the continual process of what we call "storying" and "*restorying*" whereby, over the years, we construct meaning from the maze of events and relationships that make up our lives. Prescriptively, it set forth practical strategies and ethical guidelines for "coauthoring" one another to restory in fuller, more life-affirming ways—a process to which we assigned the playful yet serious label of "therapoetics."

The present book has the same two dimensions. In fact, we began to envision *Ordinary Wisdom* well before *Restorying* was complete. Certainly by the time we reached the final sections, we found ourselves wondering about the implications of a storying-restorying model for conceptions of wisdom. Within each of us independently, and amid the discussions we enjoyed collaboratively while writing it, the conviction had grown that all of us are in our own way wise, regardless of our level of education, our type of intelligence, the knowledge and information we have acquired, and the purity or piety, fortune or fame we have (or have not) achieved. Sooner or later, as do many who work in this field, we became convinced that there is often not only incredible courage and inspiring strength but also genuine wisdom in what are otherwise ordinary lives—lives with their share of success and failure and their portion of pleasure and pain; lives that, by those who live them, are frequently diminished as "nothing special," but are nonetheless unique, that trace a particular path and tell a particular tale. Such wisdom, we have come to believe, is *extra*ordinary and needs owning and honoring as such.

Few fields are in a better position to meet this need than one as interdisciplinary as gerontology endeavors to be (Randall, in press). Meeting it is perhaps all the more urgent at the dawn of a new millennium (which somehow renders every issue urgent), as the baby boomers in our increasingly aging population awaken to the multiple challenges of achieving "a good old age." Since we are boomers ourselves, our agenda in writing this book is not only academic, then, but autobiographical as well. The questions that compel us in our midlife years possess a personal and not merely scholarly significance: As we travel our paths and weave our tales, are we learning anything of note? Are we growing truly wiser as we age, or only older? If wiser, then wise in what ways?

Questions like these are not unique to us. They are universal. Nor are they of interest only to gerontologists or to people who are "old." They are important to people of any profession and any age. Nor do they concern our physical being alone. Naturally, like everyone else, when each of us thinks about aging, we have concerns about our health and about the often troubling transformations in our bodies. But the physical-biological-medical story is not the whole story of human life, despite its dominance in present-day culture—not to mention in gerontology itself. Since it essentially leaves wisdom out, we are convinced there is another story that has to be heard. Such a story rises out of the concerns we have about our memories, minds, and hearts as well. It relates to our concerns about our relationships with others and with the wider world, about what difference our lives might ultimately make, and about the insight we might be acquiring and, ultimately, passing along. Sketching that story is the aim of this book.

In summary, our descriptive agenda is to lay out the parameters of "ordinary wisdom" by reviewing a selected range of perspectives, present and past, that have been put forward on wisdom per se. At the same time, we want to point to other conceptual resources, specifically other metaphors, than those on which, implicitly or explicitly, we have hitherto relied to envision what wisdom is. The metaphors we have in mind are as old as humanity itself. They are life as story, life as journey, and life as adventure. Exploring the fascinating implications of these time-honored images is central, then, to our prescriptive agenda. One of the things at which we look, for example, is how, instead of stifling one another's wisdom in lopsided, coercive relations where one of us wields authority *over* the other (as is too often the case), we can learn to coax it forth in respectful, cooperative relationships of authoring *with*—or of what we call *co*authoring.

Fortunately, we taste such a relationship rather regularly ourselves, certainly when engaged in a project as considerable as this. Because neither of us could have completed it on our own, we have literally coauthored it. Thus we see the book as a bridge: first of all, between ourselves (our ways of thinking, our styles of writing) but also, we trust, between ourselves and our readers. More specifically, since our readers are apt to come from a variety of backgrounds, we see it as a bridge between the several quarters in which the question of wisdom is—or ought to be—asked. From many of these, we shall be borrowing throughout. Besides gerontology, they include philosophy, psychology, theology, and ethics, plus literature, education, history, and art. We also see the book as a bridge between premodern and postmodern paradigms for thinking about "the self," between the concerns of mainstream psychology and current interest in "soul," and between academia in general and the vast, largely uncharted region we call simply "everyday life."

In short, we have written this book as a bridge between three domains at once: theory, practice, and experience. Theory, as regards conceptions of wisdom, irrespective of their origin; practice, as regards being with one another in ways that honor and elicit one another's wisdom, irrespective of our age; and experience, as regards what all of us presumably wish: to grow in insight, integrity, and grace; to age in a way that leaves a permanent legacy, that makes an ongoing difference, that advances and enriches our race.

For a book to build this many bridges is a tall order. Lest we be dismissed at the outset, then, for biting off more than we can chew, we need to make clear what, at bottom, we hope to achieve. While we shall no doubt be raising more issues than can be tidily resolved and opening up questions where perhaps, previously, no questions existed, our purpose is not so much expository as introductory in nature. Rather than presuming to *explain* wisdom, we have a humbler plan in mind. It is to bring together ideas and insights from fields gerontologists are just beginning to visit in order to identify fresh starting points and terminologies simply to *talk* about wisdom, ones that are more rooted, we believe, in the soil of every-day life. In doing so, we hope to add to the efforts of others committed to the broad project of rethinking how we age (Prado, 1986). Specifically, we hope to contribute to the project of rethinking *wisdom* and of reviving it as a legitimate topic for a truly soulful science of human life—a topic that is not lost inside a statistical chart, confined to the doctrines of religion, or kept safely at bay through either cynical contempt or obsequious awe.

The completion of this project is of course beyond our ability here. What follows is but one part of a grander adventure that some of us are pursuing under the banner of narrative gerontology (Kenyon & Randall, 1999; Kenyon, Clark, & de Vries, in press). Taking its cue from the narrative root metaphor (Sarbin, 1986a), narrative gerontology begins with the premise that lives are storied through and through. Furthermore, the stories we tell are not mere data with which to support abstract theories about the psychology or sociology of aging. They are integral to how we interpret our world and identify ourselves within it. If you will, the stories we tell are the stories we *are* (Randall, 1995). With such thoughts as its starting point, then, narrative gerontology sets out in a decidedly different direction from the central subfields of which our discipline is comprised, a direction that leads us to look, moreover, at the whole of life and not just the phase we call "growing old." Because we live in time and time lives in us, to live is automatically to age. Accordingly, we hope to point to a fuller, more fruit-ful vision of what it means not just to *age* but also to *be*.

By way of a note to the reader before we begin, we are aware that differ-ent parts of what follows might read differently from others. Given that there are two of us writing, this should come as no surprise. Both in person and in print, each of us has our preferred approach to developing ideas, our characteristic voice, our habitual way with words. As much as possi-ble, we have tried to minimize these differences and make the whole some-what smoother than the sum of its parts. How successful we have been will be up to our readers to decide. Overall, however, we see this pooling of tal-ents as a positive step. Not only are we presenting two books in one, but, more important, we are validating the volume's central theme. Like any-one else, each of us is just an ordinary person, with a voice, a vision, and a wisdom that are rooted in the experiences—and stories—of an ordinary life.

ACKNOWLEDGMENTS

It is our wish to acknowledge the encouragement we have received in undertaking this project from numerous colleagues, both at St. Thomas University, where the two of us teach, and in the wider gerontology community. In particular, however, we want to honor the influence of Dr. Jan-Erik Ruth. A colleague and close friend, Jan-Erik had become intrigued by many of the same questions we are pondering here. He was also one of the first to call openly for a *narrative* gerontology. Were it not for his sudden and saddening death in 1997 during his tenure at St. Thomas as Visiting Chair in Gerontology, he would undoubtedly have contributed to the writing of this book.

1

Ordinary Wisdom

One of the greatest Buddhist traditions calls the nature of mind "the wisdom of ordinariness." I cannot say it enough: Our true nature and the nature of all beings is not something extraordinary.

—Sogyal Rinpoche (1994)

Wisdom is bright, and does not grow dim. By those who love her she is readily seen, and found by those who look for her. Quick to anticipate those who desire her, she makes herself known to them.

—The Book of Wisdom (6:12–14)

GETTING AT WISDOM

People who dare to write books on wisdom run the risk of being considered fools. When the topic is ordinary wisdom, they are probably only ordinary fools, no more fools than anyone else, but fools nonetheless. Admitting this limitation straightaway, we have nowhere to go but up. Moreover, what is up, what we aspire to attain in the pages that ensue, is nothing less than a fresh perspective on one of the loftiest, most venerable of concepts. In a moment, we shall say more about what sort of perspective that is. For now, we need to acknowledge a few of the obstacles that immediately impede our ascent.

First is the semantic minefield through which the mere mention of "wisdom" obliges us to trek. How do we distinguish wisdom from what are conceivable equivalents, such as common sense or understanding; insight

or intuition; experience, knowledge, or maturity; intelligence or cleverness? Furthermore, as a supposed attribute of character, its meaning can
vary enormously with the context of its use. The teacher we deemed wise
in Grade 9 may seem, in hindsight, a burned-out cynic. Conduct considered wise in the world of men can appear as patriarchal posturing in the
world of women. What passes as wise in one culture, one era, or one creed
may, in another, be either sentimental twaddle or dangerous delusion.

To complicate matters even more, as a virtue to which we ought to aspire, wisdom has been cloaked in paradox. As with humility or goodness,
we are discouraged from seeking it head-on. Instead, it is a pearl of great
price that comes as a by-product of pursuing something else. Thinking we
are wise is like realizing we are falling asleep. The instant we congratulate
ourselves on how sage we have become, we taint any insight we have
managed to attain.

Finally, there is the sheer inconceivability of wisdom as a philosophical
idea. Indeed, more than an idea, it is commonly perceived as an ideal, perpetually beyond our reach, making the concept of *ordinary* wisdom seem,
then, a contradiction in terms. In many religious traditions, sacred writ ex-
alts wisdom as lost in the impenetrable mists above the summit of human
potential. Witness the longing of Job: "But where shall wisdom be found?
And where is the place of understanding? Man does not know the way to
it," he laments, "and it is not found in the land of the living" (Job 28:12–13).
Even though the hold of formal religion has weakened for many, wisdom
remains enshrouded in otherworldly clouds. Like truth or God, it functions as a limit-word, marking the very frontiers of language, simultaneously inspiring us and yet reminding us how far we fall short. Thus, it
has typically been easier to stress what wisdom *is not* than to state what it
is. At best, it has been considered a topic not for serious philosophy but for
folk psychology, despite the etymology of the former as *philo-sophia*, the
love of wisdom.

These are some of the obstructions we might expect to encounter as we
journey into wisdom, at least as it is traditionally conceived. We shall trace
some of those concepts in the chapter that follows. However, a number of
these obstacles have a way of eroding, if not dissolving altogether, when
wisdom is viewed from the perspective that is central to this book. Wisdom, as we view it, is to be understood less in intellectual or ethical terms
than in aesthetic, even poetic, ones. It is a function not primarily of moral
virtue or of cognitive competence, however much these dimensions are
nonetheless involved in and have dominated thinking about wisdom since
earliest times. Rather, it is a function of biography, of the tale we tell of our
journey through time. In short, it is a function of our lifestory—a single
word, like history, that underlines for us the unbreakable bond between
our story and our life.

Since we all have—or, as we see it, *are*—such a lifestory (Kenyon &
Randall, 1997), wisdom is thus an ordinary thing. It is not *extra*ordinary, as
it has tended to be portrayed. It is something that all of us possess, regardless (even because) of the humanness of our lives. It is something accessible to us all, despite (even because of) the failures and faults that are part of
our past, the conflicts and struggles that beset us in the present, and the
mistakes and misfortunes that may be our lot in the future. As we view it,
wisdom is linked to the capacity to "read" the ever-thickening, perhaps
ever more distilled, certainly ever-changing "text" of our own experience,
whatever its content or form. It has to do with the insight and the meaning
that such reading can yield. Discovering our own ordinary wisdom is thus
like savoring a great novel, not ultimately for the twists in its plot or for
how it unfolds in the end, but for the meanings it mediates en route and for
the revelations to which it can lead.

A TOPIC WHOSE TIME HAS RETURNED

If wisdom as traditionally viewed is as problematic as we have just indicated, then it is no wonder that in recent times it has fallen from grace as a
concept for serious debate. Why, then, are we writing about it, and why
now? There are at least five factors, we believe, that make wisdom a topic
whose time has returned.

First, in the twilight of modernity, which militarily and ecologically can
be accused of bringing us to the brink, more affirmative postmodernist
thinkers (Rosenau, 1992) are revisiting terms that had considerable cur-
rency in premodern times but have slipped from favor in recent ones.
Among these is wisdom. Related to this development is a growing appreciation for the purposefulness of nature itself, no longer dead and passive
to our observation but a living, intentional entity (Lovelock, 1982) with a
wisdom all its own (Augros & Stanciu, 1988; Capra, 1989). As well,
changes in the authority of the "master narratives" (Fulford, 1999) of organized religion and the monopoly on "truth" that each of them claims have
liberated a sense of the wisdom with which less mainstream, perhaps
more "primitive," spiritual traditions can edify us all.

Second, from another angle, the computer revolution that has transformed our everyday world has evolved to the point where we can envision an artificial intelligence that is more than mere shuffling of data or
processing of information but that partakes of knowledge, perhaps even of
wisdom (see Schank, 1990). Hence, from a strictly cognitive perspective,
there is the need to consider what wisdom might be, how it is we get it, and
how it works. At the same time, critics of cognitive science and its obses-
sion with the model of mind-as-computer are saying that folk psychology
may have merit after all (see Bruner, 1990).

Third, other developments in the broad field of the human sciences have created a climate in which wisdom can be entertained as a topic for scholarly contemplation. These include a revival of interest in psychobiography, in life history, and in the "study of lives" (see Runyan, 1984; Ruth & Kenyon, 1996a); a resurrection of respect for "soul" (Moore, 1992); and inquiries concerning the importance of articulating one's "personal mythology" (Campbell & Moyers, 1988; Feinstein, Krippner, & Granger, 1988; Atkinson, 1995).

Fourth, developments in the wake of existentialist or humanistic psychology, and of related movements that celebrate human potential, have contributed to an increased appreciation of the wisdom within us all. In feminist circles, and in the realm of popular education, this means an appreciation for the benefits of consciousness raising and a sense that all knowledge is ultimately constructed, including the unique knowledge that each of us constructs about ourselves. In adult education circles, it means an awareness of the importance of such things as "biographical learning" (Alheit et al., 1995), "the poetics of learning" (Randall, 1995), "perspective transformation" (Mezirow, 1978), and "critical reflection" (Brookfield, 1990). In spiritual circles, it means a sensitivity to the value of the revelation and transformation that can happen in fellowship, in confession, and in pastoral care; and in therapeutic or counseling circles, the value of finding answers in our own experience to the problems we may face.

Last in this list of reasons for the current re-interest in wisdom is the emergence of the field out of which we write: gerontology, the study of life-span development, or aging. With the population of our world and our society aging every day, more and more of us are asking whether aging leads inexorably to deficits of various kinds; whether it takes us only to decrepitude, despair, death, and to what Gabriel Marcel has described as "the scrapping of what has ceased to be of use" (Kenyon, 1980). We are asking, in other words, whether one of the things that happens in human development, beyond the basic activities essential to survival and reproduction, is in fact the proverbial wisdom of age. (Although the wisdom of youth is also a worthy subject and no less proverbial, it is beyond our scope here [see Meacham, 1990]). As we will see in what follows, the spread in both gerontology and geriatrics of approaches such as life review, guided autobiography, and reminiscence has opened the possibility that each person's lifestory is the vehicle of its own ordinary wisdom (Atkinson, 1995; Birren et al., 1996; Haight & Webster, 1995).

THE INSIDE OF AGING

Gerontology is a relatively new field. It is also a thoroughly multidisciplinary field. As such, it is of considerable value to the study of wisdom in two ways. First, it is concerned, in part, with being older, whatever we take that phrase to mean. Second, it contains a rich dialogue not only among different social science disciplines but also between the social sciences generally and the humanities (Bengtson & Schaie, 1999; Birren et al., 1996; Cole, Van Tassel, & Kastenbaum, 1992; Kenyon, Birren, & Schroots, 1991).

In this regard, one of the purposes of this book is to contribute to the development of theory in the study of aging, especially in the area of psychogerontology and of the emerging perspective we already mentioned, namely "narrative gerontology" (Kenyon, Ruth, & Mader, 1999; Kenyon & Randall, 1999). Later in this chapter, we shall say more about narrative gerontology, about adopting a narrative perspective on aging (Randall, in press), and about the narrative turn in the human sciences as a whole. At this point, and on a more practical level, we want to stress that our purpose in writing this book is to address a gap of which more and more gerontologists are becoming acutely aware. That gap concerns the *inside* of aging (Ruth & Kenyon, 1996a, 1996b).

As we have just indicated, the field of gerontology is evolving in exciting directions. However, until recently in its short history, it has been dominated by what has come to be called "the medical model," which basically looks at the outside of aging. This means that there has been a focus on the biological aspects of aging to the virtual exclusion of its biographical ones, on its physiological aspects at the expense of its psychological ones, and on its sociological aspects to the eclipsing of its aesthetic ones. Moreover, where psychological aspects have been the focus, the approach has been predominantly quantitative more than qualitative in nature. It has been a matter of measuring deficits and technical abilities (Holliday & Chandler, 1986), thereby marginalizing subjective practices such as life review and reminiscence. With notable exceptions, such as the work of Robert Butler (1963) and Eric Erikson (1963), reminiscence was viewed until approximately twenty years ago as a sign of dementia or of "spinning our wheels." At best, such practices were considered pleasant and possibly helpful activities but ultimately tangential or even irrelevant to what gerontology, as a social science, ought to be about.

In contrast to such a view, what we are attempting to do here is to contribute to the growing interest in wisdom by finding out about the meaning of aging and wisdom as it is experienced on the "inside." As Plato noted in *The Republic* (Cornford, 1968), "I enjoy talking with very old people. They have gone before us on a road by which we too may have to travel, and I think we do well to learn from them what it is like, easy or difficult, rough or smooth." As we will discuss in Chapter 2, this is not a methodological issue of, say, narratives versus statistics. Rather, it is a matter of employing the appropriate lens to see what it is we want to understand. In the case of wisdom, we will not see it without stories. Through the lens of "the stories we are" (Randall, 1995; Kenyon & Randall, 1997), we would argue, we will be able to gain some wisdom on wisdom.

We would even go so far as to say that without paying attention to lifestories, a serious disservice is done, both to older persons and to society at large. When we discount people's stories, we devalue their experience and therefore deny our world a source of edification and renewal—intellectually, ethically, interpersonally, and, in the end, spiritually too. The tragedy this denial entails is akin to shelf after shelf of unread novels, whose worlds are thus unexplored and whose wisdom goes to waste. As the novelist Alex Haley says, "When an old person dies it's like a library has burned down" (cited in Polster, 1987, p. 96).

Having said this, however, we want to stress that ordinary wisdom concerns much more than older persons. It is not an age-specific topic. Although many of the insights we invoke in this volume originate in literature that focuses on older adults, ordinary wisdom is more than a theoretical concept in the study of aging. It is a practical, potential reality in everyone's life, regardless of age. It is accessible to us all, not only because, technically, we all begin aging at the moment of birth, but because soon thereafter we become biographically active and so begin weaving (and living) a unique story from whose inherent wisdom the world can only be enriched. In the next section, we will explore the crisis of meaning in today's world that adds to the five reasons for the re-emergence of wisdom that we have just discussed. Such a crisis makes the discussion of ordinary wisdom particularly pertinent.

THE CRISIS OF MEANING IN POSTMODERN TIMES

As we enter the new millennium, we are constantly hearing that we are entering a new world, that we are becoming a global village, an information society, a digital world, or a postmodern age. This transition, we are told, and indeed are increasingly experiencing, signals a major shift from a more stable modern society, where people could find meaning and construct their identity on the basis of a number of larger myths or master stories, to something else. The something else involves a fundamental questioning of and, for many, a scepticism toward these grand narratives by which people could previously live. Let us take a short look at four of them.

The first grand narrative is that of the family. For increasing numbers of people, reliance on traditional family structures has been replaced by high divorce rates, something that applies increasingly across the life span. Furthermore, we have many single parents, children with two sets of parents, children raised by grandparents, and so on.

The second grand narrative is that of work. Increasingly, people feel that they cannot find a sense of meaning and personal identity in their work due to such things as rapid change that, almost overnight, can affect an entire institution, an entire industry, or even an entire economy. In addition to this, there is, with exceptions of course, a widespread feeling that our work is not valued, that we can be replaced by many other "human resources." There is also more and more stress placed on workers who do remain in their jobs following widespread downsizing or rightsizing. Loyalty and a mutual relationship between employer and employee are disappearing as well and, with them, a respect for the importance of ethical, compassionate, or wise behavior. Given that work is a fundamental way in which people define themselves in the world, the effects of these changes are only beginning to be felt and are potentially devastating, both for individuals and for our culture as a whole.

Many of us are disillusioned with organized religion and, for various reasons, adopt a set of secular, materialistic values. The traditional belief that we can find our place in the world by identifying with the third grand narrative, religion, has weakened considerably. This outcome may be due, in part, to the many scandals that have become apparent in certain denominations or to rigid doctrines that reflect less and less the daily reality that many of us are attempting to negotiate. This latter situation is sometimes referred to as the tension between "churchianity" and the experience of spirituality itself.

Finally, many of us feel that our lives are managed, increasingly, from the outside and that we have little opportunity to affect important matters, either in our own lives or in the lives of those we love. This fourth grand narrative of outer management comes in several forms, including the large-scale changes in the workplace, as we have just discussed, as well as health care and education. Moreover, we feel that our lives are directed from the outside in the sense that the life span is divided, both socially and bureaucratically, into stages of childhood, adolescence, and adulthood. For example, while legislation concerning mandatory retirement and age discrimination has come a long way, we still live in an essentially ageist society. Witness the "empty-desk" syndrome, whereby a person's job is eliminated in piecemeal fashion until he or she no longer has a reason to come to work and, so, eventually and "voluntarily" retires. For older persons who suddenly find themselves in this social stratum, this creates serious problems of both identity and meaning.

The erosion of our confidence in these various master narratives underlines the importance, we feel then, of appreciating our individual narratives as valid vehicles of wisdom. Indeed, it is our sense of their importance that has prompted the writing of this book. In the meantime, the crisis of meaning that we have just outlined, as gerontologists such as Tom Cole (1992) and Harry Moody (1991) have stressed, stems from one particular outcome of postmodernism, namely, a sense of separateness, or a lack of relatedness. This sense of separation belies a widespread sense of meaninglessness and a spiritual malaise. We can identify three levels of this separateness.

First, for many people, "the story of my life" consists of a lack of meaning beyond the material realm. Coupled with a denial of death, there is an exclusive emphasis on the *via activa*, that is, on a life based on achievement and control. Such a "way of life" is well described by Jan-Erik Ruth as that of a careerist (Ruth & Öberg, 1996). Though this way of life is by no means considered a problem by everyone who chooses to live it, such a view tends to create a separation from our deeper nature as spiritual beings.

Second, we are separate from the social aspects of who we are, or from the larger stories we live within, which we shall consider in Chapter 3. Insofar as our lives are managed by social policy from the outside, we feel powerless to influence the unfolding of the social story that nevertheless remains part of our identity. Even the language of postmodern society emphasizes this separateness in that we are called "clients," "consumers," "employees." The federal government of Canada, for example, calls its permanent employees "indeterminates." These designations make it easier for a society to distance itself from persons and their stories in order to implement unpleasant policies and decisions.

Third, we are separate because we see our own lives as individual. Such a view is sometimes called privatism. We identify ourselves as unique and apart from others. As a consequence, we have little sense of community, little collective understanding of where we are going as human beings, and little common perception of the meaning of aging. As Tom Cole (1992, p. xxii) argues extensively in *The Journey of Life*, since the mid-nineteenth century, Americans (and we would expand this to include those of us in the West in general) "have come to view aging not as a fated aspect of our individual and social existence but as one of life's problems to be solved through willpower, aided by science, technology, and expertise." From this perspective, the meaning of life becomes the meaning of *my* life as a unique individual. The process of aging becomes my problem—and perhaps even my *fault*—for not living right. This results in a kind of loneliness, in having no place to "be ourselves," no context in which we can let down our emotional defenses and feel sufficiently trusting to tell our stories.

In describing this sort of scenario as a spiritual malaise, we are dealing with a phenomenon that is associated specifically with meaning, or rather with the lack of it. It is precisely for this reason that the time-honored notion of wisdom becomes an eligible candidate for contributing to a better quality of life; that is, it can help us discover new meaning in the midst of change that is so rapid, so overwhelming, and so fundamental that it seems like chaos, change that is causing and will continue to cause much confusion and suffering. It is our view here, however, that contrary to one postmodern view, we have not lost our identity as human beings; we have not lost our center (see Gergen, 1992).

Prior to offering a preliminary characterization of ordinary wisdom, which will provide a framework for the rest of what we have to say, let us first consider the epistemological context out of which this book has emerged.

THINKING THROUGH METAPHOR

Aside from the grand narratives we discussed in the previous section, there is also a vibrant debate in the human sciences—indeed, a veritable crisis of meaning—concerning the nature of knowledge itself. This crisis is based on the postmodern conviction that all knowledge is ultimately constructed; moreover, it is metaphorical at base. In other words, language does not convey literal truth but consists largely of images and interpretations. In the words of George Lakoff and Mark Johnson (1980, p. 3), "our ordinary conceptual system, in terms of which we both think and act, is fundamentally metaphorical in nature." One implication of this conviction is the serious calling into question of the assumption of modern science that objective knowledge will arise from employing "the scientific method." In contrast, the postmodern perspective is that there is a hermeneutic or interpretive dimension to all knowledge. This means that all formal theories in science, as well as all philosophical and religious systems, are, essentially, stories. As such, they are comprised not only of facts, but also of values, perceptions, and interpretations.

Besides common scientific metaphors such as "mind as computer" or "human beings as machines," examples can be found in various therapeutic approaches. Each is based on a set of metaphors, which use something more well known to explain something less well known, specifically, some aspect of human functioning. Witness Freud's use of sexual symbolism as a way of decoding dreams and fantasies or Jung's creation of the notions of animus and anima. In addition to these metaphors, we have humanistic psychologists talking about peak experiences and behaviorists talking about little black boxes (see Schroots, Birren, & Kenyon, 1991).

The emphasis on both metaphor and story has been characterized as the narrative turn in the human sciences (see Birren et al., 1996; Polkinghorne, 1988). What this turn represents is an opening up of the epistemological and methodological territory in many areas. To focus on one example that is pertinent to our purposes, we will briefly discuss the emerging perspective that we mentioned earlier: narrative gerontology.

From this perspective, all theories of aging, as well as all formal strategies for intervention, are fundamentally narratives. They are stories about how we age. If you will, they are "storied." This is where the term *hermeneutic circle* becomes operative, the insight behind which being that "there is nothing below the narrative structure, at least nothing experienceable by us or comprehensible in experiential terms" (Carr, 1986, p. 66). To put it simply, all we have are stories and metaphors; our task is to sort out the better stories and the more effective metaphors from those that are less so. From a narrative gerontology perspective, then, there is no constraint to the employment of any particular method in our inquiries; the appropriate method is a function of the phenomenon in which we are interested. As we have alluded already and will discuss more fully in Chapter 2, this view is in distinct contrast to the modern tendency to make the problem fit the chosen method.

It is this tendency that has constrained the continued telling of the story of wisdom and has led to a widespread belief that we are missing out on important aspects of the process of human development and aging. On the other hand, contributing to a broader and more multidisciplinary exploration of the phenomena of aging are perspectives such as narrative gerontology, critical gerontology (Cole et al., 1993), qualitative gerontology (Rowles & Schoenberg, 2000), plus historical interpretations of cultural and scientific gerontology (see, for example, Cole, 1992).

Narrative gerontology makes it possible for us to explore stories of aging, new and old, that might reflect potentially meaningful outcomes of the human life span, that is, what happens to us along the way and where we are going, both individually and as a species. It is out of this context that we focus our efforts here on the metaphors of story and journey. We use these two metaphors as lenses to understand something about both wisdom in general and ordinary wisdom in particular. In this regard, we hope to make a modest contribution to answering three underlying questions: What is wisdom? How should we study it? and How can it be facilitated?

ORDINARY WISDOM VS. EXTRAORDINARY WISDOM

Wisdom is a topic with a long history. In one form or another, it appears in most cultures around the world. However, as we will discuss in Chapter 2, for a number of decades during the past century, it was relegated in the West by philosophers and social scientists alike to a list of forbidden subjects. Among the reasons for this is wisdom's historical, and in a sense automatic, association with being older. Unfortunately, until fairly recently in our own culture, being older has not commonly been considered a time of potential growth; indeed, quite the contrary. In addition, wisdom can be seen as the victim of a generally accepted methodological narrative, namely, the scientific method, particularly its emphasis on investigating exclusively quantifiable and observable behavior, or, if you will, visibly moving targets (Holliday & Chandler, 1986; Kenyon, Ruth, & Mader, 1999). These two factors—the association of wisdom with being older and the focus of science on quantifiable phenomena—have temporarily curtailed the continued recounting of the story of wisdom. Fortunately, however, there is emerging a whole new interest in wisdom and in its connection with experience and age (Manheimer, 1992; Sternberg, 1990).

As the eminent American gerontologist James Birren (1988) has pointed out, wisdom is one of the potential endpoints for human development. As with many other phenomena related to aging, it is not a natural outcome of living longer, but it does require a degree of experience. On the one hand, wisdom qualifies as a potentially positive outcome of aging that deserves serious attention. On the other hand, we are at the beginning stages of understanding the nature of wisdom and the characteristics of wise persons.

One basic agenda here concerns the characterization of wisdom itself, a challenge that involves comparing traditional interpretations with current attempts both to define wisdom and to operationalize it. For example, we need to make important distinctions between wisdom and other phenomena such as cleverness, specialized forms of intellectual functioning, and multiple intelligences (Gardner, 1993), some of which are admittedly measurable by experimental means.

Since this book is about the investigation of ordinary wisdom—that is, about the possibility that we all have a wisdom story—a useful way to begin is to distinguish between wisdom's ordinary and extraordinary manifestations.

EXTRAORDINARY WISDOM

Many people believe that wisdom is a rare quality, reserved for the specially gifted or the chosen few. Furthermore, many feel that the very idea of an ordinary person inquiring about the nature of wisdom smacks of arrogance. It is possible, of course, that wisdom is something we ought not to attribute to ourselves, since doubt, or knowing that we do not know, may be an important component of it (Meacham, 1990). However, we are not thereby precluded, we feel, from making a modest inquiry into such an important human phenomenon.

In her deliberations on the subject of wisdom, Marie-Claire Josso (1998) has observed that, insofar as we can understand *something* of the wisdom traditions, it is because we already have some wisdom within us, either potentially or actually. Lending support to Josso's observation is an intriguing study done by Holliday and Chandler (1986). Within and among groups of young, middle-aged, and older persons, Holliday and Chandler found strong agreement, or high inter- and intracohort correlation, in how such persons distinguished between wisdom and related concepts such as intelligence and how they characterized wisdom itself. Further support is available simply from looking closely at our own lives. Surely some of our actions and decisions could be categorized as wise.

With these preliminary remarks in mind, let us engage in a cursory characterization of extraordinary wisdom and then, following this, explain our approach to ordinary wisdom. As it is characterized in various traditions, and as we shall elaborate in Chapter 2, extraordinary wisdom has at least six dimensions.

First, it involves a degree of intellectual understanding. This is the *cognitive* dimension of wisdom. The interesting question here, of course, is how intelligent we need to be in order to be wise.

The second is the *practical-experiential* dimension. Wisdom has to do not only with abstract ideas or theories but with everyday life. It is knowledge of the way the world works. Moreover, in addition to knowledge itself, wisdom in many traditions involves some form of practice.

Third, there is an *interpersonal* aspect to wisdom in that it entails a perception of the larger story we live within (Kenyon & Randall, 1997; Randall, 1995). Wise people are able to put their own "stuff" aside, to see things from another's point of view, and to bring to situations a more panoramic perspective.

The fourth aspect of wisdom is its *ethical-moral* dimension, which is concerned with what the ancient Greeks referred to as "knowing and doing the good." This dimension deals with wisdom-related intentions and actions.

A fifth aspect of wisdom is its mode of *idiosyncratic expression*. There appear to be as many faces of wisdom as there are human beings, a quality that, of course, creates particular challenges to the task of identifying wise persons.

Finally, there is the *spiritual-mystical* dimension of extraordinary wisdom. That is, it involves a special experience of, and/or insight into, the nature of the cosmos and the human place within it. Wisdom often involves an acceptance of both life and death. Perhaps most important, it involves the ability to find meaning in suffering and loss.

ORDINARY WISDOM

These characterizations of wisdom, as helpful as we believe they are, raise many questions: As some authors, contemporary and historical, have asked, is wisdom one thing or many? Also, how should we study wisdom in order to understand it and identify authentic instances of its expression? Furthermore, is ordinary wisdom different from extraordinary wisdom in kind or only in degree, in actuality or only in potentiality? We will discuss these questions and others throughout this book. In the meantime, we will provide a preliminary characterization of ordinary wisdom that can be extracted from extraordinary wisdom.

There is considerable variance of opinion as to the actual mechanism of wisdom, that is, how wise people become wise. For example, some attribute the process to karma or to grace, to personal effort or to chance, or to some combination of all of these, as is captured in the saying that "God helps those who help themselves." Nevertheless, the underlying feature of wisdom is that it constitutes a particular way of being in the world (the practical-experiential dimension). Moreover, it is our own unique way of being; our personal, inside wisdom story (the dimension of idiosyncratic expression). However, that wisdom story, though personal, is coauthored in the larger story we live within (the interpersonal dimension). As we consider again in the Epilogue, it is this latter characteristic that therefore makes it possible for us, however stumblingly, to facilitate wisdom in one another's lives—to certain degrees at specific times in particular ways— through the process of storytelling and storylistening (Kenyon & Randall, 1997). Because it is a wisdom *story*, and because story is our principal form for creating meaning through our interpretations of experience, it has an intellectual component as well (the cognitive dimension).

Aside from attempting to understand and share each other's wisdom stories at the individual level, just as we do with narratives in general (Ruth & Kenyon, 1996a, 1996b), we can also study ordinary wisdom at the cultural level by investigating shared life themes, cultural patterns, and sources of meaning (Cole, 1992). By looking at the common station-stops on our human journey, we can identify sociocultural contexts from which ordinary wisdom arises, or *could* arise. An important question in this regard concerns directionality; that is, are we always restorying in the direction of wisdom, either accidentally or consciously, with more or less facility and resources, and at different times in our lives? In moving to the content of our wisdom stories, we would offer, then, the following preliminary insights.

Ordinary wisdom is about finding meaning in life and suffering (the spiritual-mystical dimension). It is about accepting, owning, and valuing our lives and our lifestories, including both our unlived lives and our untold stories. Ordinary wisdom does not manifest once and for all, however, but in the form of a journey. Moreover, it is a journey fraught with doubt and confusion, paradox and tension, ambivalence and fear. As Sogyal Rinpoche (1994, p. 104) notes: "Anyone looking honestly at life will see that we live in a constant state of suspense and ambiguity. Our minds are perpetually shifting in and out of confusion and clarity. If only we were confused all the time, that would at least make for some kind of clarity. What is really baffling about life is that sometimes, despite all our confusion, we can also be really wise." As we will elaborate in Chapter 4, it is nevertheless within this human situatedness, with its quality of opacity and of limited control, that it is possible for us to "sentir bien dans notre peau et comfortable dans notre etre en relation avec autrui" (Josso, 1998, p. 17), that is, to feel good in our skin and in our relations with others.

Ordinary wisdom, we would also say, is not about being perfect—"perfect," that is, in the sense of reflecting all of the qualities of extraordinary wisdom. Even those people who we may agree are candidates for extraordinary wisdom are, in some aspects of their lives and lifestories, often all too human. Rather, ordinary wisdom is about the possibility that, at certain times and to certain degrees, many of us are wise in our intentions, actions, and choices (the moral-ethical dimension). It is about the possibility of becoming *more* wise both by looking at our own lifestories and by listening to the stories of others. As Birren and Feldman (1997, p. 48) express it, "By telling your life story you reveal your own life's wisdom, and that's why autobiography has such an impact on people."

A further and critical aspect of ordinary wisdom as we discuss it in this book is its intimate relationship with the metaphors of both story and journey. Our ordinary wisdom, we could say, is realized through our stories read as journeys and, simultaneously, through our journeys told as stories. By means of this perspective, we can appreciate that we have to have been good travelers to have gotten this far in life. In other words, we tend to forget how good we are (see Birren, 1987; Birren & Feldman, 1997). Furthermore, the metaphors of story and journey give us lenses through which to see that ordinary wisdom, with some extraordinary characteristics, may be more common than we have recently thought and, also, that it is possible to facilitate ordinary wisdom through restorying. Or is it the case that no life is ordinary and that all lives are extraordinary? In other words, is it possible that even lives that could be considered tragic possess an integrity and a wisdom all their own?

In later chapters, we come back to such provocative questions, as well as take up the issue of how ordinary wisdom can be facilitated. We also provide examples of ordinary wisdom that only become visible when we focus on lifestory. The majority of these examples reflect studies with older adults and raise fascinating questions. For example, regarding the issue of direction, is there a transition in aging that brings with it an increase in such things as existential meaning, wisdom, and acceptance? Also, is there a relationship between the suffering, disillusionment, and loss that we face as we travel through life and a movement from having to being, a movement that reflects wisdom? It is to such a relationship that Florida Scott-Maxwell (1968, p. 47) would seem to refer in her book *The Measure of My Days*, written when she was well into her eighties. "The hardness of life I deplore," she says, "creates the qualities I admire."

THE PLAN OF THE BOOK

Before we embark on our adventure into ordinary wisdom, a quick outline of the book is clearly in order. In Chapter 2, we survey the fate of wisdom across the centuries and consider how it has fallen from grace since ancient times. In light of theorizing in cognitive science circles, as in gerontology too, the chapter also raises the questions of what wisdom is and what the criteria are by which we can identify it in people's lives. The chapter also focuses on the distinction between traditional portrayals of wisdom as some extraordinary thing and as what we are calling ordinary wisdom.

Chapters 3, 4, and 5, which are effectively the heart of the book, look at the concept of ordinary wisdom in greater depth. What all three chapters have in common is a conviction—which is a hallmark of postmodern times—concerning the centrality of language in how we construe and construct our worlds and, within language, the centrality of metaphor. In large measure, it is by metaphor that we live and experience, that we act, speak, and think. Some metaphors, however, are more fundamental or more radical than others. They are called "root" metaphors. Root metaphors are grand metaphors, which are both broad in scope and rich in implications, or entailments (Lakoff & Johnson, 1980). They are the sort we invoke, for instance, when we think about life as a whole, metaphors such as life-as-story or life-as-journey. As we introduced earlier, these are the two metaphors that we will in fact be entwining throughout this book, like themes in a musical score. The reason we entwine them, in a sort of alternating point-counterpoint manner, and the reason we cannot consider them in isolation is that most stories recount journeys of one sort or another—as in the case of an autobiographical story, or what Dag Hammarskjöld (1957) calls "the journey inward." By the same token, most journeys eventuate in stories.

Chapter 3 looks at the first of these two metaphors, the narrative root metaphor, as a means of fleshing out what we call "biographical aging." It considers, among other things, the literary dimensions of everyday life, the role of what we call "narrative intelligence" (Randall, 1999) in storying our lives, the way our stories take control of our lives, and the complex interpretive process whereby we read (or can learn to read) for meaning in the novel of our lives.

Chapter 4 takes the second and even more time-honored trope, the metaphor of life as journey, and explores it as a means of helping us understand the nature of spiritual aging. This aspect of the aging process is currently being given more serious focus than it has been given in the past, in both research and practice alike. For its part, Chapter 5 looks at how these two metaphors converge in the metaphor of life-as-adventure, a particular genre of story that, incorporated into our perspective on life, inspires both courage and hope, plus an openness to lifelong learning. In these ways, Chapter 5 illuminates the nature of ordinary wisdom in ways we find particularly empowering.

Throughout all that we will be saying, we will be attempting to point to ways of being with one another, both formally and informally, that can lead us beyond separateness and meaninglessness. Such ways, we hope to show, can also point us beyond both negative and positive stereotypes of growing (and being) older toward a basically age-irrelevant environment in which we are coauthors and fellow travelers who naturally evoke the ordinary wisdom—or the wisdom story—in each other's lives.

2

Wisdom on Wisdom

The core teachings of the great wisdom traditions live in an enduring present. They are relevant, powerful, and accessible. The insights that arise from their core practices yield a paradigm of resistance, creativity, and profound renewal for our time.

—Charlotte Spretnak (1991)

At other times and in other civilizations, [the] path of spiritual transformation was confined to a relatively select number of people; now, however, a large portion of the human race must seek the path of wisdom if the world is to be preserved from the internal and external dangers that threaten it.

—Sogyal Rinpoche (1994)

HOW WISDOM FELL OUT OF FAVOR

As we indicated in Chapter 1, there are at least four reasons for the eclipse of the wisdom tradition in recent decades. The first reason is the coincidental movement of psychology to the analysis of behavior as opposed to persons and the movement of philosophy to the analysis of concepts and propositions. As a result of these movements, wisdom, as well as other inner states and metaphysical topics, was relegated to a list of forbidden subjects. In the words of Steven Holliday and Michael Chandler (1986, p. 2), "As they are commonly understood, truly wise persons are thought to deal in essences, to avoid impromptu actions, and to often demonstrate their competence by refraining from acting at all. The impenetrability, unflappability, and cross-legged immobility of prototypically wise people make them all but opaque to a psychology whose attention continues to remain focused primarily upon moving targets." In other words, if you cannot see it with your eyes, it is not there. While this situation has improved, we would argue that there is still a long way to go in terms of opening up the black box of mainstream social science.

The last statement brings us to a second and related reason for the lack of attention paid to wisdom in many scholarly and professional circles. In the transition from the modern view of science to postmodern views, it is becoming increasingly clear that many gerontologists and other social scientists, particularly in North America, have attached meaning to—indeed, live—a specific theoretical and methodological story. It is the scientific method story. For some decades, the effort was made to make the social sciences as credible or as pure as the natural sciences by adopting the methods of the latter. Moreover, this story is not only lived by individual professionals but also extends to the social context in the training of graduate students and the priorities of funding agencies. In this way, a scientific instrument, or what Manheimer (1992) calls a reporting narrative, has become an ontology. While it is a feature of the postmodern world to have a variety of reporting narratives, the modern emphasis on the scientific method has, in some cases, developed into an unreflected dogmalike story with its own immune system, as it were, one that sometimes silences other voices.

From a postmodern perspective, any theory or method is, at least in part, socially constructed. The process of theory construction involves "hidden references to the structural conditions that are imposed on us" (Alheit, 1995, p. 63). As a result of this situation, sometimes the method comes to guide the research problem or the phenomenon to be investigated, rather than the problem suggesting the appropriate method to be adopted. For example, a number of orientations are contained in various empirical and theoretical perspectives in the field of aging (Kenyon, 1988); that is, there are several disparate starting points for the scientific study of aging that lead us to different and competing conclusions about human nature in the later years. Aging can be defined as a series of problems or as a developmentally interesting phenomenon with significantly different emphases and outcomes for research, for practice, and ultimately for the quality of life experienced by older persons. None of this sounds problematic as yet. A variety of metaphors and images for aging, and of basic assumptions about it, would seem to be a desirable situation.

The problem, however, is that these assumptions are often implicit. While they guide research and practice, they tend to do so in an unreflected manner. Moreover, a particular set of them can dominate an entire field of study. For example, in the early periods of gerontology, a preponderance of perspectives demonstrated the myriad ways in which, as we age, we fail and decline. Since then, it has been shown that many of these views are of course fraught with methodological and theoretical problems. In many cases, it was as if the researchers were looking only for decline. Thus, decline was all they found. The significance of this issue becomes apparent when we consider that scientific findings are a critical component in the formation of public and personal perceptions of aging. They also exercise a crucial influence on our decisions concerning appropriate intervention strategies with older persons. For example, if we assume that we all decline intellectually as we age, then adult education for older adults, or any sort of search for wisdom, is not even on the table for discussion as a possible direction for study and practice.

What we are saying is that, since wisdom could not be investigated behaviorally or experimentally, in effect, it was deemed to be no longer there. In Zen Buddhist terms, this is a case of mistaking the finger pointing at the moon for the moon itself. Such a view constitutes a rather inappropriate and narrow application of Wittgenstein's dictum concerning the obligation to remain silent about that of which we cannot speak. Perhaps it is our language that sometimes needs enriching rather than reducing reality to what that language accommodates. It is ironic that two main representatives of this tradition are Wittgenstein and Whitehead. While the early work of these two thinkers represents logical positivism at its best, their later work has been claimed to be representative of postmodern thinking and even the wisdom of age (see Manheimer, 1992). To put it bluntly, they could not, in the end, remain members of the club that they had helped to found.

Aside from the scientific discussion of the decline of wisdom, a third reason for the contemporary lack of wisdom studies concerns the association that we tend intuitively to make between wisdom and age. As we have just mentioned, until very recently, aging was viewed by many gerontologists and others as an unremittingly bad thing, as a process characterized by loss, decline, detriment, and death. In the words of Holliday and Chandler (1986, p. 3), "The traditional linkage between wisdom and aging which seems to have characterized the thinking of many earlier civilizations has become something of a mockery in a technological era that finds so little utility in the elderly and has elevated the notion of planned obsolescence to previously unimagined heights." Due to these powerful ageist assumptions and negative stereotypes, it is difficult for many people to imagine that an older person could exhibit such a subtle and special form of ability as wisdom. After all, many nowadays have little significant contact with older people in any meaningful intergenerational context, such as work or education.

The loss of the intuitive connection between wisdom and age is no doubt connected with scientific reasons; however, it is also different in that it involves the personal metaphors of aging that scientists and others bring to their professional context (Kenyon & Randall, 1997). A scientist or a professional may carry negative stereotypes of aging, which are then reinforced in the scientific climate that we just discussed. This can become a closed circle where things such as wisdom are not even considered a possible theme in the story of aging.

The fourth reason for the dearth of a contemporary wisdom tradition is that not only has social science been characterized by an almost exclusive emphasis on the scientific method story, but, as a culture, we have bought into the idea of scientism. We look to science for the answers to all of our problems. Anything that is less than scientific or not professed by an expert is suspect. Thus, knowledge that originates in the humanities, for example, or even in our own lifestories is not to be trusted. Under these conditions, wisdom disappears as a legitimate topic of inquiry, since it does not lend itself to technical forms of knowledge and does not provide a quick fix, despite the claims of some contemporary New Age literature.

While the foregoing describes some of the factors that have precluded the consideration of the otherwise time-honored notion of wisdom, we should note that, as we write, the climate is changing. The postmodern transition in science and probably the crisis of meaning in postmodern times that we discuss in Chapter 1 are giving rise to new interest in ideas such as wisdom and human spirituality.

Moreover, gerontologists and life span psychologists are focusing more on the potentials and even benefits of aging. This emphasis is characterized by healthy collaborations between the sciences and the humanities and by a broadening of the methodological story to include more qualitative or narrative studies and even emerging combinations of experimental and statistical methods with biographical approaches (see Svensson, 1996; Reker & Chamberlain, 2000). As Chandler and Holliday (1990, p. 127) note, "Psychologists and others in growing numbers also have come to doubt the correctness of any view that automatically equates knowledge with the empirical-analytic truths of science. Such critics are perhaps to be forgiven if they question the conclusion that all of the seemingly untrackable problems of contemporary life will be solved by still another technological breakthrough and continue to hold out some hope that there are still deeper and wiser ways of understanding these problems."

DIMENSIONS OF WISDOM

To provide a preliminary account of extraordinary wisdom our approach will be thematic. As we indicated in Chapter 1, we will elaborate six dimensions of wisdom that can be distilled from traditions that are particularly relevant to our respective interests, backgrounds, and experiences. We will then apply these insights to a rendering of ordinary wisdom that will be filled out in the following chapters through the lenses of story and journey.

The reason for this approach is that we are not interested in providing an exhaustive analysis or even a survey of wisdom, something that others have done to some extent already and probably no one could do completely. Rather, we want to approach wisdom from a perennial philosophy (Huxley, 1962) perspective. What we are saying is that wisdom traditions, although expressed "in widely varying storyforms that rise from different cultural frames of reference and different languages," as Fowler (1995, p. 273) sees it, "share what they have seen and experienced, and it all comes out to be the same experience, the same insight."

In recent times, we are seeing more literature emerge, for example, that looks at God as having either no costume or all costumes. As one of the Chinese hermits interviewed by Bill Porter (1993, p. 96) observes, "Practice is like candy. People like different kinds. But it's just candy. The Dharma is empty" (see also Hanh, 1995, for an excellent discussion of a rapprochement between Christianity and Buddhism). In what follows, we will highlight particular aspects of various traditions as we attempt to profile a phenomenon as rich and diverse as wisdom. Nevertheless, "the purpose of examining various spiritual paths . . . should not be to pluck out bits here and there to mix in a planetary stew, for each tradition possesses its own integrity" (Spretnak, 1991, p. 8). Rather, the task is to understand something about this complex and subtle phenomenon as a basis for seeing which parts of it might apply to our ordinary aging selves.

Cognitive

It is difficult to argue against the claim that there must be some degree of cognitive functioning associated with wisdom, as in fact we consider in more detail in Chapter 4. However, the question could be asked as to how intelligent we need to be in order to be wise. The links between concepts such as intelligence, cleverness, and expertise, on the one hand, and wisdom, on the other, need to be carefully examined. It is laudable that there are contemporary attempts to study wisdom within the cognitive tradition (see Sternberg, 1990); however, we need to address issues such as the atheoretical nature of psychometric notions of intelligence.

In the case of wisdom, one of the early figures in the psychometric tradition was Wechsler (1958, p. 143), who referred to the notion of sagacity as "the ability to deal with life's situations in terms of past experience." The problem with this interpretation is that, in the final analysis, sagacity amounts to what is reflected in the statement that once you know how to ride a bicycle, you never forget. For Wechsler, sagacity as a kind of practical wisdom has little by way of an intelligence component about it, let alone of wisdom. It is a wispy remnant of the past by which older people stumble their way through life on the basis of long-held habits. Part of the reason for this view is the underlying assumption that, since the aging body declines, so does the aging mind. This is only one of many possible mind-body views that have been debated for centuries by philosophers and others. Unfortunately, it is also the one that characterizes powerful negative stereotypes of aging.

The work of Wechsler (1958) points to the importance of examining the basic assumptions, or the story, contained in a given scientific perspective on aging. The cognitive tradition has significantly rehabilitated the notion of intelligence and has made major contributions to the study of aging. However, it has not yet developed theory that would link with its methodological narrative. Thus, caution is the order of the day. This applies both to theoretical matters and to the way in which we decide to study wisdom, or the methodological story that we adopt. For example, is it appropriate, as some have thought, to attempt to study wisdom by using hypothetical or fictive situations, such as, a priest must offer advice to a devout couple dealing with an unwanted pregnancy (Csikszentimihalyi & Rathunde, 1990)? While this situation qualifies as an existential dilemma that might require some wise counsel, it lacks ecological validity (see, for example, Ruth & Coleman, 1996).

The point here is that wisdom, if it is anything at all, is not only, or not most importantly, about what amounts to abstract problem solving. It is about involvement and decision making in a real-life biographical encounter. It is more about what we *did* do than what we *would* do. Wisdom requires that, in the end, we jump or leap, and whether an action is deemed to be wise or not is often not known until after the fact. This existential dimension of wisdom is difficult to capture within the psychometric story of intelligence. Such a dimension also suggests that lifestories may complement our investigations. In fact, without such stories, it is difficult to imagine how we will even "see" wisdom.

Wisdom emerges only in a specific situation, by looking into people's eyes, so to speak, and even then we cannot evaluate a wise outcome until afterward. This criticism is sometimes directed to medical ethics committees in that the philosopher on the committee plays the role of explicating and clarifying various positions and arguments but then does not vote in the actual decision-making process. Our suggestion here is that having to put it on the line separates wisdom from intelligence and other cognitive abilities.

It is laudable that researchers such as Paul Baltes and Jacqui Smith (1990) are attempting to use psychometric methods to gain an understanding of experienced judgment, or expertise, in uncertain matters of life. This is, arguably, an important aspect of wisdom. However, the effort to link these insights to wisdom through specific psychometric abilities like crystallized intelligence is, at this moment in time, a significant conceptual leap. Furthermore, for Baltes and Smith (1990), wise people as experts are rare. They may have had to be exposed to specific kinds of training in life, such as teaching or counseling, and may not be wise in their own lives but can be wise for others. As we will go on to consider in what follows, it is highly questionable whether this view captures the richness of the existential dimensions of wisdom, or even if it is wisdom at all that emerges. As Jim Birren and Laurel Fisher (1990, p. 331) point out, "The various aspects of wisdom must apply to real people in real situations in real time."

One further study worthy of note is that of Ardelt (1997). In it, wisdom is connected with life satisfaction in that people who are assessed as "wiser" are found to have higher life satisfaction in the face of adverse life circumstances such as illness and poverty. While Ardelt's study again reflects an interest in wisdom that is greatly needed, and while it does move beyond a purely knowledge-based definition of wisdom in that it includes affective and reflective factors, we still should be cautious about how valid these findings are. For example, wisdom is said to be expressed in people who, through interviews, are characterized by descriptors such as "behaves in a sympathetic or considerate manner" or "has warmth; is compassionate" (p. 17). As we have just said, laboratory assessments of this type lack real-life expressions of wisdom. And, as we shall discuss later, this is a stereotypical face of wisdom, which *may* be wisdom but could also be deception—of self and/or other—or ego inflation. Nevertheless, if there are certain identifiable patterns of thinking and feeling that do promote higher life satisfaction, then they deserve further attention.

Wisdom will no doubt tell us something about intelligence, but we need to be wary about what intelligence can tell us about wisdom. This is particularly true in our own culture, which is characterized by values of control and domination and where we often glorify people who are shrewd, clever, and intelligent. As Rinpoche (1994, p. 123) explains, "Our society promotes cleverness instead of wisdom, and celebrates the most superficial, harsh, and least useful aspects of our intelligence."

A further question concerning wisdom from a cognitive perspective is whether it is something that, if one had it, would one *know* that one had it. As Ron Manheimer (1992, p. 434) explains, in commenting on a study concerning wisdom conducted by Vivian Clayton and James Birren (1980): "Their discovery that younger generations project a link between growing older and growing wiser, though older people do not, is a profoundly suggestive result of their study. It echoes the famous Socratic denial of the attribute." The question, then, is do we measure wisdom by assessing how little wisdom a person claims to have, and how do we know whether they are telling the truth.

The foregoing discussion points us to the role of doubt in any conception of wisdom. Wisdom as a form of mature intellectual functioning may have less to do with how much knowledge we have and more to do with knowing what that knowledge is worth. "The facts a wise man knows are known by everybody. Wisdom consists, partly, in understanding the significance of what everybody knows" (Kekes, 1983, p. 280). Holliday and Chandler (1986) argue that the failure of traditional models of cognition to accommodate things such as the ability to tolerate ambiguity, doubt, and confusion makes understanding adult cognition, and, we would add, wisdom, rather difficult. From this point of view, a wise person would not necessarily know a lot—in particular, "know" in the sense of achieving high test scores on psychometric instruments—but would demonstrate a balance between knowledge and doubt. Conversely, a lack of wisdom would be "illustrated by the error of believing that one can see all that can be seen, that one knows all that can be known" (Meacham, 1990, p. 183). This error is commonplace in contemporary science and society. Meacham (1990, p. 187) sums up this view in the following statement: "Wisdom is thus not a belief, a value, a set of facts, a corpus of knowledge or information in some specialized area, or a set of special abilities or skills. Wisdom is an attitude taken by persons toward the beliefs, values, knowledge, information, abilities, and skills that are held, a tendency to doubt that these are necessarily true or valid and to doubt that they are an exhaustive set of those things that could be known."

Historically speaking, the clearest example of a cognitive wisdom tradition is the Greek tradition embodied by Plato and Aristotle. For example, even though life expectancy was rather short during the times those thinkers lived, if one did manage to live longer, the appropriate task and potential ability connected with being older was to contemplate the divine cosmos and seek wisdom. Plato thought that one should study philosophy, which he saw as the vehicle to overcome the illusions of life, only after the age of fifty. A contemporary thinker who reflects these views is Carl Jung, who is known as the psychologist of the second half of life. Nevertheless, it is important to emphasize that in the Greek tradition, the disciplines of knowledge were not discrete as they are today. Thus, the philosophical or rational study of wisdom was carried out for the purpose of acting correctly; it had a moral dimension and was not wisdom as knowledge for its own sake. Even in its theoretical form, it was practical and experiential (Holliday & Chandler, 1986).

Practical-Experiential

Wisdom is, to some extent, about thoughts and ideas and mental capacities; however, not for their own sake. The type of knowledge associated with wisdom is practical, related to the world, and based on experience. Furthermore, in most wisdom traditions, wisdom itself is a practice. Whether we look at the sweat lodges of the Native American tradition, the meditation practices of Buddhism and Hinduism, or the prayer regimens of Islam and Christianity, the emergence of wisdom is associated with a form of regular spiritual cultivation. As Spretnak (1991, pp. 8ff) notes, "a consideration of the wisdom traditions might stimulate spiritual practice, for they are entirely process-oriented, the teachings being mere supports for the experience of the practice."

In most traditions, wisdom thus involves an element of contemplation or personal reflection. This aspect of wisdom is a basic feature of our analysis here, namely "reading" for our unique wisdom story. In fact, in some traditions, there is really no contradiction between the hermit in the cave and the wise person who is politically active. Interesting examples of this are the Chinese Taoist and Buddhist hermits who, at various times in history, have been called on to lead their country or to serve in political office (Porter, 1993). The hermit tradition began in ancient China and continues today. As Porter (1993, p. 23) notes, "detached from values imposed by whim or custom, hermits have remained an integral part of Chinese society because of their commitment to their culture's own most ancient values"; in other words, to its spiritual and wisdom tradition. Whether one served in public life or lived in solitude, something that is considered more a matter of temperament than philosophy, "the aim remained the establishment and extension of harmony in the world" (Porter, 1993, p. 33). In other words, both paths follow the Tao and one need not be in a cave to be a hermit. Hermits have influenced the entire culture as springs of pure thinking and pure living that sooner or later find their way to town (Porter, 1993).

The difference between these wisdom traditions and postmodern life is that we have left out the receiving side of wisdom in favor of dominance and control through technical arrogance. In the traditions we have just discussed, and focusing on Buddhism in particular, there is a highly developed logic and a system of argumentation and debate. While clarity of thinking is a goal of Buddhist practice, this clarity does not emerge from thinking alone or from the manipulation of concepts and insights in books. Rather, it emerges from silence, which provides the vehicle to make our own whatever truths are available. From this point of view, it is the inability to sit still that has resulted in the postmodern spiritual malaise and the state of separateness that we described in Chapter 1. We have lost touch with our own wisdom that is, ultimately, there for the taking.

Interpersonal

In most traditions, wisdom is firmly embedded in relationships and social practice. This is the case explicitly in Judaism and Christianity in the West. It is also a dominant aspect of Islam, as well as of Confucianism as it is expressed in the cultures of China and Korea. In these traditions, the focus is on the concept of filial piety, or duty to family. Particularly in Confucianism, filial piety is said to be the main guiding moral principle, one that defines the very meaning of being in the world. For example, wisdom is derived from meaning in life as measured by the amount of good an older person does for family and society and from serving as an example for the younger generation.

The same insights are found in the Hindu tradition. There one progresses through a series of life stages that involve different degrees of emphasis on family and social commitments, on the one hand, and personal contemplation, on the other. The highest stage is represented by a person who, through the journey of his or her own story, is engaged in the world but not for solely personal ends (Chethimattam, 1982).

Wisdom as an interpersonal phenomenon is also found in the works of Eric Erikson (1963). There are similarities between his rendering of life-span development and the Hindu conception in the sense that a person travels through an inner journey that is inextricably tied to the world, for example, in the stage of trust versus mistrust. Later in life, the developmental task is about generativity or stagnation, that is, contributing to family and the world. In the final stage, the task or crisis involves putting the story of one's life together in such a way as to "respond to the need of the on-coming generation for an integrated heritage" (Cole & Winkler, 1994, p. 44). Wisdom, for Erikson, arises out of being able to transcend or detach from one's self-interests as an individual and therefore "balance the despair of the knowledge that a limited life is coming to a conscious conclusion" (Cole & Winkler, 1994, p. 45).

A focus on the interpersonal and social dimensions of wisdom is also evident in the early secular wisdom traditions dating back to ancient Egypt and continues to this day in the form of modern folk wisdom. In the words of Holliday and Chandler (1986, pp. 12ff), "the secular wisdom literature suggests that wisdom is social and interpersonal in nature, and that wise people exhibit exemplary understanding and behavior." Or, as Bianchi (1995, p. 197) puts it, "a person of wisdom understands human responsibility to the inward, the interpersonal, and the worldwide facets of existence." In taking this one step further, Robert Atkinson (1995), in discussing the work of Rollo May, identifies four symbols for the postmodern world that comprise a new mythology and focus for personal and collective wisdom. They are the symbol of one world, the symbol of interracialism, the symbol of women's liberation, and the symbol of an economic system that values the worker.

A contemporary author who focuses on the social and interpersonal nature of wisdom is John Meacham (1990). We discussed earlier his argument that a wise person would demonstrate a balance between knowledge and doubt. According to Holliday and Chandler (1986, p. 30), for Meacham, "wise people would be expected to excel in the application of their knowledge within a meaningful social context, to excel at asking questions, to be concerned with the nature and limitations of their knowledge, and to exhibit a balance of social and interpersonal qualities." We will discuss later the question concerning the generalizability of this form of wisdom expression. We note again at this point, however, the movement away from more cognitive interpretations of wisdom, that is, in terms of pure forms of knowledge accumulated over time.

A further intriguing point that Meacham (1990) raises concerns the issue of wisdom and age or wisdom and experience. Although this point applies to all people, in an ageist society, we are at risk of experiencing a decline in wisdom in the sense that we cannot be wise unless we are free to express our doubts and insecurities. Wisdom presupposes an ability to become detached from knowledge, success, power, and importance, which are the very things that we gain as adults and try to hang onto as long as we can. We need an environment that allows us to share our doubts and to hear the doubts of others. Otherwise, as Wilhelm Mader (1996, p. 59) argues, "there is a recourse to familiarities to fill the gap," and "repetitions are the indicators and fulfillers of this new state of self-regulating processes." As we experience loss with age, that is, we attempt to hang on to the biography we have already developed, even though it becomes loose around the edges and may even involve a paralyzing scepticism (Meacham, 1990). According to Meacham (1990, p. 209), "it is through the supportive and sharing relationships within a wisdom atmosphere that one gains the courage to engage in confident and wise action even in the face of one's doubts."

Ethical-Moral

A fundamental aspect of wisdom has to do with good intentions and appropriate actions. As the ancient Greeks put it, the wise person knows and does the Good. Among other things, this means that evil is not associated with wisdom and neither is ignorance. As Ardelt (1997, p. 16) notes, "reflective thinking and a diminished ego-centeredness lead to a deeper comprehension of the contradictions, imperfections, and negative aspects of human nature, a process that is likely to make a person more caring, empathic, and compassionate toward others." Whether someone lives a life of solitude or a life that is active and public, it seems to be the case that "sooner or later, wisdom gives rise to compassion. Sooner or later, the Tao comes to town" (Porter, 1993, p. 208). Moreover, wisdom is associated with being able to both "walk the walk" and "talk the talk"; that is, although no human being is perfect, wisdom is not only about insightful ideas or intellectual erudition. It is also about the ability and courage to act appropriately, to be part of the dilemma of involvement (Kenyon, 1991).

Furthermore, wise people can treat each situation with its own uniqueness. Being doctrinaire or applying universal principles does not appear to be part of wisdom, whereas contextual ethical insight does. We may have

knowledge of various precepts and commandments, which are often applied blindly across the board, but it is wisdom that makes these precepts
alive. It is this distinction that points up the difficulty of understanding
wisdom on the basis of the fictive situations we discussed earlier. In agreement with the cognitive tradition, wisdom does often emerge in important
matters of life. However, the matters in question are in *my* life or *your* life,
and they are here and now. Although he does not use the term *wise*, Donald Polkinghorne (1996b) addresses this insight in his discussion of the
process of counseling. Advanced or expert practitioners employ what he
calls "narrative understanding" to arrive at appropriate decisions concerning their biographical encounters with a client, whether it be to take a
walk, buy some new clothes, or set up a suicide watch on the client's be-
half.

However, unlike the expertise we referred to earlier in the context of cognition and wisdom, this action goes beyond logical and intellectual modes
of thinking and the application of universal principles. As Polkinghorne
(1996b, p. 732) notes, "the process through which these unique ideas arise
for responding to different clients occurs largely outside of awareness and is
not available to reflective inquiry. When questioned, expert practitioners
often cannot explain why they chose to act in the way they did; the helpful-
ness of their response can only be determined by examination of its consequences." These practitioners are wise, we could say, in that they have the
intention, and take the action, to allow the client to discover his or her own
wisdom story. In other words, in the encounter, that wisdom story is
coauthored, a process we will consider further in later chapters. The key is
that there is much more at work here than technical knowledge.

Idiosyncratic Expression

The fifth dimension of wisdom concerns its modes of idiosyncratic expression. Depending on the tradition under discussion, we can identify
many different faces of wisdom. This is one of the features of wisdom that
makes it so difficult to study. Wisdom might express itself as "cross-legged
immobility" (Holliday & Chandler, 1986), such as is represented in the
lives of Porter's Chinese hermits, in the late-life political activism of a
Bertrand Russell, or in the eccentric behavior of a Zen lunatic. Wisdom can
also express itself in words, such as in a well-written autobiography or in a
touch, in a look, or even in silence and simply *being there*. This subtlety of
the face of wisdom becomes further complicated when it is combined with
the dimension of intentions that we just discussed, an extreme illustration
of this being the psychopathic person who may behave "wisely" but not be
at all engaged in doing the good. As John Kekes (1983, p. 286) points out, "a
fool can learn to say all the things a wise man says, and to say them on the

same occasions." We will discuss the faces of wisdom in more detail in Chapter 4.

Spiritual-Mystical

Wisdom is fundamentally a spiritual phenomenon, since it has to do with meaning: meaning of life, of relationships, of ourselves, of the cosmos. The range of meaning extends from concern with everyday judgments in the cognitive tradition to the experience of ultimate enlightenment in the Buddhist tradition to union with God in the Christian tradition and everything in between. For example, in medieval Christian times, the more secular wisdom tradition of the Greeks underwent significant change. "Now the journey had become a pilgrimage to God," in the words of Tom Cole (1992, p. 10). In the Western Christian tradition, this view continued in some circles until the late nineteenth century. Again quoting Cole (1992, p. 158), "The old Protestant vision of life as a voyage, with its emphasis on introspection, on receiving experience as well as molding it, on reconciling past and future in the present, on yielding one's life up to its Maker, provided an inwardly viable ideal of continuity and meaning."

It is difficult to find a wisdom tradition that is not focused on this life and this world. We may speculate about death and wonder about the afterlife, and some traditions do apparently possess specific mystical views and beliefs concerning the human telos; however, no matter how esoteric these views are, there is usually an emphasis on how to live in the here and now. Wisdom comes in the form of knowing how to live, not in knowing what happens when we die, although these beliefs are not totally discrete in a particular wisdom tradition. This is reminiscent of the story about the student who asks the Zen master, "What happens to us when we die?" The Zen master replies, "I don't know." The student, upset, says, "But you are a Zen master." The master replies, "Yes, but I am not a dead one."

Contrary to a stereotypical view of it, which claims that, similar to existentialist philosophy, it is a life-denying philosophy, Buddhism is an excellent example of a wisdom tradition that addresses the fundamental human need to find love and meaning in the face of death. Beginning with the life of the Buddha, we see a sine qua non characteristic of wisdom in its extraordinary form, as well as its ordinary form. That basic characteristic is acceptance. The Buddha's first realization, the moment he became a traveler, was experienced when he encountered what have come to be called the four signs: an old person, a sick person, a corpse, and a wandering monk (Rinpoche, 1992). It was this experience that helped him eventually to accept and to see through the story of physical decline and suffering and to embrace the wisdom of a simultaneous potential spiritual ascent.

For the Buddhist, the process of aging has profound value. It represents the bodily record of the passage of time and a life of experiences. Aging reflects a movement toward more life and not less, and toward freedom from anxiety and confusion, which allows things such as joy and peace to arise. This outcome is not automatic, though, for it requires that we be willing to look at our life in meditation, as we discussed earlier, and to accept or make friends with all that we are within (Kirthisinghe, 1982). Moreover, this claim is not restricted to existentialism or Buddhism. As the narrative psychologist Dan McAdams (1994, p. 166) notes, "whether we are Christians, Jews, Muslims, agnostics, or 'other,' we are each alone responsible to engage in the heroic battle for meaning, waged on a precipice above the void."

In discussing wisdom, and as we will consider in more detail later, it is important to distinguish between acceptance and resignation. Philosophically and psychologically, these two terms have very different meanings. *Resignation* means giving up to something that is a fait accompli. It has a depressive connotation and is associated with despair. In contrast, *acceptance* involves a giving in but not a giving up. In the Taoist wisdom tradition, as it is practiced in arts such as tai chi, acceptance is expressed as yielding and adhering. Eugene Bianchi (1995, p. 223) explains: "One deals with persons and events in adaptive but effective ways, just as water naturally conforms itself to an obstructing rock by going around it. The Taoist elder, who has learned to enter into the life of wu wei, became a model for others. As a teacher and paradigm, such an old person served the community, showing others important turns on the path to wisdom." In such traditions, wisdom is a function of being able to, as we say, go with the flow. In the final analysis, therefore, acceptance is a life-affirming experience. However, wisdom in the form of acceptance does involve loss. As evidenced in all traditions, the process of spirituality is, paradoxically, one of growth through diminishment or, using Taoist language again, of investing in loss. We are invited and often pushed by life to lose the old and smaller story of both ourselves and our world in favor of a new and larger one.

The key is that this diminishment has nothing to do with passivity or with what, in terms of gerontological theory, is called disengagement. Rather, depending on the tradition, whether it be through prayer, meditation, or other forms of restorying our lives, including accidental ones, we find wisdom and meaning *in* the human condition. As Bianchi (1995, p. 181) notes, "to find significance in diminishments calls for faith and hope. One has faith that beneath, through, and beyond the diminishments there is a life-giving power that will draw special good for humanity and the world of nature from the diminishments." Other spiritual terms associated with wisdom, which we will consider in the following chapters, are *humility* (knowing less and being more), *communion* and *presence* (Kenyon,

1996a), and *generativity* (McAdams, 1996), not to mention *love* and *compassion* and even *humor*.

FROM EXTRAORDINARY TO ORDINARY WISDOM

The foregoing characterization of wisdom raises some intriguing questions. For example, is wisdom one thing or many? In other words, as we consider the six dimensions of wisdom we have just discussed, can we say that they all add up to a kind of ideal type of wisdom? Conversely, can we reduce them to one essential characteristic? Is wisdom in the final analysis a special form of knowledge, a quality of relationships, or a spiritual insight into the nature of things? These are questions that have been asked for some time and will no doubt be the focus of inquiry in the future as well. Different traditions emphasize different aspects of wisdom, yet it is possible that they all end up in the same place—the perennial philosophy again. Because wisdom is connected to people, wisdom traditions may reflect different temperaments and, as we call it in Chapter 3, different storying styles.

In this book, we will not be providing any direct answers to these weighty philosophical questions. And yet, we will be providing support for the view that wisdom is intimately related to how each of us sees the world and our place within it. In other words, we are less concerned with what wisdom is from the outside and more concerned with what it is from the inside. Whether wisdom is one thing or many is a question for future research. However, this need not hinder our more practical purposes of identifying ordinarily wise persons and discussing conditions for facilitating a wisdom environment. We now move to a characterization of ordinary wisdom based on the dimensions and traditions we have just considered as well as on examples of ordinarily wise people. As we do, we hope to contribute to the adventure of understanding the nature of wisdom, a phenomenon that deserves equal measures of caution, humility, and wonder.

From our review of wisdom traditions, we can state with confidence, then, that there is such a thing as wisdom and that there are indeed wise people, examples of whom, both historically and presently, can be readily provided. The interesting question becomes, therefore, whether wisdom is something that is attributable only to the extraordinary and specially selected few. Or are such people merely more obvious examples of something that is part of the human heritage and human destiny in general? In other words, is wisdom a question of degree and not ultimately of kind? If we follow authors such as Baltes and Smith (1990), who focus on wisdom in terms of cognition, then we arrive at the view that wisdom, as expertise, is reserved for the few, since experts are rare. Moreover, it is strongly associated with age, since it takes many years to become an expert. The implication here is that only older people can be wise and that very few of them are. In other words, very few of us learn from life and from our experiences.

At another extreme, Buddhists are wary of prejudging who is wise on the basis of age or presumed expertise, since the doctrine of reincarnation implies that one's teacher in a former life may be one's student now. Moreover, wise teachers may disguise themselves in very ordinary costumes in order to benefit those whom they are trying to help, this being another example of the dimension of wisdom that we describe as its idiosyncratic expression. Thus, while there are clearly identifiable extraordinary faces of wisdom that are culturally accepted as guidelines or role models, this does not exhaust the possible range of wisdom stereotypes—or "storyotypes," as we shall call them in Chapter 3.

There are special roles and special persons to whom we attribute extraordinary wisdom: shamans, monks, gurus, priests, experts, and so on. These representatives of wisdom are often claimed to possess transcendental knowledge, which can come from personal experience and training, about human life and death and about the cosmos. At the same time, most wisdom traditions tell us that we are all made of the same stuff, that we are all Christs or Buddhas. It follows, then, that we all may potentially possess this extraordinary wisdom in varying degrees and at different times in our lives. In Chapter 1, we discussed the fact that if we can identify wise people, it is because we have something of this extraordinary quality in us, even though most of us may not recognize it, may not have looked for it, and may have trouble living it.

Why, then, do we say that some people are extraordinarily wise? Sometimes it is because they make what we think are wise judgments (cognition), because they are contemplative (practical-experiential), because they are compassionate (interpersonal), because they have special insight (spiritual-mystical), because they have high values or are courageous (ethical-moral), or because they laugh a lot or look peaceful (idiosyncratic expression). In the chapters that follow, we hope to show that many of these same dimensions of wisdom can be found in our own lives. Once we focus our lens properly, therefore, we may see many more wise people around us. That is to say, wisdom is both extraordinary and ordinary at the same time. In addition to this, we also hope to show that there is a potential for more wisdom in the world, whether this be attained by following existing wisdom traditions, such as those we have just outlined, or by facilitating the personal and societal conditions that will better enable us to see and celebrate our lives as both stories and journeys.

3

Biographical Aging:
Life as Story

Biologically, physiologically, we are not so different from each other; historically, as narratives—we are each of us unique.

—Oliver Sacks (1985)

We turn our pain into narrative so we can bear it; we turn our ecstasy into
narrative so we can prolong it. . . . We tell our stories to live.

—John Shea (1978)

THE POETICS OF WISDOM

In the last chapter, we reviewed the ups and downs of wisdom as a topic
for official consideration in philosophy and social science. In the process,
we sketched the shape of ordinary wisdom and indicated what we see as
its principal dimensions. As this exercise should have made clear, wisdom
is still a meaningful concept. That it has fallen from grace is through no
fault of its own. It is not wisdom that is the problem so much as the limiting
frameworks within which we have attempted to conceive it and to cast our
questions concerning it. Our aim in this book is to address such limitations
by enlisting alternative ways for envisioning what wisdom is.

Exploring a topic this venerable, yet still this uncharted, requires that we
stock up on all available resources. Chief among such resources has always
been metaphor, our main linguistic link between the familiar and the unfamiliar, the known and the unknown (Ortony, 1979; Lakoff & Johnson,
1980). In the last chapter we alluded to the restrictiveness of the metaphor

that has implicitly guided much of cognitive science in its conception of wisdom, namely mind-as-computer or thinking-as-computation (Bruner, 1990; H. Gardner, 1985). We are ready, then, to ponder the extraordinary potential of two more ordinary metaphors to point to the wealth of the wisdom within us. They are life as *story* and life as *journey*.

As we have already indicated, these two tropes are intimately entwined: Journeys generally issue in stories and stories commonly recount journeys. In this chapter, however, we shall focus on story per se. In the next, we shall concentrate on journey, and in the one after that, on a blend of the two, namely life as *adventure*. In the Epilogue, we shall return briefly to story again as we envision a "wisdom atmosphere" (Meacham, 1990) or, as we call it, wisdom environment, in which age is essentially irrelevant and in which, through respectful coauthoring, we naturally evoke the wisdom in each other's lives.

The thesis of this chapter is simple: Wisdom inhabits lifestory in the same way that meaning pervades literature. This means we can approach a discussion of it through the gateway of poetics as much as of psychology, by the route of aesthetics as much as of ethics. Equally simple is the corrollary of our thesis: We access our own wisdom only by telling "the story of my life"—that is, by getting it out and then stepping back from it to investigate and interpret it: in short, to *read* it. Such a thesis has a common-sense ring to it. It strikes us as essentially right. Each of us has a unique story—scarcely anything seems more obvious—and because of this story, each of us has a unique message. Each of us has a set of questions to pose to the world and a collection of lessons to pass on to others. Each of us has our own special truth. Though in the world of lives around us, and in our own lives as well, there is surely much foolishness and failure, there is unlimited wisdom as well. For all of our stumbling, as Rinpoche reminded us earlier, we still manage to be wise. As appealing as our thesis may be, however, it is deceptively subtle. On analysis, "the story of my life" proves as extraordinary a concept—indeed, as odd a concept—as we can probably imagine.

Our plan in this chapter is to explore the poetics of wisdom through a host of intertwining insights and issues. Unfortunately, they are so intertwining that dealing with them one at a time is not only incredibly difficult to do but highly arbitrary as well. Once we consider the poetics of anything, once we adopt a "narrative perspective" (Randall, in press), we encounter a paradox that is intrinsic to story's "strange logic" (Brooks, 1985). A story may unfold in linear fashion, event by event, but, like life, it concerns a multitude of matters at once, such as relationships, politics, learning, and faith. In addition, far from being separate components, its constituent aspects (Forster, 1962), such as plot, character, and theme, are different dimensions of a common dynamic whole, none of which can be considered on its own. The same holds for the topic of wisdom. We cannot talk about wisdom without talking about intelligence in its many (and not strictly cognitive) forms. Moreover, we cannot talk about intelligence without talking about learning. Nor can we talk about learning without talking about memory. Nor can we talk about any of these without also talking about language and imagination, personality and identity, time and the self.

Despite the difficulty then of proceeding in a logical manner, we begin with a brief discussion of biographical aging. Then we assess the merits of the metaphor that is implicit in the concept of such aging, that of *life as story:* a metaphor we later extend to speak of the *novelty* of a life. Next, we examine the process of textualization whereby a life is transformed into a life*story* in the first place. After considering the role of what we call narrative intelligence in the everyday storying of our lives, we also look at the narrative structure of so-called autobiographical memory. Specifically, we look at how it is a repository not of facts ultimately but of a peculiar brand of faction (Steele, 1986), which looks to the future as much as to the past and which mediates its own type of truth (Eakin, 1985). We then look at the levels on which the very notion of lifestory can be taken, for, as we have suggested, its meaning is not as obvious as we might assume. In particular, we focus on what we call the "inside" story.

Next, we touch on how our personal stories—and thus the wisdom they embody—are invariably shaped by the various larger stories we live our lives within. This will prepare us for speculating briefly in the Epilogue on how various narrative environments (Bruner, 1990) either invite or inhibit the expression of our ordinary wisdom and, in the process, uniquely coauthor it in both content and form. Then, taking lifestory as essentially a genre of literary story, we get to the chapter's core, where we consider the question of the wisdom in stories, beginning with the question of how stories mean and moving to the related question of how lifestories mean. This will prepare us in Chapter 5 to discuss what is involved in reading our lives for the unique wisdom that lies, as it were, in our story, our whole story, and nothing but our story. In that same chapter, we will peek at the implications of seeing life—even late life—as an adventure, a journey into the unknown, a process of continual, sometimes intentional, restorying (Kenyon & Randall, 1997).

Evident in this chapter are the six dimensions of wisdom we identified in Chapter 2. Indeed, these serve as a framework for the entire book, helping us to see that extraordinary and ordinary wisdom are different only in degree, not in kind. The cognitive dimension will be reflected in our discussion of narrative intelligence and of autobiographical memory. The practical-experiential dimension will emerge in our focus on lived stories, in contrast to abstract problem solving. The interpersonal dimension will be apparent as we discuss the larger stories we live within, while the dimension of idiosyncratic expression will become obvious as we consider both the inside story and the novelty of our lives. The moral-ethical dimension will surface in our consideration of the parabolic nature of lifestories; and the spiritual-mystical dimension, in our emphasis on the meaning-creating that is central to a life when we view it from the standpoint of story.

BIOGRAPHICAL AGING

One of our guiding assumptions is that human beings change—and age—not just physically and physiologically, and not just socially and cognitively, but in ways that until recently have been left largely unexamined. We age biographically as well (Birren et al., 1996). We age with respect to our inner, subjective experience, both over time and of time—past, present, and future. We age with respect to the memories we fashion from, the interpretations we place on, and the meanings we ascribe to the events and circumstances of our lives. We age with respect to the images and metaphors, the myths and stories, by which we construct our beliefs and conduct our affairs. We age with respect to how we author and narrate, how we read and revise, the stories by which we live.

Seeing aging from this angle is a profound shift from most mainstream gerontological thought and stems from a very different starting point. It is not a nomothetic (Runyan, 1984) one, whose goal, like that for instance of traditional psychology, is prediction and control (Sarbin, 1994, p. 7), but rather a narrative one, whose goal is understanding. In other words, the starting point is rooted in the metaphor of story (Sarbin, 1986b). To appreciate such biographical aging, or such "biographicity" (Alheit, 1995), is to begin and end, then, with the view that "we interpret reality through our stories" (Schank, 1990, p. 44). It is to consider what psychologist Jerome Bruner (1987) calls the development of autobiography, which is to say, "how our way of telling about ourselves changes, and how these accounts come to take control of our ways of life" (p. 15).

Where studies of other aspects of our lives—whether the psychological or social, the medical or biological—give us essentially an outside view of the aging process, a sensitivity to their narrative aspects, or their biographical aspects, gives us, then, an inside view, for "biography is the way the world *is* for someone" (Ruth & Kenyon, 1996a, p. 5). Memories of our life as a child, of the ups and downs of our career, our marriage, our family; recollections of past achievements and disappointments, of happy times and tragic times; dreams of where our life might lead us still . . . *our story* is what we have. In a sense, it is all we have. It is what we are. Indeed, "the story *is* the Self" (p. 7, emphasis ours). "No story, no self," states Bruner bluntly (1999, p. 8). Such sensitivity to the narrative nature of who we are opens up the exhilarating possibility that autobiographical development—what Freeman (1993) calls "rewriting the self" and we have termed "restorying" (Kenyon & Randall,

1997)—is endless. Old age thus need not be seen as a useless appendage to an otherwise meaningful life but as the final, yet unfinishable, phase in the process of self-creation (Randall, 1995), in the art of living, or in what Mary Catharine Bateson calls composing a life (1989, 1993).

To think in terms of biographical aging is to participate in what we described earlier as the narrative turn in the human sciences. It is therefore to press past perceptions of aging construed in terms of statistics or the medical model or the often confining categories of modern social science. Instead, it is to entertain insights that originate equally in philosophy or history or literature—in short, in the humanities and the arts. Only by drawing from such disparate fields, we believe, can we open a space that is sufficiently wide for the topic of wisdom to be acknowledged and explored. Within that space, wisdom has to do with meaning-making processes that are not only lifelong in duration but essentially aesthetic—or, as we would say, poetic—in nature. These processes, at work in all of us all of the time, shape insights into ourselves and our world that are unique and therefore extraordinary in nature; insights that can be liberated, moreover, as we learn to read the many-layered texts that have accumulated within us throughout our otherwise ordinary lives.

LIFE AS STORY

As more and more scholars are voicing from more and more corners, "story" and "narrative" (and, like many, we interchange the two) have much to recommend them as conceptual tools. Besides gerontology, the corners in question include psychology, psychotherapy, and psychoanalysis, as well as theology, sociology, anthropology, history, and philosophy. This popularity in itself, plus the degree to which story can be seen as integral to emotion, action, and experience, indeed to selfhood itself, qualifies narrative eminently, we believe, for the status of what philosopher Karl Popper calls a "root metaphor" (Sarbin, 1986a; Kenyon & Randall, 1999). In support of such a status, Theodore Sarbin (1986a, 1994) proposes that human thought and action are ultimately guided by "the narratory principle"; indeed, our very survival depends on it. "Survival in a world of meanings," he argues, "is problematic without the talent to make up and to interpret stories about interweaving lives" (1986a, p. 11). For evidence of this principle, he says, "we can reflect on any slice of life":

Our dreams . . . are experienced as stories, as dramatic encounters, often with mythic shadings. It is a commonplace that our fantasies and our daydreams are unvoiced stories. The rituals of daily life are organized to tell stories. The pageantry of rites of passage and rites of intensification are storied actions. Our plannings, our rememberings, even our loving and hating, are guided by narrative plots.

We agree with Sarbin's claim. Since another of our guiding assumptions is that metaphor is essential to thinking about anything (Schroots, Birren, & Kenyon, 1991; Lakoff & Johnson, 1980), we take *story* as our starting point in thinking about wisdom. Given that stories, storytelling, and story interpreting have been under our noses since the dawn of civilization, it is rather ironic, however, that it is only recently that we have seen them as clues to how we make sense of our world. In contrast, hardly had the steam engine been invented but Freud was writing about the "drives" and "mechanisms" that run the human psyche. In the same way, the development of the digital computer coincides uncannily with the rise of cognitive science and its conviction that human thought—including memory and ultimately wisdom—comes down to "the processing of information" and is at bottom a business of "input" and "output," of "encoding" and "storage" and "retrieval" (see Bruner, 1990).

Story's recent emergence as an aid to understanding human nature becomes less of a mystery, however, when we remind ourselves not only of its endurance but also of its omnipresence. Notwithstanding nostalgic (though not unwarranted) laments over the decline of the storytelling traditions of days gone by (Benjamin, 1969), one look around us quickly confirms that story per se abounds more than ever. Hardly a moment of our day is not bombarded with stories of this sort or that, whether through movies, news, or magazines; through ballads, ads, or books; or through the story-sharing that is the core of conversation and thus the heart of human interaction. And this goes for the story-*forming* as well, insofar as we are constantly constructing "likely stories" about each other's lives, positive or negative, and then behaving as if these stories were true. All of this says nothing, of course, of the strange stories that assault us as we dream.

Story is everywhere. It is closer than breathing, as Tennyson might say: too close to see, too immediate to identify, too near to analyze with easy dispassion. It is to you and me as water is to fish. We breathe it with each breath, think it with each thought, believe it with each belief. We live by story and in story, and story lives in us. The same claims could scarcely be made of computers or machines. What is exciting, then, is to be able to employ something so intensely familiar for such an immensely long time to ponder a topic whose delineation has eluded us equally long: the topic of wisdom. Obliged until now to draw on metaphors whose conceptual potential is comparatively pale, with story we have a fresh opportunity to consider what wisdom is.

But what is story? One thing is certain: It is not nearly as familiar as it seems. As with realities such as energy, life, and time, everybody knows what story is, yet the question, What is a story? is as hard to answer as it is easy to ask (Leitch, 1986). As noted by writer Ursula Le Guin (1989, p. 37), "through long practice, I know how to tell a story, but I'm not sure I know what a story is." While something so ubiquitous ought to be obvious, it remains a "conceptually elusive entity" (White, 1980, p. 13f). Nonetheless, perhaps we can say something about story, or at least if not what it is, then what it does, what functions it fulfills.

Story is a structure for time. Whether it be told formally or informally, with words or pictures, in gestures or speech, through history or fiction, movies or news, rumors or dreams, a story is a vehicle for recalling the past, processing the present, and imagining the future. It is a medium for meaning as well. Thus, like wisdom, it has a cognitive dimension. It is our principal means of making sense and of communicating that sense to others. If you will, it is how we humanize our world, how we fashion a home within it. And it is how, for better or for worse, we are entwined with each other in bonds of family and friendship, compassion and competition, treachery and trust. It is to the social universe what gravity is to the physical one: the strange force that, more or less, holds things together. Given that story plays such a grand role in the midst of our everyday lives, it should come as no surprise, then, that we wish to invoke it as a metaphor for life and have enlisted it for our inquiry into wisdom. But how do we get from life to lifestory?

FROM LIFE TO LIFESTORY

As we have begun to see, pivotal to the postmodern critique of modern science are two important insights concerning the nature of knowledge. The first is that we have no knowledge of reality in itself. What we know is what is mediated through our senses, on the one hand, and through language, on the other. Our senses filter the world for us, leaving in this but leaving out that, while language articulates and interprets those data that our senses perceive. This insight has profound implications for our conception of both the process and product of the scientific method in the natural sciences and social sciences alike. Contrary to what we may have assumed, what that method yields is not truth in some direct, objective form but only an interpretation. It is not the whole story of the nature of things but merely an edited, expurgated, always provisional version.

Another way of putting this is to say that the world is mediated to us by means of a process of textualization, that is, by turning the data of our senses into accessible images and words. It is through such textualization that we experience both the world around us and our existence within it. Indeed, our experience is precisely that: our experience. It is not the world as it is, in all its blooming, buzzing confusion. It is not the raw facts but only our internalized interpretations of such facts as those to which we can attend. Reality as we can know it is thus a representation, one that is textual and textured all the way down, insofar as our interpretations are texts themselves in turn.

The same principle applies to ourselves. We can experience our own existence only by transforming it into text. In a sense, life as text (McAdams, 1994)—or the text analogy (White & Epston, 1990)—is prior to life as story. We are present to ourselves, available to ourselves, accessible to ourselves, only as a set of (infinitely interpretible) texts. This is how we know ourselves, indeed, all we *can* know of ourselves. We have no direct, unmediated grasp of anything about our lives—least of all, of their so-called facts. The faculties of memory and imagination by which we apprehend such facts inevitably refract them, as does the very language by which, using these faculties, we tell ourselves (and others) what is going on. Insist Jerome Bruner and Susan Weisser: "It is only by textualization that one can 'know' one's life" (1991, p. 129).

An overall image for this textualizing process is Bateson's metaphor we referred to earlier, that of composing a life. Taking this metaphor and working from the premise that "there is no such thing psychologically as 'life itself'" (Bruner, 1987), what we call our life is thus not some set of physical-social-psychological givens that we passively receive but a complex creation that we actively fashion. It is a tapestry we continually weave from the threads of chance, the strands of circumstance, and the fabric of relationships that comprise our existence on a day-to-day basis.

A second insight is twofold. The structures of language are, first, socially shaped and, second, narrative in nature (Turner, 1996). Pulling these points together, our experience of both the world and ourselves is socially constructed *through* narratives (Rubin, 1996; Gubrium & Holstein, 1998). In a later section, we shall consider the first part of this insight: the social construction of our stories by the larger stories we live within. As for the second part, all language, we could say, has narrative roots. We mean much more by this, however, than that we must use language to narrate our experiences. We mean that story structures reach down into and are, in fact, inseparable from the structures of language itself. The basic subject-verb-object arrangement that, in English at least, underlies the average sentence essentially tells a little tale: about someone doing something. As one scholar sees it, language is "the child of the literary mind" (Turner, 1996). In short, we know our life only by narrativizing it, by narrating it (McAdams, 1996), by construing it in narrative terms (Bruner, 1996). Indeed, "know" and "narrate" possess the same etymological root (Mancusco & Sarbin, 1983).

Deep in our memory and imagination, we continually transform events into episodes, circumstances into sequences, situations into plots. It is thus that the stuff of our life becomes the story of our life. Indeed, from a narrative perspective, this is what memory and imagination are: the means by which we continually story our lives in time—past, present, and future. Accordingly, our sense of our self, our self-concept, or our identity (McAdams, 1996) is thoroughly narrativized, as are our emotions (Nussbaum, 1989; Singer, 1996), our actions (MacIntyre, 1981; Ochberg, 1995), our decisions

(Tappan & Brown, 1989), our values and relationships, and even our mode of experiencing itself (Crites, 1971, 1986). None of these can be explained apart from an appreciation of the stories we are. Bruner captures this insight succinctly when he asserts that "a life as lived is inseparable from a life as told" (1987, p. 3). Or, as we would say, a life is inseparable from the story of a life. But as we look more closely at the life-lifestory link, we must ask how we story our lives in the first place.

NARRATIVE INTELLIGENCE

Central to the transformation of life into lifestory and of raw events into experiencable episodes, we would propose, is narrative intelligence, a capacity on which psychology has been remarkably mute. Although we have been telling stories for eons, the actual skills involved in doing so have received comparatively little attention. As a concept, intelligence is of course only marginally more manageable than wisdom. Yet, for some reason, the study of it has been tackled with great enthusiasm as not merely manageable but measurable as well, at least in terms of particular types of cognition, especially logical and numerical ones. As we have seen, it is to these that many of our modern conceptions of wisdom have tended to be tied. Researchers such as Howard Gardner (1990), however, have opened the way for intelligence (and, by implication, wisdom) to be conceived outside of the strictly cognitive realm. Indeed, he believes we must talk in terms of multiple intelligences instead, of which he cites seven: linguistic, musical, logical-mathematical, bodily-kinesthetic, spatial, interpersonal, and intrapersonal. "At the core of each intelligence," he says,

exists a computational capacity, or information-processing device, which is unique to that particular intelligence, and upon which are based the more complex realizations and embodiments of that intelligence . . . phonological and grammatical processing in the case of language; tonal and rhymthic processing in the case of music . . . each intelligence has one or more "raw" computational cores. (p. 278)

Since Gardner's important work, other types of intelligence have also been proposed, of which emotional intelligence (Goleman, 1995) is a popular example. Given the increasing attention being paid to the narrative root metaphor, another one that must be considered, we believe, is narrative intelligence. Closely linked to Gardner's linguistic and personal intelligences, narrative intelligence, we suggest, possesses its own kind of computational core.

In support of such a capacity is the thesis of Jerome Bruner (1986, 1987), which states that there are two fundamental modes of thought by which we make sense of our world: paradigmatic (or logical) thought and narrative thought. Where the former has been the mode most espoused in philosophy and science, and the most venerated in formal education, the latter is the principal mode in both the literary arts and, more important, in everyday life. In his novel, *Scar Tissue*, philosopher Michael Ignatieff (1993) advances a similar distinction: between propositional intelligence and autobiographical intelligence.

Related to narrative thought is narrative knowing, which Donald Polkinghorne (1988) sees as the fundamental method by which we make sense of our world, our surroundings, our relationships, and ourselves. Linked closely to this, of course, is what John Robinson and Linda Hawpe (1986) call narrative thinking—or, simply, storying (p. 123). Still another is narrative imagining, which, according to Mark Turner (1996) in *The Literary Mind*, is "the fundamental instrument of thought . . . our chief means of looking into the future, of predicting, of planning, and of explaining . . . indispensable to human cognition generally." Indeed, arguing compellingly that action is only possible at all because of our unconscious ability to compose small stories to explain what we are doing and what is going on, Turner insists that "the everyday mind [is] essentially literary" (p. 47). As if this were not enough, some educators have called for nothing less than a complete revamping of our K–12 educational system to involve what Richard Hopkins (1994) calls narrative schooling. With narrative being connected, then, to knowing, thinking, imagining, and even schooling, surely it is a short semantic leap to suggest we connect it to intelligence too.

Put simply, narrative intelligence entails, firstly, the ability to follow a story, "followability" being a basic criteria for defining what a story is (Kerby, 1991). Following a story means being able to make sense of it, being able to "read" it. In addition, we propose, narrative intelligence involves the capacity to formulate, or tell, a story too. Such a definition of narrative intelligence, as the capacity both to follow and to formulate stories, parallels what Roger Schank (1990, p. 6) says of intelligence per se: "Knowledge," he writes, "is experiences and stories, and intelligence is the apt use of experience and the creation and telling of stories." Against the background of such a conviction, in fact, he effectively dissolves the familiar distinction between episodic memory and semantic memory by calling the former story-based and the latter generalized event-based (p. 119).

This latter category is akin to what Neisser (1986) calls repisodic memory. Such memory is formed through the repetition of so many similar episodes—such as dealing with dogs or flying in planes—that a kernel of knowledge eventually settles out; for instance, dogs usually bark and planes normally land. In any case, some people are obviously in greater possession of this capacity than others insofar as they seem capable of following and formulating stories of considerable complexity and depth. But without the ability to follow a story at all, we would argue, human beings would be unable to function, unable to make sense of their ever changing circumstances, unable to comprehend the actions of others or to carry out their own actions in a coherent and more or less purposeful manner. Narrative intelligence is thus essential to composing a life. Insofar as we can live at all only by storying our world, we must all be narratively intelligent to at least a minimal degree.

As we have said, what a story is, is not easy to say, nor shall we dare a definition here. However, we routinely think of a story—any story—as possessing certain central elements, such as plot, character, point of view, genre, and theme. Accordingly, narrative intelligence could be said to involve such specific and intertwining subabilities as our ability to emplot, to characterize, to narrate, to genre-ate, and to thematize. Although we have elaborated these abilities elsewhere (Randall, 1999), a quick survey of them will assist us here.

Emplot

To emplot is to edit. It is to notice some aspects of a given event but to ignore others. It is also to summarize, which means to distill actual events into manageable, memorable form. Over time, however, these same summaries become overlaid by and lost under our summaries of subsequent events in turn. Of greatest importance about this inveterate editing is that we obviously forget far more than we remember. Most of our life is consigned to the cutting floor. The question of what we remember versus what we forget, and of why we remember what we remember and forget what we forget, is absolutely central to biographical aging. None of us deals with "a completely remembered life" (Phillips, 1994, p. 69). Indeed, it is impossible to know what such a life would even look like, let alone whether it is something we could actually live.

To emplot is also to compare and contrast what is happening in the present with remembered happenings in the past and anticipated ones in the future. Indeed, says David Carr (1986, p. 60), "the present is only possible for us if it is framed and set off against a retained past and a potentially envisaged future." To emplot, then, is to correlate our past to our present and future, and not to be stuck in one time-sense alone. A person who lived exclusively in the past, present, or future would experience incalculable difficulty functioning "normally" in the everyday world.

To emplot is to link individual events into coherent, interrelated sequences. It is to construct explanatory accounts to interpret what is happening in a given context or situation in terms of origins and outcomes, influences and results, causes and consequences. It is to sense the connectedness among otherwise disparate occurences and discern cause-effect relationships between them. For example: I went to the grocer's this morning, bought this pasta I'm preparing for supper and that I'll finish for tomorrow's lunch.

To emplot is also to perceive events in the first place. It is to see situations, relationships, lives, individual days, and so forth, as having their distinctive beginnings, middles, and ends (Polster, 1987), as going or leading somewhere, as unfolding in some kind of direction or toward some kind of conclusion.

To emplot is to intuit the basic story line in the accounts by which others explain what is happening and to keep it more or less straight in our minds, interconnecting the events they recount so that they constitute dynamic, coherent wholes that we can thereby comprehend. To emplot is to recognize conflict (inner, outer, interpersonal, intrapersonal, and so forth), to identify its possible sources and elements, and to seek, desire, or envision some sort of resolution to it. To emplot is to determine what is relevant or expedient in a given situation—that is, what furthers or frustrates a particular, desired outcome and is, in that sense, good or bad—and so edit from our immediate awareness any details we may deem unimportant and inconsequential.

Characterize

To characterize is to form a working picture of what other people are like and, by means of this picture, to imagine their thoughts and feelings and to predict their possible actions and reactions in particular situations. Highly developed, this ability manifests itself in us as a talent for either mimicking other people or feeling compassion for them or both.

To characterize is to reformulate our pictures of other people in the light of new evidence about them and so not stay stuck with first impressions. It is to compare and contrast our picture of one person with pictures we have formed in the past of others and then to construct a theory, fair or not, as to what type of person they are. In more developed forms, it is to appreciate the storied uniqueness—or novelty—of each new person so as not to pre-judge them completely but, rather, to try and learn their whole story before settling on an official version of what they are like.

To characterize is, most importantly, to form a working picture (a moving picture, as in ever revisable) of what we ourselves are like, a self-image or a self-concept or a personal myth (Atkinson, 1995; Feinstein, Krippner, & Granger, 1988; Keen, 1993). It is to see that we are the hero of our own story, in the sense not so much of "heroic" as of the one who is ultimately the central character amid our own unfolding life plot. It is also to compose comparable characterizations of ourselves that we recall or imagine having been in the past and that we guess or envision going on to become in the future.

Narrate

To narrate is to communicate to others what has gone on in the past, is going on in the present, and may go on in the future in a relatively sensible manner—that is, with a sensitivity to what they will understand in terms of logical connections between one event and another, between causes and effects, and so on. Again, some of us seem to have more developed abilities in this regard than do others. As Henry James once said, "stories seem to happen to people who can tell them" (Bruner, 1987).

To narrate is to use the basic storytelling conventions of the linguistic or cultural context in which we are trying to communicate and so recount events in ways that maximize our audience's engagement in what we are saying, that is, in terms of background information, cause-effect relations, and so on.

To narrate is to summarize the central action of a given occurrence after the fact, in a way that captures its core dynamic of development, thickening, and narrowing, and that, depending on our audience, includes neither too much detail nor too little. To narrate is also to portray ourselves as an "I" or "me" who is a protagonist or character in the midst of the activities we narrate (Berman, 1994) and yet know that it is both connected to and distinct from the other "I" or "me" who is doing the narrating.

Genre-ate

To genre-ate is to construe events in our lives, in other's lives, and in situations around us in such a way that we can discern the difference between, for example, a good mood and a bad mood or between optimism and pessimism. Given Shakespeare's observation that "nothing is either good or bad but thinking makes it so," to genre-ate is to perceive or interpret a person or event as basically tragic, comical, romantic, adventurous, or ironic (see Bruner, 1996; Gergen & Gergen, 1983).

Thematize

To thematize is to sense certain recurring patterns of meaning—motifs, metaphors, or myths—running both through particular situations and through lives overall, whether our own or others'. It is also to be aware of how such patterns are introduced, developed, alluded to, dealt with, and resolved (see Csikszentimihalyi & Beattie, 1979; Kaufman, 1986). It is to identify symbols at work amid the unfoldings of our lives and to be able to play with theories as to their application or relevance. It is to read a series of statements or behaviors, gestures or events (our own or others') as mediating a particular message or meaning or point.

These various operations—emplotment, characterization, narration, genre-ation, thematizing—are fundamental to narrative intelligence, we believe, and thus to how we continually story our lives. Though we would argue that such intelligence is basic to us all, and is effectively hardwired into the apparatus by which we make meaning out of our existence (see Campbell, 1989), it seems reasonable that its experience and expression can be expected to change as we pass through the natural stages of psychosocial development. In early childhood, for instance, the sort of story we can follow from others' lips and formulate with our own is generally less complicated and less sophisticated than what we can follow and formulate at subsequent stages—say, in adolescence, early adulthood, or middle and old age. For this reason, we do not normally inflict Shakespeare's plays on four-year-olds, while the exploits of *The Hardy Boys* seldom sustain serious debate among tenured professors exploring the finer points of literary theory. As we mature, we tend to put away childish stories. That we also tend to put away the childish stories by which we understand our own lives is the possibility this chapter assumes.

The maturation of our narrative intelligence is presumably tied to our development in a variety of areas at once, from a gradually expanding vocabulary to an increasing degree of personal independence (which requires us to explain many things for ourselves) and of general complexity in our everyday lives. Sooner or later, such an increase pushes us to increased alertness to the nuances and levels of meaning in what others say, not to mention in our own thoughts and feelings as well. But if we learned no literary competence (Culler, cited in Spence, 1982) whatsoever in school, if we learned neither how to tell nor how to read (or listen to) stories, if we remained literarily illiterate, we would be seriously impoverished in terms of the exercise of our own native, narrative intelligence in interpreting and navigating our world.

It is understandable that much attention has been paid by educators, psychologists, and cognitive scientists to the acquisition of basic narrative grammar (Mancusco, 1986) in childhood, since in that phase of the life cycle we stand on the threshold of a lifetime of making meaning, and telling stories is the principal means by which such meaning gets made (see also Gardner, 1982; Turner, 1996). However, how many studies trace the development of or changes in our narrative intelligence across the whole life span in the way, for example, that changes in hearing capacity have been studied, or in eyesight or short-term memory? The growing number of studies that are considering the stories of people suffering from dementia is, of course, a welcome trend (see Crisp, 1995; Holst, Edberg, & Hallberg, 1999; Hallberg, in press) in this regard, and it is helping to impress on us that, regardless of our mental state, we do not cease being stories.

In general, however, given the critical importance of narrative intelligence in making our way through everyday life, it is only fair that we exercise an equal curiosity about what happens to our narrative competence toward the end of the life span as we exercise with respect to its beginning—taking into account changes in, for instance, our general linguistic competence, the range of our vocabulary, both our fluid and our crystallized intelligence, and so on. It seems only fair that we pay as much scholarly attention to the processes and implications of language erosion—in the latest phases of life, for instance—as we do to those of language acquisition. Yet, ironically, our study of the development of narrative grammar tends to stop with early adolescence. Do we know anything about how individuals change throughout the rest of their lives in terms of story understanding and storytelling, above all in relation to their own lifestory?

While narrative intelligence, like any other intelligence, may unfold on its own through predictable stages and may not, strictly speaking, be teachable at all, we would submit that it can nonetheless be stretched and refined. Certainly, this is part of the rationale for including the teaching of literature in educational curricula: as a means of what Northrop Frye (1963) would call educating the imagination. Despite pressure from more pragmatic pedagogies that make not literacy paramount but rather numeracy and technical training, such education—education in the literary experience (Rosenblatt, 1983)—serves the purpose of enriching and expanding our narrative intelligence. No doubt the literary imagination per se (its origin and development) is a mystery—that is, how writers conceive and compose good stories—but we propose it is different not in kind but only in degree from the basic narrative intelligence that all of us possess.

It seems reasonable, then, that there is in fact a spectrum of narrative intelligence with respect to the storying in which all of us engage each day. While none of us is entirely lacking in curiosity about what will happen next or what sort of person someone is and why they did such-and-such to so-and-so, it is obvious that for some people, the deliberate and detailed exercise of their narrative intelligence is central to what they do on a day-to-day basis. In this category are detectives, lawyers, journalists, historians, psychoanalysts, biographers—all of whom are committed, to varying degrees and for differing motives and for different audiences, to determining what has happened in the past and, more or less, what will happen in the future, that is, to determining and telling the whole story (even, we could say, the truth).

If we take the foregoing as a sketch of narrative intelligence, the question arises, then, as to the nature of narrative wisdom. As we saw in Chapter 2, there is a cognitive dimension to wisdom, which suggests that intelligence and wisdom are in some way related (see Kramer, 1990), even if neither can be satisfactorily defined. Common sense says that wisdom is a kind of intelligence-plus, intelligence of a higher order or on a more intuitive level. Accordingly, we might be not only musically intelligent but also musically wise—as might a seasoned composer or a veteran violinist, whose talent has matured beyond mere technical correctness to communicate musical themes with a subtlety and richness that was impossible for him hitherto. In the same way, it is conceivable that we could be mathematically wise as well, or kinesthetically wise, and so on, while being decidedly dim with respect to other types of intelligence. Since our thesis here is that we must all, to some degree, be narratively intelligent, the question is whether we might all be narratively wise as well—even autobiographically wise (see Brady, 1990). But what might this mean? What is autobiographical wisdom? Since such a question is central to this chapter, indeed to the book as a whole, we propose to answer it through a consideration of the narrative dimensions to autobiographical memory.

STORY TIME: PAST AND FUTURE IN AUTOBIOGRAPHICAL MEMORY

The formation and function of memory have consistently mystified theorists. As recently as 1990, one of them admitted that the nature and structure of memory remains at the frontier of research (Schank, 1990). Others have suggested that the very concept of memory as a specific faculty by which we navigate our world is without foundation. Memory, says one, "is only a metaphor, a dim surrogate for past time that can never be recovered, never embodied, never made to sit still" (Albright, 1994, p. 39).

Despite such views, there has been no dearth of efforts to tame the mystery of memory. As a result, distinctions such as "short-term" and "long-term" memory; "sensory," "primary," and "secondary" memory; or "procedural," semantic," and "episodic" memory have become common components in the lexicon of modern psychology, indeed in gerontology too (Baltes & Smith, 1990). Our feeling here, however, is that, as helpful as such distinctions have proven in understanding the processes of remembering, many of them reflect the "mathematization of memory" (Casey, 1987). The culmination of this process is the widespread conviction that memory can be conceived of in terms of the operations of a computer, that is to say, as a matter of encoding, processing, storage, and retrieval. However, more and more scholars have become disenchanted with the computer model (Conway, 1990; Schacter, 1996; Neisser, 1994; Freeman, 1993) and its assumption that the mysteries of remembering can be captured by such mechanical terms. Instead, they have turned to consider another type of memory: autobiographical memory, a phrase which, like memory per se, refers both to individual recollections and to the collection of such memories as a whole. Since it is impossible to summarize the theories that have been advanced concerning autobiographical memory or to catalogue the experiments on whose results they are based, we shall limit ourselves here to a survey of some central features of it that have been identified in recent research.

In contrast to semantic memories, which are memories for information that is untied to particular life events, individual autobiographical memories are, first of all, self-referential. We are conscious of them being about us; they have a certain "mineness" about them. Whether as participants in the field or observers on the sidelines (Schacter, 1996, p. 21), we ourselves are in the midst of the episodes they are about. They are thus, second of all, the basis of our sense of self. Third, they cover the entire span of a life, stretching from our earliest images of ourselves as children— whether our own images or others', which we have adopted as if they were our own—to impressions from the immediate past. In this respect, autobiographical memory constitutes long-term memory par excellence. Fourth, and of special importance for our purposes here, such memories are not objective photocopies of events as they occurred at the time but only as we have experienced and interpreted them, both during and after the fact.

This last point highlights the difference between what has been called a passivist approach to understanding memory and an activist one. In the former, "remembering is reduced to a passive processs of registering and storing memory impressions" (Casey, 1987, p. 15). In the latter, as most theorists of autobiographical memory tend indeed to stress, memories are not recordings of original events but reconstructed copies of those events that capture what they meant to us at the time—or mean to us now. They are re-collections (Brewer, 1996) of the past that are—to use Bateson's (1989) term—composed in the present on an essentially improvisational basis. In a sense, we make ourselves up each time we open our mouths. The present is the key. We do not recount such recollections without concern for the context in which they are heard but in light of present circumstances, present audiences, and present agendas—agendas that can change from moment to moment as we wrestle with the range of possibilities that, in the future, we hope, expect, or fear may unfold.

This is the hermeneutical circle at work. What it means is that, subjectively speaking and as we will consider further in Chapter 4, we live not by clock time primarily but by story time and journey time. It is these latter modes of time, not clock time, that give us access to our ordinary wisdom. In his reflections on the temporal dynamics of his own autobiographical consciousness, novelist Philip Roth (cited in Freeman, 1993) captures this point rather nicely for us when he says that "you search your past with certain questions in mind—indeed, you search out your past to discover which events have led you to asking these specific questions . . . you construct a sequence of stories to bind up the facts with a pervasive hypothesis that unravels your history's meaning" (p. 118). Indeed, where memory is concerned, all three dimensions of time are involved simultaneously. As memory theorist Daniel Schacter (1996, p. 308) puts it, "Our memories are the fragile but powerful products of what we recall from the past, believe about the present, and imagine about the future." In view of this presentness (and futureness) of the past, therefore, Ulric Neisser (1994) urges that the whole concept of autobiographical memory be taken with a grain of salt: "The self that is remembered today," he argues (p. 8), "is not the historical self of yesterday, but only a reconstructed version." While Neisser may go further than we would wish to go here, we must at least accept that autobiographical memories are fundamentally inaccurate in the sense of being exact replicas of actual events. Instead, they are reconstructions whose veridicality is always distorted because of, among other things, the emotions by which they are surrounded.

This, then, is a fifth feature of autobiographical memories. They are memories of episodes that, both at the time and subsequently, have had emotional significance for us, whether positive or negative, happy or sad. The relationship between emotion and memory, however, is the relationship between chicken and egg. The one is so entwined with the other that it is impossible to determine which elicits which (Singer, 1996; Ruth & Vilkko, 1996). Do certain memories trigger certain moods, or do certain moods summon certain memories? While the question may be impossible to answer, it is at least possible to ask. A view that has otherwise held sway under the influence of the medical model, however, effectively rules the question out, implicitly divorcing our feelings from the actual events of our lives by seeing them as epiphenomenal to our physiological state, with little validity of their own.

In our search for clues to the memory-emotion link, the computer metaphor and its accompanying terminology prove, in any case, particularly lacking. The intent in invoking them, which is to break memory down into measurable components and predictable processes, has been noble indeed. But it has also, we could say, been naive. More than that, its overall effect has been to strip memory of the very complexity and emotionality that gives it the delicate yet enduring role—the fragile power (Schacter, 1996)—that we experience it to possess in our day-to-day lives.

To take autobiographical memory seriously and to appreciate its connection with our emotions, certainly to understand its relation to wisdom, requires that we attempt to reclaim some of its mystery by shifting from a computer analogy to other analogies instead. A rather different view of both memory and emotion is elicited, for example, when we work with the analogy not of a computer but of a compost heap.

As unflattering as it may sound, such an analogy lurks behind the comment of artist Anne Truitt (1987) concerning what she calls "the detritus of my history." It is also implied in what philosopher Edward Casey (1987) calls "the thickening of memory," which includes how it is "sedimented in layers" and has a "concentrated emotional significance, ranging from feelings of regret or nostalgia to the sheer pleasure of recognizing a long-absent friend" (p. 265). Though biochemical processes are surely implied here, the advantage of the analogy that undergirds such understandings of memory is that it honors its incredible fertility and its consequent aliveness—forever fermenting and transforming itself from original events into, eventually or potentially, fruitful insight. At the same time, it opens the way for us to appreciate the link between feeling and forgetting. Our emotional life may only be able to emerge in all of its subtlety and unpredictability and depth, in other words, as a rich mulch gets fashioned from the multitudinous remembered material that is laid down inside us, layer by layer, and then progressively buried beneath the weight of the past. We become, as it were, more sedimental as we age. If it is fair to say that we compose a life, is it then perhaps fair to suggest that we compost one as well?

In any case, despite their dubious technical accuracy, and possibly even because of it, our autobiographical memories still seem to serve as a more or less reliable basis for a sense of self. As Schacter puts it, psychologists agree that "people are generally accurate when reflecting on the broad outlines of their past lives" (1996). "There is a fundamental integrity to one's autobiographical recollections," echoes Barclay (cited in Schacter, 1996 p. 95). Although autobiographical memories may be "complex constructions, . . . they are not therefore simply fabricated, self-serving fictions" (p. 94). While they may not be true, they are not, strictly speaking, false either. Helpful here is the proposal made by psychologist Robert Steele (1986) that memories be seen as a peculiar cross between raw fact and pure fiction, a kind of hybrid for which he reserves the term *faction*. Also helpful is Donald Spence's (1982) distinction between historical truth and narrative truth. These distinctions notwithstanding, it is still difficult to dislodge a certain ambivalence toward memory. In the words of André Maurois (1986), it is "a great artist." Or as poet P. K. Page (1997) observes, it is a "trickster figure . . . a fiction writer offering alternative versions of what you had once imagined written in stone: the immutable *facts* of your life"—what, echoing Sartre (1956), we are calling here our "facticity." We shall return to some of these unusual and perhaps unsettling insights in Chapter 5 when we consider the process of reading our lives.

The sixth point is that autobiographical memory is social as well. The socialization, or social construction, of autobiographical memory begins early in life. "Early in life," write Bruner and Weisser (1991), "we learn how to talk about our lives. . . . We learn in the circle of the family. . . . We learn the family genre: the thematics, the stylistic requirements, the lexicon . . . procedures for offering justifications and making excuses, and the rest of it" (1991, p. 141). It is in the context of our family that we first hone our skills in "the narrative construal of reality" (Bruner, 1996), skills we instinctively apply to how we remember reality as well. In the words of David Rubin (1996, p. 2), "Parents teach their children the culturally appropriate genre for telling their memories in a socially interesting and informative way, one that gives them and their parents both a sense of the importance of sharing their memories and access to their personal histories." These "ways of telling," Bruner (1987) has said, "and the ways of conceptualizing that go with them become so habitual that they finally become recipes for structuring experience itself, for laying down routes into memory" (p. 31). Our principal tool in telling and conceptualizing our past, of course, is language, which "cannot help but deform and distort one's memories of the past" (Freeman, 1993, p. 87). In other words, "it replaces them, by putting something else in their stead"—that is, the words themselves by which we re-member past events. Thus there is always slippage (Gubrium & Holstein, 1998; Spence, 1982) or a "gap [that] can never be bridged . . . between experience itself and the words we employ to describe it" (Freeman, 1993, p. 88).

A seventh and extremely significant feature of autobiographical memory relates to what we have just discussed concerning its reliability as truth, and that is its storied dimension. In talking about such memory, not *storage* but *story-age* is the operative term. As we have already suggested, however, and as we shall continue considering under "the larger stories we live within," autobiographical memories are recorded, recalled, and recounted not in a vacuum or void but according to narrative structures (Rubin, 1996) that are integral to the narrative environments (Bruner, 1990) of the various contexts in which we have storied our lives across the years, among which our family is first. These storying conventions (Becker, 1999)—these forms of self-telling, as Bruner (1987) calls them, or narrative templates—will undoubtedly vary from one narrative environment to another. However, the fact that they are more or less shared enables us to communicate our experience to others. At the very least, we share the same basic rules of grammar and syntax and a tacit agreement as to the meanings of words. If we did not, we would be deemed not only incoherent but probably insane (Rubin, 1996). As Bruner (1987) puts it, "life stories must mesh . . . within a community of life stories"—or "interweave," as Sarbin says. They must be "interknit," say Kenneth and Mary Gergen (1983). In essence, "tellers and listeners must share some 'deep structure' about the nature of a 'life,' for if the rules of life-telling are altogether arbitrary, tellers and listeners will surely be alienated by a failure to grasp what the other is saying or what he thinks the other is hearing" (Bruner, 1987, p. 21).

A final feature of autobiographical memory is related, once more, to its presentness. Because the present—from which we interpret the past—is always changing, the past is, in effect, always changing as well. For this reason, "the past is a foreign country" (Hartley, 1953), a point that is as true of our personal life as it is of our collective one. The past can never be fully known, which makes the autobiographer's task (not to mention the historian's) an endless one indeed. In a sense, we are all exiles from our past (Salaman, 1982) and, consciously or otherwise, are continually in search of it, continually journeying into it, continually questing (Wakefield, 1989). We shall return to this feature in Chapter 5, when we consider life as adventure.

In summary, then, autobiographical memory is the memory we have of our life as a whole (Rubin, 1986, 1996). As types of memory go, it is the richest there is. Besides being the longest, it holds clues to aspects of our lives that the computer metaphor is simply ill-equipped to account for. Among these aspects are not only our emotional life but also our spirituality, our sense of personal meaning (Conway, 1990), indeed our very sense of self. Included in these aspects is our wisdom as well. As we shall see when we consider how lifestories mean, however, wisdom cannot be understood in relation to memory alone—any more (oddly enough) than autobiographical memory can be understood in relation to memory alone, at least as memory is usually conceived: as something oriented exclusively toward the past. The view we are advancing here, in other words, is that autobiographical memory is ultimately more like story memory than like anything else.

By *story memory* we mean two things. First, individual autobiographical memories are essentially stories—an insight we shall return to soon. Second, autobiographical remembering functions in much the same way as does the remembering required in reading, or following, a story: whether a fictional story, such as a movie or novel, or a nonfictional story, such as a biography or autobiography. From these two points follow two controversial notions. First, whether we are talking about formal, written, public autobiography or about the informal, felt, internal variety that is being continually processed within us, autobiography concerns the past and future alike. Second, both outer autobiography and inner autobiography (and, however ambiguously, the two are linked) are as much about fiction as they are about fact. The first notion has to do with our experience of time, the second, with which we have already flirted, with the issue of truth. Since the whole issue of truth would take us well beyond the scope of our inquiry here (see Pascal, 1960; Spence, 1982), we will focus for now on time.

As we shall see later in cataloguing the story material within our inside story as a whole, many such stories are not memories of the past at all but visions and anticipations, fantasies and fears, directed to the future. This is a key point. Like a novel, an autobiography is a complex narrative entity that recalls not past events alone but, in a real sense, both present and future ones too. While writing our autobiography—or merely thinking the autobiography that lies unwritten within us (Eakin, 1985)—we make meaning by moving back and forth between the remembered past, the experienced present, and the expected future. Our past cannot be understood on its own terms but only in light of our present *and* future—and, of course, vice versa as well. It is for this reason that we propose autobiographical memory be thought of as the inside story of our life. The inside story of our life, we also propose, is like the inside story of a novel.

In the course of reading a novel and being drawn into its unique story world, we must rely on memory to keep the story straight. To accomplish this, however, memory must continually sort and select. It must edit, consigning to the cutting floor the vast portion of events and scenes and characters we encounter on each page. Otherwise, we would be unable to form a sense of the unfolding shape of the story as a whole. As it were, the individual trees would obscure our view of the forest, making us immune to the atmosphere that the author intends us to feel. This means that, once again, there is a link between forgetting and feeling. To have a sense of the story, just as to have a sense of our self, we must forget as much as we remember, or at least must summarize things so much that we are left with only enough traces for us to understand what has gone on before. Sven Birkerts (1994) gets at this insight in his observations on what he calls a "certain equivalence between life memories and reading memories," both of which he finds "subject to the same inscrutable laws." "[A]s in life," he says, "so in art. Just as most of what happens to us dissolves, becomes part of an inner compost known in generalized terms—'my high school years,' 'boot camp,' and so on—so most of what we have read loses definition and becomes a blurry wash" (p. 107).

This is one thing about story memory: it must not be perfect. We *have* to forget. The second thing is that, insofar as it is by memory that we keep the story straight, what we are keeping straight is the trajectory of the story as a whole. It is not just what we have already read but the parts of the story that still lie ahead. If it were the former alone, our experience of the story would be only half an experience, like hurtling down the highway staring in the rearview mirror at the scenery receding behind us, yet ignoring the road in front. Speculative though it may be, we need a sense of where things are going as much as of where things have gone. If each night, when we picked up the novel with which we have been reading ourselves to sleep, we forgot where the plot line was headed at the point we left off, the story would cease to make sense. We have to remember the future. A sense of the future is integral to our understanding of the past.

In reading, moreover, we must undergo a forward-backward dynamic that, when we think about it, is as peculiar as it is familiar. Literary theorist Peter Brooks (1985) calls this dynamic "the anticipation of retrospection" and views it is as "our chief tool in making sense of narrative" (p. 23). By means of it, he says, "we read in a spirit of confidence, and also a state of dependence, that what remains to be read will restructure the provisional meanings of the already read" (p. 25). Relating this insight to our experience of our own life—that is, of our inside story—we undergo the same dynamic so continuously and so automatically that we rarely notice it. Yet, by enabling us to orient ourselves in time, it makes it possible to make sense of the ceaseless flux of our daily existence.

For philosopher David Carr (1986), "the present is only possible for us if it is framed and set off against a retained past and a potentially envisaged future" (p. 60). As Neisser and Fivush (1994) express it in their introduction to *Remembering the Past*, people are "temporally extended in both directions: into the past via memory and into the future via anticipation" (p. 16). Self-narratives, echoes Bruner (1994), are not dependent on memories per se. When we sigh in the face of a certain circumstance, for example, that, alas, "It's the story of my life," we are making a statement, therefore, about patterns we project into the future as much as we perceive in the past. What we are saying is not only "That's the way my life has gone," but also "That's the way it always *will* go." *That's my destiny, my karma, my fate.*

Such insights into our two-way experience of time corroborate an idea we have already introduced, which is that, ultimately, we live more by story time than we do by clock time (Kenyon & Randall, 1997)—not to mention digital time. In light of this idea, we propose that the very concept of autobiographical memory be seen as something of a misnomer, insofar as, in practice, it concerns our inner awareness of our life as a whole and not just our past per se. Such an awareness—which Barrett Mandel (1980) calls the autobiographical consciousness, Michael Ignatieff (1993) autobiographical intelligence, and we ourselves our inside story—concerns our present and future as much as our past. Certainly, in the grip of this awareness, we can find ourselves grazing desultorily from one to the other and back. If we insist on retaining the term *autobiographical memory* let us think of it, then, as the means by which we attempt to keep our story straight: the story by which we steer our way through time: A story that is about the future as much as it is the past (Crites, 1986). As far as our ordinary wisdom is concerned, therefore, time is not tensed for us but truly open.

THE LEVELS OF LIFESTORY

So far, we have seen that our individual memories are more factional than they are factual, that the very notion of autobiographical memory is problematic. We have seen that memory per se plays less of a role in our lives than we may assume, that we live by our sense of the present and the future as much as we do by our sense of the past. This licenses us to launch wholeheartedly, we feel then, into a story approach to life and, by extension, a story approach to wisdom as well.

Few concepts are as familiar as the story of our life. We each assume we have one and that everyone else has one too. At the same time, few concepts are as difficult to define (Kotre, 1990). If story itself presents a conceptual challenge, as we have seen, then we should hardly expect lifestory to be any less challenging. Indeed, as a concept, it is as complicated as it is commonplace. Yet if we are going to conceive ordinary wisdom in terms of the narrative root metaphor, we must try to understand what a lifestory means. Elsewhere (Kenyon & Randall, 1997; Randall, 1995, 1996), we have argued that it has meaning on a number of levels at once: outside, inside, inside-out, and outside-in. To help our line of thinking here, a summary of these distinctions is in order.

The outside story of our life is, technically speaking, the whole story. It is the sum of all the events of our existence—events of whatever type: molecular, biochemical, physiological, psychological, conscious, political, and so on. We cannot know this whole story in itself, of course, for it is too vast. Witness the last long drive we took and how few details of it we could later recall. Our outside story is essentially outside our ken, for we are inside it, as an infant is within a womb.

Our inside story, on the other hand, is that portion or dimension of our existence that we are able to experience. Indeed, experience itself, insists Stephen Crites (1986), "is a vast story-like construct." Our inside story, if you will, is what makes it inside us, metaphorically speaking, whether as a memory, a thought, a perception, a fantasy, or a feeling. Taken together, these comprise "the story of our own lives which we narrate to ourselves in an episodic, sometimes semiconscious, virtually uninterrupted monologue" (Polkinghorne, 1988, p. 160), that is, in our view, misleadingly labeled as autobiographical *memory*. To the degree we can quantify the difference between them, this inside story is of course tiny in comparison with the vastness of our outside story. Yet it is vast in its own right. There is so much inside us at any given time! We need only think of the flood of memories that is set loose within us as we leaf through an album or reminisce with a friend.

Our inside-out story is our inside story as we express it to others— whether intentionally or not; whether in our gestures, actions, or words; whether formally, as in an autobiography, or informally, as in casual conversation. We can never express all of our inside story, of course, anymore than we can experience all of our outside story—only particular portions in particular situations to particular people in particular ways. We can only express a *version* of our inside story, and different audiences will, inevitably, elicit different versions at different times. Furthermore, the very act of putting our thoughts into language refracts the original experience, which means we can never say totally or exactly what we remember, think, or feel.

Finally, what we call our outside-in story is not our story of ourselves but another person's impression of us, based not just on our words but, again, on our actions and gestures as well. Once more, there are as many versions of the story of our life as there are people with whom we deal, from those who know us intimately (or think they do), such as parents, partners, or friends—or our official biographer!—to those who know us only in fleeting or superficial fashion, whether colleagues, customers, or clients—or the proverbial stranger on the train. Some of these versions are freeing and affirming and seem to bring out the best in us, while others are crass caricatures: stiff, stifling "storyotypes" (Randall, 1995) to which their originators stubbornly stick but which, so to speak, "misunder-story" us each time they are thrown in our face. Of course we have no way of knowing exactly what versions others may be entertaining of us nor how these versions may change from one encounter with us to another. We can have no idea, really, how they story us, how they experience us. All we have is our outside-in story of their outside-in story of us, or our impression of their impression. To put the point bluntly, in our everyday interaction, we never deal with each other straight on but only through stories of stories of stories.

Such distinctions—between outside, inside, and so forth—have broad application. Not only can an entire life be seen to have both an outside story and an inside story but so can each event within a life. Putting aside the thorny philosophical question as to what constitutes an event in the first place (see Becker, 1959), there is always both an outside perspective on a given occurence—the raw facts, as it were—and an inside perspective—the feelings behind the facts and our interpretations of the facts. Put another way, there is the event in itself, apart from us, and there is what we make of the event, or how it is "privately composed, made sense of," and so "becomes an event" for us (Kegan, 1982, p. 2). In the same way, as we shall see later, each larger system we live within, be it our family or community or class, also has an outside story and an inside story.

Overall, such a schema helps us to appreciate the range of levels on which, daily, we experience reality. At the same time, it helps us understand why it is not always clear, even to ourselves, what we mean by our everyday allusions to the story of my life. As we can now see, we may mean (or think we mean) a number of levels at once—both the raw events of our life and those events we remember (which can constitute a quite different story); both the stories we have trotted out to others and those that others have projected onto us, to which, for better or worse, we often defer as the *real* story of who we are. When we think of our lifestory, however, it is far more than merely our expressions to others that we have in mind (which on some level we may not even trust), and more than others' impressions of us (which we frequently resent). It is ultimately our experience of ourselves: our inside story—however much it is shaped and penetrated by (our versions of) others' outside-in stories of us; however much its contours are determined by the oft-told tales by which we present ourselves to others, inside-out; and however much its composition is guided by the forms of self-telling (Bruner, 1987) that are integral to the larger systems within which we live. Certainly, when journalists assure us they have the inside story on a particular news-making event, we sit up and take notice, for the phrase is so enticing. When we apply it to our own lives, we begin to be enticed by how interesting we actually are.

THE INSIDE STORY

On close examination, what is inside us—our experience—is in fact a vast range of material. "Every time an old person dies," says novelist Alex Haley (cited in Polster, 1987), "it's like a library has burned down." While there is surely much information and knowledge lining the shelves of that library, the simplest exercise of trolling for memory (Birkerts, 1994) quickly reveals that it holds many stories as well. Memory, insists Schank (1990, p. 16), "is memory for stories and the major processes of memory are the creation, storage, and retrieval of stories." Sir Francis Galton and later Herbert Crovitz learned in their respective studies of autobiographical memory, for example, that mention of the simplest word, such as "apple"or "bike," triggers not abstract definitions so much as specific recollections: the time at age ten when we stole the apples from Farmer Brown's orchard or the time we first learned to ride a bike on that beaten-up, hand-me-down with the crooked front wheel (see Schacter, 1996). We cannot separate our sense of the meanings of many words from the memories we associate with them. As Schank flatly says: "memory is story-based" (1990, p. 12); indeed, we are veritable "repositories of stories" (p. 40).

As we have seen in looking at autobiographical memory, individual memories are not still-life photographs of specific events but rather narrative reconstructions, storied re-creations that, to a greater or lesser degree, we improvise in the present (Schacter, 1996). There is little in the sense of a direct, straightforward, event-memory connection; a fictionalizing element is always involved. In short, memories *are* stories. Thinking of our memories as stories first and memories second might unsettle us, however. Certainly, this simple equation represents a significant conceptual shift. Nonetheless, it is a shift that we take so much for granted that whenever someone says, "I've got some *stories* I could tell you about X," we automatically assume they mean memories of X. Having made our point, then, what are some of the main categories of stories that we carry around inside us?

The first categorization may come as a surprise, although we alluded to it above when we were considering the nature of autobiographical memory. It is between the stories we have about the past and those we have about the future. Supporting it is the simple point that while all of our memories are stories, not all of our stories are memories. As for the past, of course, we have stories about situations from as far back as our childhood and as recent as the moment just finished. These past stories can indeed play a powerful role in our lives, but our stories of the future commonly play just as significant a role. Our future stories run the gamut from vague visions of what if or what might be to our wildest fantasies and darkest fears. They include both our long-range dreams—about life when we graduate or marry or retire—and our short-range plans—about what to have for supper, what to watch on TV, what to do next week. In his important book *Remembering*, Edward Casey (1987) reminds us that, in fact, many of our memories concern not the past at all but things we have to do in the future: "I mustn't forget to put the garbage out in the morning" or "I must remember to include copies of those receipts with my tax return." By the same token, some of our stories of the future are, technically, stories of the future *of the past*. They are hypothetical speculations on the consequences of possible courses of action in relation to a dilemma we have already faced or a decision we have already made. Historian Niall Ferguson (1997) calls such speculations counterfactuals. In his view,

we constantly ask . . . "counterfactual" questions in our daily lives. What if I had observed the speed limit, or refused that last drink? What if I had never met my wife or husband? What if I had bet on Red Rum instead of Also Ran? . . . [W]e cannot resist imagining the alternative scenarios: what might have happened, if only we had or had not. . . . Nor are such thoughts mere day-dreams. . . . [T]he business of imagining counterfactuals is a vital part of the way in which we learn. Because decisions about the future are—usually—based on weighing up the potential consequences of alternative courses of action, it makes sense to compare the actual outcomes of what we did in the past with the conceivable outcomes of what we might have done. (p. 2)

The line can thus be fine between memories of the future and speculations on the past. The key, though, is that our stories of the future—of where our lives might go, or might have gone—can play as pivotal a part as do those of the past, not only in our emotional life (inasmuch as our emotions, as we have hinted, have storied roots) but also in how, generally, we maneuver through our world.

A second categorization is between particular or specific stories and general or spread-out stories. The first type stand out as clean-edged nuggets about individual events, often recalled in sharp detail. The second type, while such events may be in the background, are overlaid by countless other similar events as well, all of which tend to merge into a sense simply of the sort of thing I *used* to do. Again, Neisser (1986) calls such stories, "repisodic" to reflect the fact that they are memory-impressions that have formed around the repetition of otherwise isolatable episodes. Although we may have made umpteen train trips throughout our life, no one of them still stands out. Instead, we have one long, composite image embracing hazy recollections of the clickety-clack of wheel against rail, of scenery fleeting past through shaded windows, of the ding-ding-ding of a thousand railway crossings, all triggered by the single phrase "train travel." Similar images are triggered by titles (Polster, 1987) such as *Going to the Dentist* or *Eating in a Restaurant*. For each situation, we have scripts (Schank & Abelson, 1977) for what to do and how to behave but few impressions of particular events.

A third distinction is between solo stories and shared stories, or between stories that are primarily about us and stories that are as much about others. In the repertoire of narrative material with which we identify our life, in other words, are stories that concern not only us in particular but also the various people with whom our lives are linked: our family, our mates, our children, our neighbors, our colleagues. We also have stories about things that have happened not to people we know but to people who are removed from us in both space and time—stories we have learned through neighborhood gossip, through newspapers, through history books. Though these stories are not stories about us directly, they are nonetheless stories about the world we know, about the roots of our clan, our community, our culture, our race. They figure in our narrative picture of the world as a whole; they inform, indeed *form*, our world.

A fourth distinction is between public stories and private stories, or between stories we tell others and stories we keep to ourselves. A related distinction is between the stories we tell, if only to ourselves, and the stories we leave untold. The latter are the stories we have not yet found the vocabulary or courage—or encouragement (as in, the right sort of listener)—to enable us to tell. They are stories of events our initial impressions of which we have buried, perhaps deliberately repressed, so deeply that, for all intents and purposes, they never occurred. However, it is out of the compost heap of these numberless stories—which we have left thus far untold, have stopped telling altogether, or could never tell in the first place—that, provided the right environment, much of our wisdom might emerge.

At the same time, it is in many of the stories that we do tell—and in the telling itself, as we shall see in Chapter 4—that our wisdom can also be discovered. One category of such stories is the sort of specific story we have come to call signature stories (Kenyon & Randall, 1997). Signature stories are the anecdotes, which in turn may be short or long, and so forth, that we have recounted about ourselves repeatedly across the years. Compared with other stories in our repertoire, they are more polished and practiced. They are the stories of things we simply cannot forget, of events that may seem as real to us now as they were when they first took place. They are stories we not only tell but somehow *like* to tell, for they portray us in ways that, for whatever reason, we prefer to be portrayed—because they flatter us, make fools of us, inspire us, or simply intrigue us. They may be stories of or leading up to what, from the vantage point of the present, are major turning points in the unfolding of our life, what McAdams (1994) calls nuclear episodes. They may also be "the time I . . . " stories, such as I'll never forget the time I . . . first went wind-surfing, first met my husband, first met my first wife, and so on.

What can be disturbing to discover, however, is that some of these stories may not be terribly true. For one thing, they can be stories about things that we ourselves did not actually, or at least consciously, experience but that others—our parents or friends, for example—have *told* us we experienced. True or not, they are stories that not only may have significant entertainment value—they shock, amuse, and so on—but also, in more or less transparent manner, reveal a great deal about us, about our fundamental self-image, or about our guiding personal myth. For this reason they are often the very stories around which we would construct our formal autobiography. They are the nodal points in the narrative line by which we identify ourselves to the world, which stand out like mountain peaks above the sprawling expanse of our memory's mostly cloud-shrouded terrain.

A fifth distinction, which is related to the one we mentioned between public and private, is between surface or presenting stories and deep or guiding stories. Surface stories are the stories that roll off our lips with little effort or thought. By means of them we present ourselves to the world, and on the basis of them, often, others form their impressions of us, that is to say, the storyotypes they believe we are. By our deep stories, however, we mean the stories by which, at the profoundest levels and for better or worse, we actually live. Captured by titles such as *I'm a Loser, I'm a Child of God, I'm an Orphan, I'm a Survivor* (Pearson, 1989), these are the authorized versions we have come to accept, deep down inside, as essential to who we are. Such guiding myths, as we suggest, are usually in the background or between the lines of our signature stories.

Overall, then, the inside of our lifestory is many stories in one—just like a novel. In fact, as we shall see, a novel provides an interesting analogy for the story of our life. On the one hand, there are the countless individual episodes and scenes that are contained in its several subplots and chapters. On the other hand, there are the various overall stories the author intended it to turn into at different stages before, during, and even after writing it, any of which might be quite at odds with what the narrator—or narrators—actually recount. Similarly, each of the characters will have—and perceive themselves to have—their own individual stories unfolding amid the novel as a whole, while each chapter will trace its unique portion of the overall plot, and each subplot will represent a particular perspective on what the story is. In turn, each reader and each critic will entertain their own range of theories as to the kind of story the story is, not only while reading it but afterward as well, as it continues to rumble around inside them, often becoming a different and more significant story each time they reread it later in their lives.

Just as the story embedded in a given work of literature is therefore far from being a singular, obvious entity (however much we may persist in thinking it is), so is the story of my life. Narratively speaking, we are multiple beings. We can trace many plotlines; we can play many roles; we can embody many themes; we can recount many tales. The story of my life is ultimately an infinite set of narrative possibilities that can be spun from a finite set of historical-biological facts. As Sartre scholar Stuart Charmé puts it, "There can be different 'versions' of the story of one's life, each presenting a different text for interpretation" (1984, p. 52). Like the surface of the planet, like the universe as a whole, then, "my life" is finite but unbounded: bounded by what actually happens (my facticity) but infinite as far as what I can make of what happens (my sense of possibility). Seeing this inherent multiplicity in the story of my life does not make our exploration of ordinary wisdom any easier, of course, for it suggests that wisdom is not singular but plural, not one thing but many. Yet once we engage the services of the narrative root metaphor, such multiplicity is a necessary variable to factor into our thinking. At the same time, it is the very thing that makes our ordinary wisdom so incredibly rich. From this perspective, then, there is an open, basically unfinished quality to human life. As we shall see in Chapter 4, human life is a journey and not a destination. There is always an opportunity to move beyond our facticity and exercise our sense of possibility.

THE NOVELTY OF OUR LIVES

Our thesis in this chapter, then, is "novel," in both senses of the word. No one has gone through quite what we have gone through. No one has been shaped by the people and events, the circumstances and conditions, by which we have been shaped. No one has processed life like we have processed life. No one sees the world as we see the world. Our view, our vision, our wisdom—and "vision" and "wisdom" are etymologically linked—is one of a kind. It is original, extraordinary, unique. It is novel. At the same time as our wisdom is extraordinary, however, each of us possesses our own. This means it is possible for us all, which is why we call it *ordinary*.

As for the second sense of "novel," what we are doing in this chapter is pushing the narrative metaphor as much as we can and proposing that a life be seen not only as a story but as a species of literary text. What sort of text? Not just a play or a short story, we believe, nor a mere anthology of stories with no intrinsic link but a sprawling, more or less continuous narrative tableau; a vast, more or less coherent story-world; a living, multileveled, flesh-and-blood novel of epic proportions—not in a singular sense, as we have just seen, but a multiple one, as many stories within one. As French writer Gustave Flaubert (cited in Polster, 1987) expressed it: "Everyone's life is worth a novel." To the degree such a perspective is valid, it makes all of us novelists, the authors of our own lives, as it were—not to mention their narrators, characters, and readers as well. Of course, many will dismiss such a perspective as too grand when invited to apply it to themselves. "My life isn't anything special," they will claim; "My story's not so different from anyone else's." We reject such disclaimers here, however, as, in secret usually, do the same people who voice them. In some instinctive manner, each of us knows that our life *is* unique. No one else could have lived it but us. However much it may seem so when seen from a distance, it is never the same old story. As snowflakes share the same general shape but, on analysis, reveal distinctive crystalline configurations, so our lives, at the genetic level though generally alike, differ widely in the details.

Contrary to the nomothetic bias in much developmental psychology (Runyan, 1984), the story, and the wisdom it mediates, is in the details of our lives. Our wisdom emerges from this personal recognition of the details—which we shall be exploring in the chapter to come—of the idiosyncracies, of the variations from the norm, not from the shared shape. Indeed, we would argue, each life course defines afresh the very genre of a life, a point that may be all the more true the more we *individuate* (to use Jung's term) or the more advanced we are in age. "The older we grow," the expression runs, "the more like ourselves we become," and the more, perhaps, we live out a distinctive "storying style" (Randall, 1995)—just as any novel deserving of the label recounts a tale that the world has never before heard and articulates a vision it has hitherto not seen. Unlike the familiar narrative formulas we find in pulp fiction, a novel stretches the very concept of story in untried directions. In his analysis of the philosophy of Jean-Paul Sartre—who described his own autobiography as a "true novel," and "a novel I believe in" (cited in Charmé, 1984, p. 79)—Stuart Charmé (1984) underlines the notion of the novelty of our lives in his insistence that "the structure of a person's life resembles a literary text." As he expresses it, "Every person is the 'author' of his life; his acts, like the words of a writer, combine to constitute a unique view of the world" (p. 47, 51).

To be sure, this view of the novelty of a life is as paradoxical as it is unique—given its implication that we are the author of a story of which we are at the same time the central character, the principal narrator, and the primary reader. By means of such a view, however, we believe we are led to a deeper understanding of the poetic complexity of biographical aging. We are also enabled to address a disorienting tendency in postmodern

psychology to dismantle the very notion of the self. For us, the notion of
the novelty of our lives exemplifies a positive postmodernism, or what has
been called a hermeneutics of recovery. From such a perspective, we are
neither entirely socially constructed (see Gubrium, in press) nor shaped
willy-nilly by forces and influences over which we have no control. Rather,
we each operate out of a unique interpretive center from which we negotiate a unique path through the maze of competing narrative possibilities for
constructing who we are. In our many-storiedness, we are ultimately one,
with a measure of agency, even authority, over the composition of our
lives. As we indicated in Chapter 1, while the self may be saturated
(Gergen, 1992) with the traces of countless other story lines, it can still be
more or less centered amid a continuous, ever unfolding narrative fabric
that possesses its own direction and integrity.

Clearly, what we are doing here is stretching the metaphor of life as
story to life as literary story—or life as literature. Practically everything associated with literature, we believe, holds insights into the inside of life,
into aspects so central to our everyday experience that they slip unnoticed
through the categories of social science. We refer to the subtle, internal,
aesthetic complexity of a life, to its dynamic coherence, to its peculiar and
inherent meaningfulness—even truth—and to its often explicitly and always implicitly moral or spiritual dimension. However, though literature
represents the known in the life-as-literature link, it is not nearly as
straightforward as the steam engine that informs Freudian psychoanalysis
or the computer behind cognitive science. Witness the vastness of the literary world and the complexity of even the simplest novel. And witness how
literary theorists themselves can find it difficult to define such essential
novelistic elements as plot, character, point of view, genre, and theme. For
this reason, we agree with the point made by Bruner that "linguistically
and in spirit as well, the modern novel may be as profound . . . as the invention of modern physics" (1987, p. 21).

Employing the countless entailments of the narrative metaphor to get at
the nature of ordinary wisdom, when each has a complexity of its own,
may seem like throwing abstraction after abstraction, like trying to tether
an ethereal horse with an ethereal rope. A more empirical approach would
seem more solid. The reality, however, is that the very topic we are pursuing requires a shift in paradigms. Since wisdom is not really a thing, we
cannot expect to do justice to it with thing metaphors, even intricate, dynamic things such as motors or computers. At the same time, drawing on
story to get at the nature of wisdom, even though a story is far less
thing-like than a computer, in no way means that we are on any less solid
conceptual ground or have defaulted to a softer, more speculative approach. For mind as computer or psyche as machine is, in the final analysis, no less a metaphor than life as story. Moreover, we are convinced, it is
ultimately more limiting, since it obscures aspects of our everyday experi-

ence that can be so familiar as to be *un*familiar, so ordinary as to be *extra*ordinary, so mundane as to be mysterious, so in-our-face as to be invisible. By being sensitive to the origin and nature, and to the dynamic shape, of a literary work—how it is composed, how it unfolds, and how it is interpreted or read—we begin, then, to catch critical clues to the wisdom that is inherent in that colossal work-in-progress, that massive work of art (Bruner, 1999), that fundamental project (Sartre, 1956) of which we are each perpetually in the middle: The Story of My Life.

The next obvious issue is how literature *means*. But before we focus on it, we need to consider an aspect of the stories of our lives, and thus of our wisdom, that we have underemphasized so far: how it is socially constructed.

THE LARGER STORIES WE LIVE WITHIN

Up to now, we may have given the impression that people story themselves in isolation, that biographical aging occurs in a vacuum, that each person's wisdom is a function of the novel of his or her life alone. If this is the impression, we need to correct it.

No novel comes from nowhere. Each is written within a particular language during a particular era by a particular author. Though it is ultimately a fresh aesthetic endeavor, it still reflects the beliefs and biases, the conventions and questions, of that author's culture and class, gender and creed. The same applies to the story of our life. As we have seen with the socialization of autobiographical memory, our story, however unique, is shaped within the narrative environment of a particular family, a particular network of relationships, and a particular community, and reflects the beliefs and biases of a specific generation and gender, culture and creed. What we are proposing here is that each of these—family, culture, creed—be thought of as larger stories. Within them, our individual lives represent particular subplots, constitute particular characters, and contribute particular conflicts and themes (Kenyon & Randall, 1997). In the words of Miller Mair (cited in Howard, 1994), "We inhabit the great stories of our culture.... We are *lived* by the stories of our race and place.... We are, each of us, locations where the stories of our place and time become partially tellable."

Such stories are what Wilhelm Mader (1996) calls "biographizers," insofar as they shape our individual biographies. If you will, we live within these stories. The events of our life occur within and are constrained by the events of their lives. Effectively, these stories are the setting in which our personal stories unfold. In fact, we live within many such stories at once, insofar as they exist in a roughly concentric or ecological relationship to each other. That is to say, a family story is nested within a community story, which is nested within a nation story, which is nested within . . . .

More important, not only do we live within them, but they live within us—so much so that where we begin and they end can become impossible to say, which is an idea we shall return to in the Epilogue.

Calling them stories instead of systems or structures, however, is not to say that they are only stories and not real. It is to underline their aesthetic-dynamic dimensions, as well as the aesthetic-dynamic aspects of our experience of them or of their effect on us. Until recently, these aspects have been largely overlooked by those disciplines that otherwise concern themselves with the formation and function of human groups, such as sociology, anthropology, and history. But like lives, we believe, groups too are storied. They are shaped in stories, defined by stories, and, as Mair might say, *lived* by stories. Moreover, like lifestories, they can be understood on different levels—outside, inside, inside-out, and outside-in— and, like literary stories, as having plots, characters, atmospheres, and themes. With respect to each of these, the process of authoring, narrating, and reading are relevant as well. Finally, like both literary stories and lifestories, larger stories may be said to mediate their own range of meanings and insights, plus, as we say, their own wisdom, by which the form and content of our personal wisdom will inevitably be shaped. In other words, insofar as "narratives are not only structures for meaning but structures for power as well" (E. Bruner, 1986, p. 144), the political dimension of wisdom is as critical to consider as the poetical one we have been considering up to now.

Another way of putting all of this is simply to say that our ordinary wisdom is in part always socially constructed, just as is the autobiographical memory from which it emerges or in which it is rooted. The term *social construction* can be translated in a more everyday way. Rather than composing a wisdom that is entirely our own, we also absorb, as if by osmosis, a wisdom that resides already in our family story, community story, creedal story, and so on. Be it ever so humble, and however much we may critique it or reject it, there is no wisdom like the received wisdom of the Randall family or the Kenyon clan. We see the world—or the world-story (Randall, 1995)—one way growing up within this family, another way growing up within that family. Our vision—our wisdom—varies, often dramatically, from one to the other. And this is so, in spite, or more accurately because, of the particular chain of events by which the story of each family has unfolded, the genre or narrative template in which these events have been cast, the signature stories that stand out within that story, and the particular tensions and conflicts by which, across the years, its plot has been riddled: conflicts that, in its own generally subliminal ways, the family has struggled to resolve (see Bruner & Weisser, 1991).

To appreciate the complexity of the storiedness of the systems we live within, we can consider the example of one type of larger story in particular, that of a specific religion. Since one of us was for ten years a parish minister, the religion that comes most readily to mind is Christianity. Co-incidentally, it is within Christianity that an approach has emerged called narrative theology (see Hauerwas & Jones, 1989; Cupitt, 1991; Tilley, 1985; Kliever, 1981; Stroup, 1981). Narrative theology, which reflects a postmodern perspective, is premised on the view that "virtually all of our convictions, nonreligious as well as religious, are rooted in some narra-tive" (Goldberg, 1991, p. 36). Literary critic Sven Birkerts (1994) captures this premise nicely when he writes that "whatever else they may be, reli-gions are grand stories that make a place for us" (pp. 196ff). As we trace how story is integral to all aspects of Christianity, we can understand why narrative theology is an appropriate approach to take.

First, story is central to scripture. While the Bible contains much in the way of abstract religious philosophy and theological reflection, it is noth-ing if not also an anthology of narrative forms: from myth to legend, from allegory to epic, from annal to chronicle, from half-history to quasi-biography, and from provocative parable to apocalyptic dream. In turn, the creeds of the Christian faith are essentially distilled recitations of the story line that threads through the Bible from beginning to end. For their part, theological doctrines are at bottom analyses and interpretations of the mighty acts of God that are chronicled in scriptural texts.

When Christians believe, then, what they believe in is some version of a particular master narrative (Fulford, 1999) about the origin and end of the universe as a whole and about everything within it, including the nature of good and evil and the difference between right and wrong. And when they witness to non-Christians, they are sharing not only this master story but also their own personal story, through which the former is naturally fil-tered, such as the tale about how once they were blind but now they see, and so on. When they admit to their sins, whether privately in prayer or discretely in confession, they are attempting to tell their whole story, to get it out and get it off their chests. And when they receive pastoral counsel-ing, they are encouraged to retell that story in light of the story of God's love—a story in which the universe is a graced place to be, with purpose in each corner and meaning in each moment, and a power that is continually turning evil into good. As well, it is only by a continual swapping of sto-ries, accurate or not, that the everyday life of the average congregation is able to proceed. At best, this storying is an expression of compassion, of people seeing the best in each other's stories and assisting each other to restory toward ever greater wisdom and love. At worst, it leads to a gos-siping, backbiting mess.

For its part, the study of church history, like that of any history, is obvi-ously a narrative endeavor (White, 1980; Danto, 1985), while church coun-cils, interfaith dialogues, and theological disputes are aptly described as battles of stories (see Hillman, 1975). As Goldberg (1991, p. 36) describes it, "[O]ur more serious disputes with one another reflect rival narrative accounts." In turn, conversion can be viewed as de-storying one's old life and restorying it afresh, a process that converts describe as rebirth or being born again (Randall, 1995). Preachers are the official custodians and conduits of the old, old story of sin, grace, and redemption, or of the drama of salvation (Haughton, 1976)—while the process of preaching is one of retelling this story afresh by interpreting particular scriptural narratives in ways that will illuminate parishioners' lives. In other words, people hear such preaching and make sense of it not *despite* their personal lifestories but *through* them. At the same time, in the process of hearing, they implicitly place themselves in a position where the lifestory through which they hear the story is not merely edified but, literally (or literarily), informed. It is formed, deep within it, by the structures of that story. It is suffused by its themes, its ethos, its vision and values, its emplotment of the world. In such a manner, for better or worse, religions have traditionally provided us with ready-made structures by which, or *in* which, to live out our lives.

This quick catalogue shows how critical it is to consider the narrative variable in the context of religion. If a narrative approach makes sense in the context of the Christian religion, then it makes no less sense in a Jewish context or an Islamic one (Goldberg, 1991). However, narrative is pivotal not just in traditions that are explicitly historical in orientation but conceivably in those at whose heart is an ahistoric myth or in those that pretend to espouse no master story at all (Cupitt, 1991). If you will, the question, then, is how do the stories—and the storying—at the heart of any religion work their way inside us, molding our memory, impregnating our imagination, and shaping how we understand and identify ourselves in both content and form? By what process of osmosis do we absorb and accept these stories as reality, as truth, as the way things are, as, therefore, inseparable from our story, both of ourselves and of our world? A still broader question is how might the various other larger stories we live within, besides religious or spiritual ones, conflict with one another in foundational ways, thereby making our inner life even more complicated and embattled, narratively speaking, than if we could somehow compose our lives in a cultural void.

Answering such questions is of course beyond our scope here, for they take us to the heart of the social constructionist perspective. There we face a paradox. We cannot talk about the processes that occur within the self in its efforts to fashion meaning without understanding how deeply it is permeated by narrative structures outside of it that would seem to prescribe beforehand what meaning is. At the same time, we cannot talk about how those structures get rooted inside us—and with them, their wisdom—without understanding how the self operates within itself, without a sense of the complexity of the self's interminably interpretive, meaning-making, storying activity, orienting itself to the countless events and circumstances and relationships, past, present, and future, that constitute its existence amid the ceaseless flow of time.

By extrapolating from this consideration of what happens in relation to Christianity, we can see that whenever we are talking about any of the larger stories within which we live, it is always difficult to say what exactly *the* story is, just as difficult, in fact, as it is in the case of a literary story or a lifestory—or a family story too. Assemble the members of our family for a reunion and ask each one to recount *the* story of the family, and we are apt to be amused by how many versions we hear—some so different from the others that we may wonder whether we even grew up under the same roof! And yet, overall, the many stories are versions of one narrative whole, however complex and multileveled it may be—just as a novel, while hosting many stories between its covers, can still be one. As we think about the wisdom in stories, then, we must not forget this multiple-singular paradox. Having said this, what about the wisdom in stories?

THE WISDOM IN FICTION: HOW STORIES MEAN

Life is inseparable from story: We live in story and story lives in us. This has been our premise throughout this book. But because it sounds odd in relation to analyses of human development that we have inherited from mainstream social science, it needs continual reinforcement. Though simple to state, it can be complex to comprehend and can quickly slip our grasp. Once we grasp it and take seriously the idea of the stories we *are*, however, we open a Pandora's box of conceptual implications that are not soon pondered. One implication we want to ponder now is that, just as the shape of a life is a story shape and the content of a life is story content, so the meaning of a life is story meaning. Tied to this is the implication that whatever wisdom a life may possess is story-wisdom, akin to the wisdom we encounter, and expect, on the pages of a great novel. Thus, every lifestory can be seen to be wise in the way that every literary story is wise. But the question then becomes: What exactly is story wisdom? Long before we look to philosophy or any other subject (including gerontology) for insight and wisdom, it is frequently literature to which we turn. But what sort of wisdom does literature involve, and how is it conveyed? To get at an answer, we need to pose the prior and broader question of how stories *mean*. Only then can we have some sense, in the following section, of how lifestories might mean.

Let us begin by saying that, though some stories seem innocuous, no story is ever innocent. Even the humblest bedtime tale seeks to drive home a point on its impressionable audience. The ad that would sell us deodorant, detergent, or beer is at bottom a morality play; its message or moral, evangelical in tone: *I purchased this product and my life was transformed*. In the same way, each autobiography is a case of special pleading; each novel, the vehicle for a particular vision; each play, the purveyor of its creator's pet views. The point is, stories always have points—agendas, purposes, aims. Indeed, the greatest stories serve several aims at once. They raise questions, focus issues, highlight themes. They conjure up worlds and usher us into their midst: worlds we would otherwise not know. They push back the boundaries of our understanding by eliciting our memories and by awakening our longings and dreams. They expand our sense of possibility by articulating insights and affirming feelings that may have lain dormant all our lives, awaiting the right words to render them real. In short, stories bathe our world in meaning. They are structures for meaning.

"Meaning," however, means different things in different domains. It means one thing in the realm of music, another in that of math, and another in philosophy or faith. What it means in that of story is a matter all its own. The meaning of "meaning" in story terms is elusive, like the meaning of "story" itself. Granting for the moment this definitional dilemma, we can nonetheless assert with some confidence that all stories mean something to us. Witness the ease with which any story, no matter how odd or avant-garde, can capture our attention. By the same token, some stories seem to mean more than others. They linger longer inside us; their atmosphere haunts us and their implications pursue us well after the movie has ended or the book has been returned to the shelf. The shelf life of other stories is, by contrast, comparatively brief. Whether their medium be the page, the stage, or the screen, they appear composed by formula; their dramatic shape is familiar, predictable, neat. Luring us from initial calm through ensuing conflict to building climax and gradual denouement, they may satisfy our narrative lust (Lewis, 1966) and provide a minimal message in the form of a moral cliché, such as Persistence pays off or Love conquers all, but the meaning we extract from them is otherwise thin. No sooner do we finish the story than we forget it. Once its plot is complete, our interest quickly wanes.

The situation is different with great literature. Events succeed events, characters are developed, themes get spun, an atmosphere is created, and the story becomes about much more than just Love conquers all. The story-world that unfolds is not merely longer but bigger as well—wider, deeper, thicker—and it works on many more levels than simply that of its central events, that of plot alone. By the time we reach its end, the story line has so entwined itself around our soul and its themes so enchanted us that we are loath to let it go. Our curiosity may be satisfied regarding how things turn out, but the story lives on. It reverberates through our minds. While, technically, it concludes, there is no conclusion at all to what it can mean; it is endlessly meaningful. Moreover, its meaningfulness for us tomorrow will vary from its meaningfulness today. Each time we reread it, the same old story becomes a different new story, as fresh as it is familiar.

All of this underlines that stories mean, and that the better stories mean more, but it stops short of answering *how* they mean. Unfortunately, this is a vast question, one to which here we can scarcely do justice with the thoroughness it deserves (see Polkinghorne, 1988). However, we can still propose, at least as a beginning, a number of interrelated points. In the next section, we can take these points as starting points for considering how lifestories mean.

First, story-meaning is *reader-related*, which is another way of saying that it is contextual. A story does not have meaning in the abstract. It has meaning only in the sense that it has meaning for us. An unread novel is meaningless text; a read one is meaningful only as it links with, or illuminates, some aspect of our own experience—for example, when we recognize ourselves in its characters or see the conflicts of our life in the convolutions of its plot. If not for autobiography, we could say, fiction would have no effect. As with the riddle of the tree falling in the forest, a story has no meaning apart from a reader reading it, a viewer viewing it, a hearer hearing it. Its meaning is a function of the experiences and expectations that we bring to the text.

Though the text may stimulate these expectations, they originate ultimately in the material of our own lifestory. We experience the text through the texts of our own lives; we read the fictional story through the true story we are in the middle of living (Beach, 1990). If you will, we get out of a story what we put into it. And what we put into it, what we *read* into it, is our own experience, our inside story, the complex web of remembered past and anticipated future that constitutes the dynamic, ever-changing interpretive grid, the gestalt, through which we make sense of everything. Story-meaning, then, is not ultimately *in* the story, or at least not solely so. Rather, we make it *out of* the story, which, in effect, functions as fodder for our imagination. We bring our instinctive meaning-making tendency to the text—as indeed we do to the the the text of each day. In a sense, we find meaning where, technically or intrinsically, no meaning exists. We do this by fashioning stories of our own: virtual stories, as it were, which, depending how carefully we read, are more or less related to the actual stories that are intended by the novelists themselves. It is these virtual stories, however, not the actual ones that we afterwards recall.

A corollary here concerns the capacity we introduced earlier: narrative intelligence. The greater the sophistication with which we can formulate and follow stories—about either others or ourselves—the easier we will find it to see meaning in stories that are otherwise hard to read. Conversely, armed with a less well-developed or less advanced narrative intelligence, we may be hard-pressed to find much meaning at all in what critics might hail as a great novel. As it were, we understand the words but we miss the point; we fail to catch the meaning. By the same token, the meaning we would catch, if we could catch any, might be a far cry from the meaning that the author initially had in mind.

Story-meaning is also, then, *individualized*. To use the term we are using throughout this book, it is idiosyncratic. The same story will be found meaningful by two different people in two different ways, though, of course, the meanings they find will invariably overlap. Otherwise, they could hardly compare notes concerning it, which is another way of stating the point made by Northrop Frye that each book "becomes the focus of a community, as more and more people read it and are affected by it" (1988, p. 5). At the same time, different meanings will be found not only by different people but by the same people reading it at different times. Thus it is that a story can mean more for us each time we read it—again, depending on where we happen to be at the time, amid our own unfolding lifestory.

Story-meaning is thus *indeterminate* too. Though the story itself must end, there is no end to the meaning it can mediate to us, no predetermined limit. There is an indeterminacy about it. What it is about, as Bruner (1996, p. 140) says, "is always open to some question." It has a built-in "ambiguity of reference." The same story can be about a variety of things at once: love, money, politics, philosophy, faith. Thus, no novel has one meaning alone but a whole range of potential meanings. Nor are such potential meanings set in advance—by the author, for instance. Certainly, there is no limit to what we can get out of it as readers.

Story-meaning is also indeterminate in that it is *not localized*. It is omnipresent. It ultimately pervades the whole of the story. The meaning is not to be found in one place alone, anymore than the story itself is to be found on one particular page. In a well-composed tale, every event, every detail, every word is significant (J. Gardner, 1985). It serves some purpose in the flow of the tale as a whole, however difficult it may be to discern that purpose at the time. As it were, story-meaning is connected. Accordingly, great literature has a sense of profundity throughout; its atmosphere is laden with significance from beginning to end. We cannot say that it has meaning here but not there or that the meaning is in this chapter, this page, or this passage but not in that. Nor is it in or tied to a particular event or conversation, though some events and conversations seem to reveal it more than others; that is, while it is spread through the story as a whole, it is not necessarily spread in an even fashion.

Critical points in the story line—turning points, we might call them—possess particular dramatic significance. As we pass through them, something about how they are crafted or foreshadowed, and also something inside us, tells us "this is an important part; pay attention." Depending on how the crisis in question is resolved, we know that the plot could thereafter unfold in a number of ways, that the characters' fortunes and futures hang in the balance. For this reason, story-meaning is also *intermittent*. We

are bound to find a story more meaningful—and thus more memorable—at some points along its plot line than at others. Certain events will
stand out as having more implications than others for how the story as a
whole turns out and for what, ultimately, it means. Still, at no point in the
story is there no meaning at all. In our readers' minds, we know instinctively—or we trust—that even those parts of the plot that feel flatter or
more plodding are going somewhere, are leading to something. They are
the lull before the action, the calm before the storm.

Story-meaning is also a *function of aesthetics*. It is linked to the complexity
of the plot, the depth with which the characters are displayed, and the
thickness of the atmosphere. The more complexity and depth and thickness then, the more meaning, potentially, we find. At the same time,
story-meaning is actual and not abstract. It is rooted in events (albeit fictional ones) and cannot be reduced to a moral philosophical proposition.
The point of the story cannot be isolated *from* the story. Justice can be done
to it not by distilling it into a single phrase, such as Love conquers all, but
only by telling the story again. The medium *is* the message. The meaning
of the story *is* the story. As the saying goes, "It's all in the telling." Perhaps
for this reason, existentialist writers such as Jean-Paul Sartre and Gabriel
Marcel frequently used fiction to flesh out their philosophical ideas: in order to root in the soil of (fictional) existence the issues and questions with
which, albeit vicariously, they wanted us to wrestle.

Story-meaning is *parabolic* (see Turner, 1996). At the same time as it asks
us to look for its meaning within it and not apart from it, the story points us
beyond its world to our world, as readers. Moreover, it points to some elusive, yet persistent world that lies beyond even that: a larger world of possibility and meaningfulness to which the story merely opens a door. The
degree of meaningfulness the story will hold for us depends in part, then,
on our ability to accept that there is such a "something more," a something
other, beyond it, of which it is ultimately but the symbol or sign. It may remain a mystery, of course, as to how exactly each story, or story in general,
illuminates our world and transforms our sense of it thereafter: our world,
that is to say, plus, or multiplied by, the version of it that the story inspires.
At the same time, appreciating story-meaning requires that, while we are
experiencing the reality of the story itself, we escape our normal reality, accept the story's world as *the* world, and also, at the time at least, lower our
awareness of the other world to which, wittingly or not, it is attempting to
point. Story-meaning requires that we submit to a suspension of disbelief,
allowing ourselves to forget that it is, after all, just a story.

Story-meaning is thus parabolic in a *moral*, even ethical, sense as well. A
story, any story, describes an ordered and orderable world. It cuts an
evaluative swath through the chaos of innumerable details and possibilities, dividing it implicitly into what is desirable and what is not desirable,
into relevant and irrelevant, into its own and not necessarily conventional

version of right and wrong, good and bad. In this sense, each work of fiction not only has a moral but is, inherently, moral (see Gardner, 1978).

Story-meaning is also *consequential*. A story consigns meaning to events by laying them out in a particular order, and so conferring on them a causal coherence. A story comes from somewhere and goes somewhere. It sequences events not in a higgledy-piggledy manner, like items on a shopping list, but consequentially, conferring on them a dynamic structure of beginning, middle, and end. Of course, individual novels may play with the convention and jump around chronologically in their presentation of events. As the filmmaker Jean-Luc Godard has put it, "A story must have a beginning, middle, and end, but not necessarily in that order" (Marchand, 1991). Nonetheless, insofar as a story needs a beginning, middle, and end, in whatever order they may be arranged, the assumption is that one event is intrinsically linked, or leads, to another.

Story-meaning is *conflictual*. It requires conflict in order to emerge. Whatever kind of conflict is in question, whether between ideas, between characters, within characters, or between characters and their environment, the struggle to resolve such conflict gives the story its distinctive atmosphere, style, and shape. Paradoxically, the conflict is what holds it together, what makes it cohere. If there are no detours and no interruptions in the straight path from initial calm to final conclusion, then the story has not only no shape and no goal but also no energy and no drive. It fails to go anywhere. It also fails to say anything, to make a significant or even just interesting point. If everything unfolds smoothly with no disappointment of expectations, if there is a middle that is not in some way muddled (Atkinson, 1995), then there is nothing of note to report. If nothing goes wrong, then there is nothing to write. A story needs trouble (Bruner, 1987; 1999). This is the law of narrative: No trouble, no tale. No problem, no plot.

Story-meaning is linked to genre as well. It is *generic*. While there is an infinite number of stories in the world, there is arguably a finite number of kinds of stories. Northrop Frye (1966) identifies five: myth, tragedy, romance, comedy, and irony. A story recounted according to the tragic mode will naturally have a different range of meanings for us than one conveyed in a comic, romantic, or ironic mode. This is not to imply that the category of genre is especially straightforward (Bruner, 1996), however, for the same story line can be converted into many modes. More to the point, in the more profound, more captivating, more engaging stories, genres become blurred, tragic themes run side by side with comic ones, and so on.

Story-meaning is *culturally rooted*. A story is deemed meaningful only in relation to the story patterns or story forms that are available in the culture from which it emerges. No story stands entirely alone, is completely novel. It must inevitably borrow from its culture's (ever changing) repertoire of acceptable, conventional, and meaningful story lines. These story lines tend to vary, of course, from one culture to another, each with its unique history and its peculiar political, economic, and religious traditions. The literature Italian writers produce is arguably different from that generated by American ones or Chinese or Iranians ones, and so forth. Similar varieties will also pertain within each culture, between particular periods. Eighteenth-century English literature tends to be different, to reflect different genres of story making, and perhaps even to mediate different meanings, from nineteenth- or twentieth-century English literature. Within twentieth-century literature, further divisions pertain, insofar as the themes and forms reflected in the literature of the Roaring Twenties may be generally different from those of the Dirty Thirties, the postwar years, postmodern years, and so on. Though the details are no doubt debatable, the point still stands: Literature is not a monolithic category. Within each culture, certain story types stand out and, with them, arguably, so do certain types of story wisdom.

One reason for this culture-rootedness is that the language in which a given novel is written is necessarily shared with the language in which others are written as well. Like its counterpart creations emerging from the same culture, it must ultimately draw on, and so be limited by, a common store of words, a common set of grammatical rules, and a common pool of proverbs, allusions, and figures of speech. The combination formed from these common elements will, naturally, be novel, just as each symphonist takes the exact same notes as anyone else yet fashions a fresh composition: same notes, different tune. However, though story-meaning can therefore to some degree be novel or unique, it can only be judged as such because it is related to, and so can be contrasted with, a common language and a common frame of reference regarding the nature and limits of meaningfulness per se.

Story-meaning is *retrospectively assigned*. We read meaning into the events of the story after the fact. To borrow from Kierkegaard, we read the story forward, but we understand it backward. The meaning of an event is inferred back into it in light of the ending of the story as a whole, or at least in light of the ending that, as we read, we anticipate or predict. As we read, story-meaning is thus always provisional, forever being revised in light of our ever-changing theories as to where the story is going and how it will eventually end. Meaning is end-related. For example, a story that ends well, in the sense of tying up loose ends, may *seem* to mean more, while a story with an ending that we see as open or unresolved may seem so confusing as to lack any meaning at all. By the same token, confusing endings can ultimately be more meaningful, insofar as they give us more to ponder. They push us to work harder at figuring things out, at making and owning the meaning for ourselves. (They may even push us to read the story again, which is a different experience from reading it for the first time. In the former case, we know how it ends but are still trying to understand what its end might mean.) The type of meaning a story conveys to us depends, in general then, on the genre of its ending. The meaning we take from a story with what we see as a tragic conclusion is colored one way, while with a comic conclusion, it is colored another way, and so on.

Finally, story-meaning is *cumulative*. It builds over time. It thickens. In one sense, there is less of it on the first page than there is in the middle or, especially (and this is significant from the perspective of biographical aging), at the end. Having engaged our imagination increasingly since its beginning, the story becomes steadily more poignant for us, and more precious. Our experience of it grows more intense. It shines, we could say, with a sharper, more delicate light. The more its end draws nigh, the harder it is to let go. It becomes more meaningful, more powerful, and, to that degree, more wise. This accumulation process is, once again, reader related. As we move through the text, a continually changing array of expectations is set off as to where the story is going and what it means. Temporally speaking, this is a highly complex process. As Peter Brooks (1985) points out, "We read in a spirit of confidence, and also a state of dependence, that what remains to be read will restructure the provisional meanings of the already read" (p. 25). At the same time, "if the past is to be read as present, it is a curious present that we know to be past in relation to a future we know to be already in place, already in wait for us to reach it" (p. 23). So it is that what one critic calls our sense of an ending (Kermode, 1966) overshadows both the middle of the story and the beginning as well. In this respect, which once again underscores the nature of story time, there is as much significance in the beginning as there is in the end, albeit a significance that, compared with the realized significance of the end, is only tacit or implicit, only promised or potential. In any case, in both story and, as we shall see, lifestory, "meaning always stands in a horizontal context that stretches into the past and into the future" (Berman, 1994, p. 178).

With these observations about meaning in terms of story per se, what can we say about the meaning of meaning in terms of lifestory? Each of the dimensions of story-meaning we have identified can shed light on the mystery of meaning within a life and, by implication, on the meaning of ordinary wisdom. Before exploring this conviction in greater detail, however, let us pause to consider an important issue.

We have been saying here that a story is by definition a structure for meaning. But surely it is possible for a story to have meaning, at either its end or its beginning, without having wisdom. Its message may be clear but ultimately insipid. Its meaning, though interesting, may be novel and nothing more, and so may not resonate for very long inside us. It connects with our experience but only superficially and fleetingly and so fails to illuminate our life, to stretch our souls. For this reason, it will probably also fail to qualify as literature. As to the exact link between meaning and wisdom in story terms, it is therefore difficult to say. But perhaps we can say at

least this: Stories that prove meaningful on an enduring basis, that capti-
vate us generation after generation, that work on several levels at once, are
the stories we might dare to label wise. It is our thesis in this chapter that
the stories of our own lives, as ordinary as they seem, are wise in comparable ways.

STORY TRUTH: HOW LIFESTORIES MEAN

At this point, our agenda is to take the various characteristics of meaning we identified in the last section in relation to stories per se and try to extrapolate them to lifestories. Lurking behind the scenes as we carry out this
agenda, of course, is the question of truth, which, like the question of time
itself, emerges as soon as we consider the *literariness* of a life, or what Hillman (1975) calls "the fictional side of human nature." While a full discussion of truth in relation to autobiography (see Charmé, 1984; Pascal, 1960;
Eakin, 1985) and narrative generally (see Bruner, 1996; Spence, 1982) is certainly pertinent to the topic of ordinary wisdom, it is, as we have said, outside of our scope to do justice to it here. Prior to getting on with the
question of meaning in lifestory, however, allow us to summarize our
thinking so far.

All we know of ourselves is a set of stories that we compose and continually recompose about the facts or the events of our lives. We have access
not to those events themselves, but only to our interpretations or our versions of them. "Our knowledge," says Schank, "is really a collection of
hundreds of thousands of stories" (1990, p. 63). Applied to our knowledge
of ourselves, this means that our identity or self-definition amounts to "the
adoption of a set of stories as [our] own" (p. 203). Besides constantly
changing in relation to the contexts and agendas that trigger our recollection of them, these stories are often, at best, only edited summaries of our
past, hasty assessments of our present, and speculative versions of our future (Kenyon & Randall, 1997). Untrustworthy as they may be, however, it
is nonetheless in terms of—or through—such stories that we dream and
worry, believe and doubt, think and feel; that we act, react, and interact. Indeed, we never think or feel about anything in the abstract, but always in
terms of, against the background of, or (once again) through our own
lifestory material. At an unarticulated level, we experience our lives and
the world around us—past, present, and future—as a set of incipient stories awaiting formulation. In essence, our lives are repositories of stories
(Schank, 1990). More to the point, they *are* stories (Randall, 1995): living,
flesh-and-blood novels of which we are at once author, narrator, protagonist, reader, and text.

Before we look at how life-novels mean, however, we ought to review
the overall ways in which a life is—and is not—like a story. On the one
hand, a life is like a story in the broad sense that it has a beginning, middle,

and end. A life is also made up of a sequence of events that unfolds over time, events of all different types and on all different levels, some that (before, during, or after) seem more important and more meaningful than others. A life can also be followed, both by the person living it and (though differently) by others looking on. A life has a central person—or character—at the heart of it. A life has a narrator too, in the sense of someone (the person living it) who can communicate concerning it by means of symbols and signs, gestures and words. A life is thus textual, and so understandable. It can be analyzed, interpreted, reflected on, or read—once again, both by the person living it and by others looking on.

On the other hand, while a life is automatically edited by the person living it, it is much more than what the editing leaves in. A life cannot be confined between two covers and consigned to a shelf, nor can it be limited to the two-hour framework of a full-length film. A life is not only about symbols or images or words, it is about muscles, bones, and blood. It is about breathing and eating, about being born and being bored. It is about disappointment and disease. It is about decrepitude and death. Sometimes excitingly, other times depressingly, a life is all too real. A story, however, no matter how great or how true to life it is deemed, is ultimately a representation, a facsimile, a fiction. Furthermore, it is not customary for most of us to think of a life as having a single author either behind it or above it, a mastermind controlling and decreeing, god-like, what to include and what to omit, what is the main plot and what are mere subplots, what is important, or relevant, and what is not, how what is included is to be sequenced and cast, and according to what genre it ought to unfold—in short, determining what *the* story is. Indeed, in a life, distinctions between author, narrator, character, and reader can seem scarcely to apply at all, or if they do, then only in the unusual, paradoxical sense that each "I" is actually all of these things at once.

Obviously, the story metaphor cannot account for everything about a life. No metaphor can. A life is not a story in some immediate manner. "Life as story" is a metaphor and not a fact. Our premise in this book, however, is that, given that we cannot think about anything except through metaphor, story is one of the richest metaphors yet used to get at what it is like to have a life and live a life. For this reason, it deserves as much exploration as we can manage. It is particularly rich, we feel, in relation to wisdom, a topic that cannot be adequately entertained using other metaphors. For now, then, the route to take is to examine meaning as it pertains to lives as stories, taking the features of story-meaning we identified last section as our reference points. We will consider a number of these features in turn, except for how lifestory-meaning is culturally rooted, which in a sense we have already considered under the larger stories we live within. Overall, the assumption we shall be working with is the same as that expressed by Charmé (1984, p. 47): "The meaning and interpretation of a person's life share certain common characteristics with the meaning and interpretation of a literary text."

First, lifestory-meaning is *reader-related*. As we shall explore more closely in Chapter 5, one of the perspectives we can have on our own life-narrative is that of reader. Just as light requires an eye to see or sound an ear to hear, a story requires a reader to read. My capacity (or my narrative intelligence) to experience my life in the way that a reader experiences a story is what gives substance, shape, and soul to my sense of my life. While my lifestory may have meaning for others who are reading it outside-in, that is, from the biographical angle (indeed, even more meaning than it may for me), it will have no meaning for me at all if my own reader side is inactive. It is possible that individuals afflicted with savant syndrome are included in this category, with a limited sense of self in the midst of the events of their own life, because they are poor self-readers (Treffert, 1989). The same category could include those who are suffering from dementia as well. Dementia represents an increasingly important area in which a narrative perspective can be fruitfully applied. For dementing persons, it could be said, this capacity to read themselves is severely impaired. They certainly cannot tell their stories in the manner that the rest of us can. What we are learning, however, is that with the help of others, it is possible for them to continue to have, and tell, a story that still has meaning, both for them and for us (Crisp, 1995; Hallberg, in press; Holst, Edberg, & Hallberg, 1999; Guse et al., in press).

Lifestory-meaning is *individualized* too. My lifestory will not have the same meaning for me as it will have for other people. No matter how well they may think they know me, they cannot read my inner text in the way in which—accurately or not—I can read it. Ultimately, they are looking at me outside-in. At the same time, everyone who has some reading on me forms a kind of community around me, analogous to that created around each work of literature by virtue of the fact that a group of individuals has read the same text and thus had a comparable literary experience. Accordingly, each of us is the center of a network of other individuals who have an interpretation of our lifestory. Each autobiographer, that is, is surrounded by a host of would-be biographers.

Lifestory-meaning is *indeterminate*. Not only is a lifestory, like any story, filled with multiple levels, numerous characters, and several subplots and themes, it is also, like any great novel, both boundless and bottomless. It is boundless in the sense that it is a world unto itself. It is bottomless in the sense that there is no limit to what we can discuss concerning it nor to the meanings we can extrapolate from it. Just as any biographer can attest to the different stories that can be spun from the same set of life events, so any journal-keeper can tell us that one slice of life, one otherwise innocuous encounter, one snippet of conversation, holds layers of possible insights into who we are, how we relate to others, and how we experience our world.

There is thus no end to the meaningfulness of a lifestory, no end to what we can read into or out of the texts of our lives. The upshot of this is that there is always something more to discover within ourselves. We can never know ourselves completely. As we will examine in more detail in Chapter 4, our story is opaque.

Lifestory-meaning is even more indeterminate than story-meaning, however, due to an important difference between lives and stories. Though our life, like a story, ends, we can never get outside of it. We can get outside of a story because we can transcend its ending. Knowing that ending makes it clearer to us, once we are done reading, what sort of story it has been, what it has been about, and what we are to make of it—the range of possible interpretations that are acceptable, sensible, and plausible. With a lifestory, however, such clarity is impossible. Thus it is that a lifestory is more indeterminate than a story-story, not only while it is still unfolding but even after it has concluded—that is, in death. Even though death confers a finality on the chain of life events, there is no end to the stories that can be read into that chain—or, more correctly, chains, since there has been no advance declaration that one chain is the main plot and others only subplots. A biographer's task is nonetheless easier when the subject is deceased than when still alive, and therefore still changing, which means that the whole story cannot yet be written.

The task of the autobiographer is harder still, as we shall discuss further in Chapter 5. Unless he or she were to die in the act of composing the last line, the whole story remains more elusive than it is for the biographer writing from the perspective of outside-in. Of course, the question can be asked if death is the end at all or merely a change of perspective. In any case, the autobiographical task is also difficult because, as narrator, character, and reader all at once, we have no single standpoint from which to state what the story is unless we tell our story according to the conventions of our culture; for example, according to a normative story line of getting married, raising a family, assuming a mortgage, and so forth. How do I tell my story? the autobiographer must always ask. Where do I begin? What language do I use? What tone do I strike? What do I include and what do I leave out? How do I decide what is important, and why?

With so many questions, the autobiographical task can easily make us dizzy, yet it is potentially a liberating and not unsettling experience. While it is true that, as a friend of ours once said, "you can get lost in your own story," this open-endedness to our inner, narrative world is the inspiration and impetus for unlimited development. For psychologist Mark Freeman (1993), who sees development to be "as various as the people who walk the earth" (or, in our terms, novel), "development may be seen as a process that can go on forever." Indeed, he asks, "Don't even the most frail and wizened sometimes achieve renewed insight into who and what they are?" (p. 48). Freeman is not talking about development in a biological or psychosexual sense, which up to now has been one of the primary ways in which development has been understood. Rather, he is talking about biographical development, which, we would argue, has no end, no final phase or stage. If you will, there is always more to learn about ourselves, which means that restorying, and indeed radical restorying, is always a possibility (Kenyon & Randall, 1997), no matter our age.

Lifestory-meaning is indeterminate in another sense as well: It is *nonlocalized*. This goes along with the intermittent nature of lifestory-meaning. While we experience some phases in life, at the time, as high in significance, we experience others as comparatively low. Yet even during these times when nothing much is happening, we seldom write them off as entirely meaningless. However much it may strain our patience to sustain it, a sense of potential meaningfulness still pervades them, once we see how things turn out. Eventually, we expect to understand something about why they have happened, what part they have played in the unfolding of our life. If we can bring no such sense to events for too long at a time, of course, the result may be a deepening crisis of meaning and, at worst, suicidal despair.

Lifestory-meaning is *parabolic*, and, like story-meaning per se, moral as well. Given that no story is innocent (Rosen, 1986), but always laden with values and intent on driving home some message or point, a lifestory, we would argue, is no exception. Each person's life may be said to inject into the world a unique set of insights and to pose it a particular set of questions for which no other person's life can ever be the vehicle. Each life cuts a swath through a realm of possibilities, achieving its own peculiar balancing act between good and evil, right and wrong. Furthermore, like the events and details included in a novel, which are always more or less consequential to the outcome of the story as a whole, the events and details of a life are not automatically valueless or flat. Indeed, it is common for us to talk about making more of some events, situations, or relationships than we do of others. We do so out of a sense, which the novelist explicitly articulates, that they are somehow more important than other events; that they are more significant; that no matter how subtle, fleeting, or delicate they may be, they have more in them. They are intrinsically deeper. We might feel too, of course, that they have happened for a reason.

This sense that certain events are thus somehow deeper and more significant than others is part of a larger sense we may have that we live our lives within a meaning-context (or larger story) in relation to which degrees of meaningfulness (greater or lesser) can be assigned. Instructive here are the words of May Sarton (1977), whose sense of the meaningfulness of even the most ordinary events leads her to speak in her journals about "undigested experience," about the importance of "living at the deepest level" (p. 131), and about "the deeper the experience, the more time [being] required to sort it out" (Sarton, 1986, p. 173).

Another way to say that lifestory-meaning is parabolic is to say that lifestory per se is parable-like. "Like a parable," writes theologian Sallie TeSelle (1975, p. 151), "an autobiography tells a particular kind of story, a metaphorical story. That is, the autobiography is intended to be a metaphor of the self" (see also Olney, 1972). If we apply TeSelle's point to the kind of inner autobiography that we are constantly, if unconsciously, composing inside of us (our inside story, as it were), then what she says is fascinating: "We read autobiographies to find out about ourselves. The other is a medium, a metaphor, into that desert, *myself*" (TeSelle, 1975, p. 146). As for what happens when we move from the inside level to that of inside-out: "We cannot look at the self directly, for like mercury it squirts away from our sight; but we can evoke the self through a similitude of it, through the metaphor we call autobiography" (p. 149). "When we write an autobiography," she says, "we move from the known to the unknown; we attempt to grasp the unknown, the mystery of the self, through the known, the myriad details of the story of one's own life. The details are *not* the self, but they ought to point to it, be a metaphor of it" (p. 150).

Lifestory-meaning is dependent as well on the *suspension of disbelief*. Objective observation of the raw data of our day-to-day life (assuming such objectivity were possible) might suggest that there is no inherent coherence to our existence, that events follow events with no intrinsic sense. If we were truly to believe this, however, we would be bound to believe that our sense of self in the midst of these events is the product of pure fantasy, with no basis in fact. Sheer psychological survival requires that we put this suspicion aside. It requires we believe that we are not mere "Humean beings" (Sacks, 1985), not mere bundles of essentially unconnected sensations, but that there is indeed an "I" that is continuous through time. It requires we believe that our life traces a story and that, complex as it is, that story makes sense; furthermore, that the events it recounts and connects have not just one factual-historical meaning but a whole range of possible interpretations, limited only by the limitations of our readerly imagination (see Spence, 1982).

Lifestory-meaning is *conflictual*. Conflict is as essential to the unfolding of a life as it is to that of a story. Not only is it essential, but it is a given. No life is without its ups and downs. No life is without its tensions and problems. From a story perspective, however, these are not difficulties; they are absolutely necessary. In a sense, the more conflict the better, for it is vital to the dynamic progression of a life. Is it an accident that to Eric Erikson (1963), for example, movement through the stages of psychosexual development depends on our success in resolving a series of "crises"? Crudely put, the principle is *no pain, no gain*.

To return to story-meaning as such, the more a novel is classed as literature, the less soluble are its conflicts, the more "open" (Eco, cited in Selden, 1989, p. 117) is its story, and the more we keep thinking about it after we have finished reading it. Thus, we find certain stories more meaningful than others. They resonate more deeply with the contents of our hearts and minds. Literarily, there is more in them. A play by O'Neill or Shakespeare, a novel by Atwood or Oates gives us much to ponder and discuss. There is no limit to the material we can draw from it. Conversely, a story written to formula is a closed book. The same insight could apply to life. "The serious problems in life are never fully solved," says Carl Jung (cited in Sarton, 1977, p. 101). "If ever they should appear to be so it is a sure sign that something has been lost. The meaning and purpose of a problem seem to lie not in its solution but in our working at it incessantly. This alone preserves us from stultification and petrifaction." Reflecting Jung's positive assessment of the place of problems in our lives is Michael Novak's (1971, p. 49) observation that "interesting people are full of contradictions." Indeed, he says, "to bring integration out of wildly disparate tendencies is the mark of a great soul."

Lifestory-meaning may require conflict, then, but conflict alone is insufficient. It requires connection as well. It requires a sense of integration, both in space—as in, I am connected to you and to my house—and in time—as in, one event leads to another. Lifestory-meaning is therefore not merely sequential but consequential too. And in this consequentiality is a certain dynamic, dramatic, aesthetic shape, one which the story metaphor helps bring into view. As we emerge from infancy, move into adolescence and adulthood, raise a family, take up a succession of professions and pursuits, it is as if the plot of our life steadily thickens. It complexifies. It includes more subplots and characters, incorporates more themes, becomes more intricate and layered. As we near our life's conclusion, of course, it may be said to undergo a certain narrowing as well, given the decrease in the number of physical options or social opportunities that are open to us. But such narrowing of our life path need not be seen as a necessary development—as in the denouement of many a literary story. Indeed, as long as they are biographically active (Kenyon & Randall, 1997), many people's inner story world may actually continue to thicken, thereby illustrating in the novel they are living what E. M. Forster (1962) says is "the idea that the novelist must cling to. Not completion. Not rounding off but opening out." May Sarton, for instance, refers to how, "as life goes on, it becomes more intense because," as she says, "there are tremendous numbers of associations and so many memories" (1981, p. 231).

In this respect, lifestory-meaning is *cumulative* as well. Drawing on Whitehead's philosophy of process to develop an aesthetic understanding of the physical universe, John Haught (1984) provides a rich image with which to understand the cumulative dimension of lifestory-meaning. "As the sea of events that make up the cosmos broadens and deepens," he writes in *The Cosmic Adventure*, "the meaning of each individual happening is itself intensified and widened. Its final meaning, therefore, cannot be determined from its own limited perspective any more than we can determine the meaning of the early episodes of a novel without reading it to the end" (p. 104). Meaning is determined, then, by virtue of the hermeneutic-dynamic interrelationship between part and whole, or as we shall see in a moment, between middle and end. Every event is potentially related to every other event in an intricate way (see Gardner, 1985), a way that increases as more events are added, and a way of which we can, theoretically, be increasingly conscious as our story proceeds. Every event is thus potentially the bearer of ever greater significance, and our life as a whole is thus infinitely meaningful. Psychologist Ira Progoff (1975, p. 11) builds on such an insight and goes so far as to say—indeed, farther than we might wish to say here—that it is "possible for all the events and relationships of our life to show us what they were for, what their purpose was in our lives, and what they wish to tell us for our future." Echoing our earlier point about the "followability" of a lifestory, he says we therefore "gradually discover that our life has been going somewhere."

In the meantime, lifestory-meaning, like story-meaning, is *retrospectively assigned*. We ascertain it by means of hindsight, by occupying the end of whatever chain of events has brought us to the interpretive standpoint of the present moment. As the present moment changes, then, our sense of our lifestory and of its meaning thus far will naturally change as well. Each time it does, it will usually seem a more insightful sense than the one we had yesterday or last year. Hence, the adage about hindsight being 20/20. But though hindsight may occasionally be perfect, it is certainly never final, for today's hindsight, like today's headline, is inevitably superseded by tomorrow's. Bearing in mind Haught's words about needing to read a novel to the end in order to determine "its final meaning," we are helped here by the description that Polkinghorne (1988, pp. 69, 150) gives of the interpretive dilemma we face in our everyday lives. "We are in the *middle* of our stories," he says, and "are constantly having to revise the plot as new events are added to our lives . . . without knowing how the story will end."

Lifestory-meaning is thus *ending-related* as well, at least with respect to our sense of an ending, or of the ending we anticipate. Lifestories, too, come from somewhere and go somewhere. Like story stories, they have particular trajectories or potential directions or, if you will, predispositions. However, we can hardly stand at the end of our own life as we can of a story that we see or hear or read. We cannot get outside of our own life-in-time in that sort of way. Individuals who have undergone near-death experiences may wish to differ, however, claiming that they have been to the end and back. Henceforth, until they die, they interpret everything that has happened in the past, is happening in the present, or may happen in the future in light of the type of ending that they have had the chance to skip ahead and taste. For the rest of us, denied such a sneak preview, our sense of the ending to our life may change on a daily basis, depending on the genre of story that we feel ourselves to be living and on the larger story we see ourselves to be living within. Each such larger story provides a built-in ending for our individual lives. In Christianity, that ending is constructed in terms of concepts such as heaven and hell, resurrection and eternal life; in Buddhism, in terms of nirvana; in atheism, of a return to the meaningless void from which our existence originally, if pointlessly, emerged.

In any case, this insight into the ending-relatedness of lifestory-meaning leads to another feature, which is that lifestory-meaning is *generic*. How a story ends affects how we experience it as a whole (Pearson, 1989), whether as a tragedy or a comedy, and so on. Putting this another way, just as a novel hangs together within itself as an entire story world, each of us may be said to live in our own little world, with its distinctive atmosphere, spirit (Owen, 1987; Randall, 1995), and genre. In the words of the novelist Guy de Maupassant (Allen, 1949, p. 126), "each one of us makes for himself an illusion of a world—poetic, sentimental, joyful, melancholy, ugly or gloomy according to his nature."

Just as, in a literary novel, these genres rarely appear in pure form, however, so they are no less mixed in life, understood as a narrative composition. As James Hillman (1989, p. 81) says, "while one part of me knows the soul goes to death in tragedy, another is living a picaresque fantasy, and a third engaged in the heroic comedy of improvement." While it sometimes happens that we see our lives in terms of a particular genre—for example, *I've had a tragic life*—and that our whole self-concept is accordingly colored, the ease with which we can assign a particular genre to a particular life tends to be proportionate to the degree we are outside of that life looking in. When we look at lives outside-in, we may readily witness distinctive, generic trajectories at work, what Ruth and Öberg (1996) call ways of life. "Though our stories are unique," writes literary critic Wayne Booth (1988, p. 289), "they fall into 'genres' that are obviously not infinite in number." Indeed, he offers us the following summary: "from high promise to happiness to misery; from beginning misery to happiness to misery; from misery to misery to maximum misery . . . ; from happiness to happiness to misery; from happiness to happiness to higher happiness . . . ; from promise to promise to sudden accidental death. And so on."

Added to our earlier investigations into autobiographical memory, these reflections on the meaning of meaning in terms of lifestory have enabled us to see that lifestory is really a peculiar brand of fiction—whether we express it in the form of an autobiography that we write for publication or in that of the internal autobiography that we are continually composing within us. The fact, however, that lifestory in either form is fundamentally faction (Steele, 1986), replete with plots, characters, and themes, has important implications for how we understand the wisdom we believe to be associated with it. We shall examine some of these implications in Chapter

5 when we expand on a notion we have already introduced, that of "reading ourselves." For the moment, let us conclude with a summary of where we are so far.

What we have been building toward throughout this chapter is the provocative proposition that wisdom fills lives like meaning pervades literature. Insofar as our lives are inseparable from our lifestories, our lives are wise in the ways that stories are wise. Although the mere suggestion that stories can be wise may be anathema to some, the wisdom of a story, we would submit, is never reducible to or expressible in terms of some gem of insight, some general platitude, or some moral conviction. It is not extractable from the story but integral to it, warts and all. Indeed, it is in the telling, and the warts themselves are the key.

The greatness of a great story, that is, lies in the questions it raises as much as in the answers it supplies. It lies in the ambiguities as much as in the clarifications, in the conflicts as much as in the conclusions, in the problems as much as in the resolutions, in the muddle as much as the end. It lies in the loose ends as much as in the tying up, in the mysteries as much as in the certainties, in the possibilities as much as in the actualities. It lies in the murky water as much as on the solid rock, in the unsaid and unseen as much as in what we read on the page or view on the screen. It lies in the poignant silences between the lines, in the loaded spaces behind the scenes, and in the dark depths beneath the words as much as it does in whatever, on the surface, might meet the eye.

The nearer we approach the end of the story, moreover, the more wise it may be said to become. If we apply such a line of thought to the stories we are, it would seem to add strength, then, to the old adage about old age, which is that we do indeed get wiser with our years. But not necessarily wiser, we would stress, in the sense of smarter or better, or of more practical, sensible, ethical, or anything else. If for no other reason, we may grow wiser simply because we approach the end, in the same way that any story becomes more meaning filled the closer we get to its conclusion. In any event, we now shift our musings on wisdom from the biographical side of things to the spiritual side, as captured by the metaphor of life as journey.

4

Spiritual Aging: Life as Journey

As symbolic creatures, we remain ever unfinished; this is our glory. The human spirit, through its conscious and unconscious life, is forever open to the unexpected, to shaping a new story.

—Eugene Bianchi (1995)

And, when the given hour shall strike, arouse us, eager as the traveler who straps on his rucksack, while beyond the misty windowpane the earliest rays of dawn are faintly visible.

—Gabriel Marcel (1962)

STORY AND JOURNEY

This chapter is about the intimate connection between ordinary wisdom, human spirituality, and the life course viewed as a particular type of story, namely, a journey. It is by journeying through our lifestories, we believe, that aspects of our ordinary wisdom can become visible to us. Moreover, that journey is essentially a spiritual process.

As to what we mean by spirituality, we share the view of Robert Atkinson (1995, p. xiii) when he says that "everything we encounter as adults that gives us a new and deeper meaning in life is spiritual." Defined in this broad way, spirituality is inseparable from the process we began talking about toward the end of Chapter 3, namely reading for meaning in the stories we are. Quoting Atkinson again, "telling the stories of our life is telling our spiritual autobiography, because this helps us discover, and become more aware of, what our deepest values are and what we can put our fullest trust in" (Atkinson, 1995, p. xiii). As we discussed in Chapter 2, however, our consideration of spirituality here is undertaken without reference to a specific theology. While we will draw examples from different sources, what we are interested in primarily is the insight that underlies various wisdom traditions, or the perennial philosophy. In what follows, then, we will look at the characteristics of the metaphor of life as a journey in order to see what journey can tell us about ordinary wisdom, and vice versa.

In this chapter, too, the six dimensions of wisdom we have been considering all along will continue to be at work. As in Chapter 3, the cognitive dimension is represented in story as the basic form of telling a life, with the added focus on journey as a particular story form. The dimension of idiosyncratic expression is reflected in the unique and inviolable aspects of each of our journeys. The practical-experiential dimension is evident in the emphasis on lived experiences as well as in the discussion of wisdom-related practices such as meditation. The interpersonal dimension is highlighted in our exploration of the paradox of intersubjectivity, which we began to consider in Chapter 3 in the section The Larger Stories We Live Within. The spiritual-mystical dimension is emphasized in what we call the storying moment and in the creation-discovery paradox of the journey. Finally, the moral-ethical dimension is reflected in the discussion of the directionality of the journey, namely, toward less separation and more connectedness in a life.

HOMO VIATOR: CHARACTERISTICS OF THE METAPHOR

The term *homo viator* is taken from the title of a work by the existentialist philosopher and dramatist Gabriel Marcel (1962). Translated literally as "itinerant man," the phrase refers to human beings as travelers, pilgrims, or wayfarers (see also Kenyon, 1991). Viewed against the background of Marcel's thinking, there are five important dimensions of life as a journey that we will consider here.

The Journey Is Personal

As we have found in looking at various wisdom traditions, the human journey is, to an important degree, both individual and inner. We each bring to our voyage our own set of past experiences, present perceptions, and future expectations. This means there is a unique, inviolable, and intimate center to each of us, or as we said in the last chapter, an inside story. The journey is of a person, in contrast to the impersonal, indeed, dehumanized images of human beings that are associated with, for example, strict behaviorism or extreme social constructionism, as we discussed earlier. In these views, there is little room to argue that people create meaning since they are understood either as systems of stimulus-response that react to an inner and outer environment or as beings whose lives are determined by social and cultural narratives over which they have no control. From a theoretical point of view, there is little meaning in the word "journey" (or in "story" for that matter) if we buy into either of these perspectives. A journey might at most be considered chaotic wandering or, even more basically, the chaotic wandering of a what, let alone of a who. We cannot see ordinary wisdom, however, unless we read a particular person's story in great detail and understand the twists and turns of the journey they have taken as imbued with unique and personal meaning. This insight has significant implications for gaining insight into our own ordinary wisdom as well as that of others, either as professionals or as informal agents of restorying (Kenyon & Randall, 1997).

The Journey Is Interpersonal

At the same time as there is a sacredness and a uniqueness to each of our journeys, we are, paradoxically, not alone. As Cole and Winkler (1994, p. 5) explain in discussing the context in which particular moral and spiritual truths about aging are shaped, and, we would add, truths about wisdom as well: "To become personally inhabited, such truths must be cut from the historical cloth of particular cultures, measured by the yardstick of individual experience, and stitched together during an evolution of the spirit that 'pilgrims' of every tradition have experienced along life's way." The key, then, is that the human journey is taken neither alone nor in isolation. Our stories, and our being, are by definition, co-authored. The world we are born into, or find ourselves in, is always a world with other people.

Relationships enjoyed on the journey can range from those of love and communion to indifference and even to what the early Sartre (1955) meant by the now famous phrase that "hell is other people." Whatever the quality of our relationship to others, we need to develop a viable relationship, since the other is already part of our own identity (Kenyon, 1996a). In terms of the language that we used in Chapter 3, both our own life narrative and that of the other are interknit. On some level, I am a character in your lifestory and you are a character in mine: This feature of the journey as interpersonal presents particular challenges in later life. In a culture that does not confirm the powers of age, but only those of youth, it becomes difficult for a person to deal with the crises of aging, because "there is no communal confirmation of the individual who is going through these rites of passage" (Friedman, 1981, p. 147).

The Journey Is Opaque

The landscape of the journey resembles a winding mountain path rather than a prairie highway or a four-lane freeway. It is like what we see when we look through a stained glass window or, in biblical terms, through a glass darkly. In essence, there are fundamental constraints to a clear or panoramic vision of the journey. As we discussed earlier in relation to life as story, we cannot know everything in advance; we cannot know what will occur further along the way. Nor can we know it in hindsight either. Human travelers are not transparent to themselves and therefore cannot read off the truth about reality or uncover the facts to form a basis for their action and decision making.

The Journey Is Transitory

The human journey is of indefinite duration and has a quality of impermanence. There are four points that help us to understand this feature. First, the fact of death makes the traveler finite. However, it is part of the opacity of the journey that we do not know when that part of our story will actually arrive. Second, we do not know if death is the end of the journey. Third, we *do* know that death does not necessarily end *our* journey, in that our story can live on in our culture and in the hearts of our loved ones. Fourth, as we indicated earlier, we live more than one kind of time. While we all are aware, and sometimes painfully so, of clock time or chronological time, we also experience story time or journey time, and such time has both a dynamic quality and an emphasis on the present moment.

These reflections on impermanence suggest that nothing lasts except the journey itself; more to the point, that the journey *does* last, that there is an everchanging landscape and always another destination, that we truly are en route (Marcel, 1962). However, as Victor Frankl (1962, p. 120) notes, "the transitoriness of our existence in no way makes it meaningless." Indeed, we would argue that the experience of ordinary wisdom that comes from viewing life as a journey generates not only meaning but also potentially positive ways of being in the world.

The Journey Is Wonder-ful

The metaphor of a journey suggests—as entailments (Lakoff & Johnson, 1980)—such characteristics as anticipation and hopefulness, as curiosity, discovery, and wonder. As Baird (cited in Reker & Wong, 1988, p. 222) explains, "part of what it means to be human is to *wonder* about what it means to be human" (our emphasis). The notion of wonder implies a going out from oneself, a readiness to learn, an openness. Underlying the characteristics of the metaphor of the journey is a fundamental affirmation of life.

A pilgrimage, for example, is not usually considered to be a negative experience, even though difficulties may occur in the midst of making it, such as bad weather, missed connections, severed relationships, illness, or loneliness. We may even go so far as to say that some forms of joy and well-being are possible on the human journey. Descriptions of peace and happiness are found in many spiritual traditions in connection with the release that occurs in meditation, in prayer, in the experience of nature, and in the acceptance of our own lifestory.

In the following sections of this chapter, we will explore how we can apply these characteristics of the journey metaphor to help us gain some insight into our own ordinary wisdom. For now, we are dealing with what is possible if life and aging are viewed as a journey. We are considering the elements of a good life or a good aging. However, it is more than a consideration of what is possible. In what follows, we will attempt to provide examples that show how the lives of many older (and younger) persons may actually reflect characteristics of this metaphor. Insofar as this is the case, the journey into ordinary wisdom that we are making in this book suggests that other systematic studies could be undertaken to clarify and support these sorts of insights within the context of narrative gerontology. As was the case with earlier research on aging that looked for disengagement and decline, perhaps too assiduously, and therefore found it (Kenyon, 1988), if we look for wisdom, we may in fact find some. In the words of Bianchi (1995, p. 7), "Middle and late adulthood present opportunities for combining the physical descent or gradual organic diminution with a spiritual ascent. The potential for this spiritual ascent, moreover, indicates more than individual development alone; it also promises a reform of social relationships toward a more sharing and just society."

CONTINGENCY AND OPENNESS: THE SPACE IN BETWEEN

The characteristics of the metaphors of both story and journey suggest that, as the philosopher David Hume (1955) would say, there is no necessary connection between the events of a life and how one "is" as a result of experiencing those events. The very qualities of the uniqueness of a human journey, its opacity, and its transitory character, are, on the one hand, invitations to existential dizziness and anxiety. On the other hand, they provide opportunity for change, for altering the itinerary of the journey. We can elaborate this insight further by considering, as we did earlier, that lives and lifestories are made up of both facticity and possibility.

The term *facticity* refers to the story that we "are," or are living, at any point in time. That story is not yet available to us as a story, however, since we are in the middle of living it. Once again, life is lived forward and understood backward. In addition to the story we are currently living, however, our facticity also includes the larger stories we live within, as we discussed in Chapter 3. These would include the structural and social dimensions of our lives that affect and/or constrain them, such as relations with our employers or policies around retirement and pensions. Facticity also includes our hereditary predispositions, as well as our basic emotional themes, or emotionality (Mader, 1996), which is part of what we mean by "genre-ation." Because these elements of our story are not quite facts, however, the term *facticity* is used. From a narrative perspective, it is very difficult to establish the facts, or the truth, the whole truth, and nothing but the truth about either a person or an event. We have access only to our interpretations, to our meanings, or to the stories we tell ourselves and others about a particular event or a specific aspect of ourselves. In other words, while we can speak of my facticity or your facticity, there is no objective facticity.

In contrast, possibility or, more accurately, our sense of possibility refers to aspects of our stories that are open to change, to restorying (Kenyon & Randall, 1997), or to a changed itinerary on our journey. As Maddi (1988, p. 183) explains: "Our sense of what is possible is intertwined with what we perceive as given, and the dynamic balance between the two gives our lives its particular flavor." It is a basic feature of both the story and journey metaphors that we cannot anticipate in advance, on the one hand, what belongs to a person's facticity and is therefore locked in and cannot be changed and, on the other hand, what is open to new meaning. In the words of Martin Buber (cited in Friedman, 1981, p. 143), even in the later years, "to be old is a glorious thing when one has not unlearned what it means to begin." From this point of view, it ultimately does not matter what has happened in our life so long as we can say that we did and are doing our best under the circumstances of our journey.

There is a fundamental contingency and openness to the human journey. There is a void aspect to it, as the Buddhists would say. That is, mistakes are made, the wrong path is taken, and unexpected crises and catastrophes occur (Riegel, 1976). Nevertheless, as long as the voyage of life continues, and as long as it is viewed as a voyage, there is movement onward. As Sogyal Rinpoche (1994, p. 95) observes, "There is no situation, however seemingly hopeless, such as a terminal disease, which we cannot use to evolve. And there is no crime or cruelty that sincere regret and real spiritual practice cannot purify."

Furthermore, as we discussed in Chapter 2 and Chapter 3, the path to ordinary wisdom, or an authentic journey, does not mean that we have this or that story, or that one path is better than another. It means that we become and are our own journey.

Let us summarize our thinking so far. At least in principle, there is a low correlation between what has happened to us on our journey and the possibility of our eventual acceptance of that journey, which is the discovery of our ordinary wisdom. While the radical contingency of, or the spaces in between, lives, stories, and journeys may create an opportunity for existential dizziness, it may also allow opportunities for the continuing creation/discovery of new meaning and for the acknowledgment and appreciation of what we have already experienced on our journey.

There is one source of evidence to which we wish to point to support the claim that people can and do live their lives as journeys and therefore discover their ordinary wisdom. It is the involvement of one of us, for almost ten years, as both participant and facilitator in workshops and courses on what is called Guided Autobiography (Birren & Birren, 1996; Birren & Deutchman, 1991; Kenyon, in press; Mader, 1995). Guided autobiography is an approach to storytelling and storylistening that is minimally directed. Amid it, the observation is often made that negative objective events, such as the loss of loved ones, war, serious illness, separation, divorce, or exile, frequently fail to figure in people's lifestories in ways which, stereotypically, we would expect. Two important points can be made in connection with this observation.

First, it seems that over time, what began as an abject tragedy has been "re-genre-ated" (Randall, 1995) into a satire, a comedy, or at least a questioning acceptance. In other words, it may be the case after all that time heals wounds. As a result of telling their stories in a nonjudgmental environment, some people who undergo tremendous suffering either continue to experience or begin to experience a meaningful and positive journey, and continue to live as travelers who are open to new experiences.

For example, a sudden and painful divorce can seem at the beginning like an experience of being thrown off a cliff or of losing the trail completely. Such an experience may require even a very independent person to seek friends and guides, at least for a time. The words of William Bridges (1981, p. 75) capture these sentiments: "I have recently and reluctantly come to the conclusion (to put it bluntly) that I am lost. Not just unsure that this is the right trail, but off any trail whatsoever. I find myself, figuratively, looking for footprints, broken twigs, any sign that someone has been over this ground ahead of me." In time, however, this trauma, which makes life impossible, can become a satire, with anger, sarcasm, and even a little dark humor built in: *She even took the keys to the tractor!* Then, a new itinerary on the journey is begun: a radical restorying (Kenyon & Randall, 1997) that involves a new partner and children who were not part of the previous path, plus a dramatically increased sensitivity to the stories of others.

This example demonstrates not only the story of the journey but also the journey of the story. In the first and acute period, the story is lived only. It is part of our facticity and dominates that facticity. It is, so to speak, the only story in town. Then, the story becomes readable or tellable, albeit painfully. At this point, it becomes open to our sense of possibility. Finally, it continues to accompany us and change with us on our journey. With the storylistening of others, it provides us with a continued source of ordinary wisdom that we recognize in others and can sometimes apply to our own life too.

The second point to be made in relation to the practice of guided autobiography is that some people have powerful experiences that fail to figure in the present descriptions they give of their journey. For instance, after the fact, they may realize that they have omitted a seemingly significant event, such as a happy marriage or the death of a loved one. Once they realize they have made it, such an omission can be deeply disturbing. But it points to the notion that as long as we are alive, the story of the journey goes on. It is dynamic, creative, and ever changing. This observation provides evidence for our earlier statement that there is no one story of my life that is set, once and for all. We might recall in this regard the point we made earlier about facticity and possibility. At one time, a particular experience or event might be locked in, as facticity. At another time, under the right conditions, it becomes open to restorying, and thus part of our own ordinary wisdom.

The view of our humanity through the lenses of story and journey is in distinct contrast to the argument of traditional personality psychology that omissions from our stories reflect repression, defense mechanisms, and/ or various types of coping strategies. While these concepts are useful and do apply in some situations, they fail to capture the full range of activities in which we human beings are involved, both psychically and emotionally.

Human beings are not only defending themselves against, and coping with, an implied nasty world. They are going out to that world in other ways as well, ways that are mirrored in new trends and constructs in gerontological research. As Jan-Erik Ruth and Peter Coleman (1996, p. 318) explain, "These constructs often reflect aspects of 'the ego's involvement in the world' (Allport, 1955), such as possible selves, goal setting, values, meaning, and purpose in life (Ryff, 1989)." The scientific story of traditional personality research is one that relies on problem-oriented themes, and on implicit, if not explicit, images of human beings as reactive rather than proactive entities. While this perspective certainly presents one important emphasis, people are also engaged in transformation and growth, or a process of what one author calls gero-transcendence (Tornstam, 1989; 1994). In sum, we need to add wisdom-related phenomena such as compassion, love, and acceptance, and as presence, personal meaning, and even serenity, to our list of concepts that are worthy of future investigation.

SPIRITUALITY BEYOND RELIGION: THE ZEN OF ORDINARY WISDOM

Earlier we considered that there is no necessary connection between the events of a life and the meaning that a person places on those events, a feature that lends a quality of workability (Riegel, 1976) or fluidity to our lives. As Marcel (1962, p. 269) notes in citing the work of the poet Rilke: "The heaviness is not in things but in us." A further indication of the potential spaciousness of the human journey is the experience of release and healing that occurs in what could be called the "storying moment," a phenomenon that has a distinctly Zen-like quality.

It is in the very perceptual turn to life as a story and a journey that new meaning and spiritual growth can take place. The telling, which is what we mean by storying moment, *is* the release, a phenomenon that is frequently observed in, among other contexts, the practice of guided autobiography. It allows our story to move from being part of our facticity, and therefore not yet readable, to being available to our sense of possibility and to our creative resources for composing a new story. Sherman and Webb (1994, p. 265) express this insight in their report of a study they made of older persons' lifestories, the focus of which was on spiritual dimensions.

Among other things, they found that those studied continued to appreciate the fact that "their self is indeed a hypothesized self, a storied self, that the self-as-being is larger than that hypothesized self; that the process of spiritual development is one of observing everyday life." As these authors put it, "reflection is fulfillment." Robert Atkinson (1995, p. 15), a narrative theorist and practitioner, expresses it this way: "We may also tell our stories as a way of purging or releasing ourselves of certain burdens. We may not even be aware that part of the story we carry within us is a burden to us until we let it go and let another person hear it." A priest friend of ours once said that he felt that he did very little in the sacrament of reconciliation. Although the expectation on the part of the person confessing is that God is listening through the priest, what provided the healing, he felt, was really the person's act of telling their story and having it listened to; that is, the healing is in the biographical encounter itself and not necessarily in what is disclosed by the storyteller. Nevertheless, as we shall consider in the Epilogue as well, the appropriate narrative environment is essential for our wisdom stories to be able to emerge and for us to then move on in our journeys.

Another Zen-like aspect of the human journey concerns its directionality. Earlier we said that there is no particular map that guides us to an authentic journey, one that is imbued with meaning and wisdom. There is no general answer to the question as to which direction we ought to proceed. Instead, the more we tell and read the text of our lives, the more we observe our journey and the more that direction will reveal itself on its own; that is, the more our unique inner wisdom will be free to be our guide.

As we have proposed elsewhere (Kenyon & Randall, 1997, p. 136), "there can be no cookie-cutter patterns, no prepackaged analytical schemas, with which to story our lives. Ultimately, we are novel. In the end, no one but ourselves can tell us who we are, or who we can become. Within the rich sprawling text of our potentially infinitely interpretable experience we hold whatever answers we need and wisdom we seek." For this reason, many traditions say that we do not go anywhere in our journeys, that the ordinariness of wisdom comes in seeing what we have always seen, though in a radically different way. As Harry Moody (1994, p. 1) points out, "We persist in climbing the ladder of human development, step by step, hoping that, like Jacob's ladder, it will one day lead us beyond the human condition to the stars, like the spaceship in *Cocoon*." We do this when, all the while, the answer may be so close to us that we cannot even see it. For this reason wisdom is said to arise—like love, hopefully—when we least seek it but are most open to it, as, ultimately, a mystery and a gift.

This description of ordinary wisdom may sound familiar. The theme of making the journey within is part of the process of wisdom, extraordinary or ordinary, in most traditions. This is true whether we look at the examined life of Socrates, the Christian perspective, Buddhism, or the tradition of Native spirituality. As George Fowler (1995, p. xv) says, "I spent years grubbing around the globe for something to eat, having all the while a pocket filled with priceless stones. Or, in the metaphor of Meister Eckhart in the fourteenth-century West and of Buddhists before him in the East, I was a man riding an ox looking for an ox to ride on." Both the wisdom traditions and ordinary wisdom, viewed through the journey metaphor, tell us that "we have a natural tendency to find our way to those experiences in life that will lead us through our own transformation" (Atkinson, 1995, p. 30).

It is in the telling, and sharing, of our lifestories that we find these precious stones, one of them being the realization that we have had to be good travelers to have gotten this far. We are all survivors, in other words, and this is something to be valued. Such discoveries lie within us, however, not without. They cannot be prescribed by others, only discovered by ourselves. Nevertheless, our unique wisdom emerges through a process that is larger than "me" as an individual. As we will consider in the next section, we both create *and* discover our ordinary wisdom.

The creation-discovery paradox of ordinary wisdom also tells us that we should not pay too much attention to our journey, since doing so can become a neurotic exercise. We need to live it as well. Staying with the Zen theme, the following story is instructive:

> A centipede was happy, quite,
> Until a toad, in fun,
> Said, pray, which leg comes after which?
> This worked his mind to such a pitch,
> He lay distracted in a ditch,
> Considering how to run.

A distinctive feature of ordinary wisdom, as we characterize it, is that we can engage in the process of restorying either inside or outside of established religious, spiritual, and therapeutic regimes. There are many forms of restorying, both with ourselves and with others. However, they all partake of a basic storying moment that has a distinctly spiritual and Zen-like quality in the simultaneity of the process of storytelling and the realization of ordinary wisdom.

THE CREATION-DISCOVERY PARADOX

The fundamental opaqueness of the traveler's perspective suggests that ordinary wisdom involves a healthy respect for that very opacity. We understand certain things, accept other things, but perhaps wonder about many things too. As we discussed in Chapter 2, wisdom is a balance between knowledge and doubt. Human life cannot be totally controlled or mastered, either our own life or that of another person. From this it follows that it is inappropriate to hold ourselves responsible for all that occurs in life. Relying again on a Buddhist perspective, which has much in common with the perspective we are outlining here, we need to make friends with ourselves. The human journey involves both ownership and forgiveness— or compassion—in relation to our shared voyage.

Progress in this regard can be made, for example, in one of life's central areas, namely, work. That progress is in the direction of "a willingness to accept authority figures as they are . . . as a mixture of good and bad, of wisdom, fallibility, and other limitations. The result is an acceptance of authority without needless rebellion or sulking withdrawal, together with an acceptance of self as an authority without guilt or bravado" (Bianchi, 1995, p. 60). Given the crisis of meaning that we discussed in Chapter 1, which involves letting go and moving the journey onward, this type of wisdom is desperately needed. Fortunately, it is available in the stories of current cohorts of older persons. If we listen to those who have been "through the mill," and if we can get beyond being indignant (which means we are assuming that the world is fair), then we realize that many of these changes in our attitudes toward work are workable indeed.

They are workable in that, when we calm down, we might see a way to communicate with someone with whom we are in a conflictual or abusive biographical encounter. Or we might see that our own anger is hurting only us and that it is possible that the other person might even be enjoying that anger. Such a realization is a significant example of ordinary wisdom insofar as it presupposes learning from experience and relinquishing control, though only in the Taoist sense that we discussed in Chapter 2, of yielding but adhering, of giving in but not giving up.

We are not giving up, therefore, when we decide to get out of the way of a tornado or a truck. As the saying goes, we are surviving to fight another day. Either that or we are realizing that there is nothing to fight for anyway and that it is time to move on to the next destination. A world of technological knowledge with a very short half-life may incline us to leave older persons out of consideration in certain contexts. Yet there is a timeless value to the ordinary wisdom we have just described, and it is there for the listening. Moreover, it is born not only out of books or out of an intellectual knowledge of fictive or hypothetical situations. It is born out of an existential context of having lived through a a segment of our journey.

There is tremendous healing possible in the very act of hearing, first, that other travelers have survived and then, *how* they have survived what are similar station stops, despite the different historical periods and the change of characters. Moreover, this wisdom is ordinary. It simply consists in the stories of ordinary, and yet extraordinary, journeys that all of us are traveling. As we noted in the previous section, sometimes the answer is so close we cannot see it.

The characteristics of life as a journey imply that it involves both a decision to travel and a willingness to accept what happens to us or what we see on that journey. In other words, ordinary wisdom arises out of a process both of active seeking and, paradoxically, of discovering through sometimes listening, letting life be, and letting go of things—that is, of unlearning. With respect to being older, this point is addressed in the introduction to a series of essays by Helen Luke (1987, p. viii): "A point comes in our lives at which we 'choose' how we go into our last years, how we approach our death. The choice may be painful, requiring (should we choose to continue to 'grow' old, instead of merely sinking into the aging process) that we let go of much that has been central even to our inner lives."

We should not underestimate what this statement implies. If we live long enough, radical changes and losses befall most of us, in our work, in our love relations, in our social life, our health, and our inside story itself. With regard to illness, for example, Sharon Kaufman (1988, p. 217) notes in discussing her study of stroke patients that "a major illness not only interrupts and transforms one's biography, it also magnifies certain themes of the biography, forces one to actively take control of the biographical process by reflective decision making, and, at least in the case of elderly persons, alludes to the end of the biography by drawing attention to one's death." The key here is that the journey need not be over or the story closed.

Similar insights are found in emerging studies of widowhood, which is an important aging issue. Some studies have shown that many widows, following periods of devastating loneliness and anxiety, emerge literally as new persons on a new journey. This is a remarkable finding, given that current older cohorts of women often identify themselves with their spouses so much that they appear not to have their own story at all. Their husband's meaning in life is their meaning in life (van den Hoonaard, 1997; 1999).

As a result of widowhood, these women discover their own ordinary wisdom and what they often experience as, simultaneously, a ripping away of the self that had been conjoined with their husband and a recognition of their own personal journey, which was previously submerged. This new journey involves them in experiences such as doing their own banking, driving a car, and dealing with service people, tasks that many of us take for granted but that, for these women, constitute a whole new world. Furthermore, they develop new relationships to family and friends, and sometimes must find new friends altogether, since they are no longer welcome in a world of couples. Such experiences of ordinary wisdom are a result of radical restorying, of not only *having* a new lifestory or having changed some elements of their previous story but of *being* a new story. There may be some continuity with their old story, but there is also significant discontinuity.

Additional sources of ordinary wisdom have been identified in studies done with victims of abuse, incest, and cancer (Silver, Boon, & Stones, 1983; Taylor, Wood, & Lichtman, 1983). As with widows, moving life on as a journey for these people involves more than simply having, or conveniently writing themselves, a new story by which to live; that is, "construing benefit from a victimizing event . . . goes much further than simply finding something positive about it. Victims often learn from their experiences and the meaning gained can greatly enrich their lives" (Taylor, Wood, & Lichtman, 1983, p. 33).

These studies, and others like them, point to our ability as human beings to find meaning, to discover our ordinary wisdom, and to continue on a meaningful journey by moving through and beyond extreme life circumstances. It is here where we can see the spiritual quality of wisdom. Ordinary wisdom is not a matter of putting a bandaid over a problem, or even of coping, in the sense of merely getting by on the basis of a clever strategy. It involves the possibility for real growth and transformation. A more well-known example of this, of course, is the work of Victor Frankl (1962) with death camp survivors. It is difficult to imagine a more extreme set of circumstances that has nevertheless given birth to much meaning and wisdom.

With respect to the comment about our inner lives, as Latimer (1997) points out, there is a particular emotional compass that we need for the journey. This involves not only having the intention to make our life and later years pleasant and having goals, but also working with our facticity, with both our handicaps and our assets. Ordinary wisdom may involve, for example, unweighting ourselves from "superfluous baggage laid on [our] shoulders in [our] childhood" (Latimer, 1997, p. 153).

A final area of interest to us in this context are near-death experiences (Rinpoche, 1994). Whatever these experiences may turn out to be from a clinical or physiological perspective, the long-term outcomes for many people who have them reflect a number of the characteristics of wisdom that we have identified. And, again, they arise at an extreme of life, when things appear to be at their worst. With remarkable consistency, we find in reports of such experiences that people develop a compassion, an acceptance of life and a lack of fear of death, a greater concern for ethical issues, and in general, joy and gratitude in being alive. These qualities that some people hope to achieve in a lifetime of spiritual practice are experienced by some NDEers (near death experience-ers) in one moment.

LOSS AND DESPAIR

As we have been discussing, ordinary wisdom involves, paradoxically, growth through diminishment and gain through loss. It involves finding meaning and even peace through suffering. We are saying that, as is enshrined in the Buddhist wisdom tradition, it is possible, and perhaps even necessary, to travel through this journey of loss and decline to en-light-enment. We can understand this concept in terms of two senses, as less darkness and as less weight. Anderson (1980, p. 182f) notes for us:

[W]hat the Tibetans mean by "enlightenment" is "growing up." They see it as a matter of discovering (we might also say rediscovering) the essential and natural wholeness that is the human being's natural birthright. And this means it is part of everybody's experience. We all go through periods when we are conscious of beginning to comprehend the world in a new way, putting the pieces together differently. As we do so, we may notice that we not only add certain things but also let go of certain things as well. In other words, some things that seemed terribly important to us no longer have their power; some things that we used to believe no longer seem true; some things that were once great fears or obstacles no longer seem so threatening; and some things we once wanted so badly we no longer want at all.

It is a basic paradox of life to *decide* to let go. However, believing in the value of letting go is not a common characteristic in Western culture, where, as we discussed earlier, attitudes of agency and control tend to dominate. As Eugene Bianchi (1995, p. 35) explains, "The preponderant conditioning of technological culture opposes the inward journey as a threat to the ethos of man-the-producer. The contemplative life is thought to be opposed to the full-time energy required for productive purposes." The question is whether these values are not becoming counterproductive in a postmodern world where adherence to this ethos causes mental, physical, and spiritual debilitation due to the scale of change that is occurring. In the words of G. Stanley Hall, "only greater easement between fifty and seventy can bring ripe, healthful, vigorous senectitude, the services of which to the race constitute . . . probably the very greatest need of our civilization today" (cited in Cole & Winkler, 1994, p. 56). Insofar as this is the case, returning to metaphors such as journey points us to important aspects of spiritual aging and thus to wisdom in its ordinariness, which can perhaps contribute to some degree of healing and well-being, both individually and culturally.

Nevertheless, while the journey is about finding meaning in suffering, letting go, and accepting, none of this takes place in some facile or mechanical manner. As we have already mentioned in considering examples of wisdom stories, discovering ordinary wisdom involves more than simply uncovering some positive feature of a negative or traumatic experience. It is a question not of having a new story to tell about the experience, but of *being* a new story.

Such a movement toward wisdom involves not only cognition but also feeling and action. As such, anxiety and even periods of despair are part of the process, which makes sense when we realize that the journey is, literally, about life and death (Kenyon, 1990). However, while the experience of despair is one thing, an *outcome* of despair is quite another. Frankl (1997) has a formula to capture this insight. It is $D = S - M$: despair is suffering without meaning.

From our perspective in this book, both meaning and some degree of wisdom are possible. Therefore, the question is what goes wrong for some people that closes their journey for them, while it still goes on at deeper levels of their story. For other persons around them, however, it goes on for as long as they are alive. The difference between a periodic derailing of one's journey, on the one hand, and despair, on the other, is described by Marcel (1962, p. 53) as the difference between someone "who is trying to feel his way in life as we feel our way along a road, who only has a flickering light to guide him, and someone who claims to be at the other side of this same life (and of his own life as well) and to be able to give out, from some abstract spot, truths acquired at a great price." From an ontological point of view, that is, if life is a journey, then the despairing person has imposed an end to that journey. Such people are denying the opacity and the transitoriness of their journeys, as well as the fact that, in making them, they are not alone. In an important sense, they have *chosen* to despair. They are no longer part of their own paths, no longer involved in their own lifestories (see Mader, 1991). They have established a final meaning of life and have decided to "disarm before the inevitable" (Marcel, 1962, p. 37).

From our point of view, this situation reflects an aging that has gone wrong and a decision not to be open to ordinary wisdom. In story terms, there is too much facticity and virtually no sense of possibility. This is not

to say that we are to blame for that decision, since if wisdom is an interpersonal phenomenon, as stories and journeys always are, then, as
Meacham pointed out in Chapter 2, and as others including Jung (see
Cole & Winkler, 1994) have noted too, there can be either a decline in wisdom, on the one hand, or, on the other, an inhibition of spiritual growth
in the later years of life due to societal values and conditions. For Jung,
"these people look back and cling to the past with a secret fear of death in
their hearts. They withdraw from the life process, at least psychologically, and consequently remain fixed like nostalgic pillars of salt, with
vivid recollections of youth but no living relation to the present" (cited in
Cole & Winkler, 1994, p. 9).

The above analysis appears to contradict one of our basic assumptions
in this book, namely, that we can never make final decisions about the content of someone's facticity and possibility, or in other words, that someone
is never going to change his chosen itinerary and move on. The situation is
that, in principle, we cannot make a claim to total and complete despair.
On the one hand, some people will always remain travelers, regardless of
the vicissitudes of their paths, and will maintain what Erikson (1979, p. 59)
calls "a dynamic balance between integrity and despair, in integrity's favor." On the other hand, there are people whose closure or isolation is, in
the end, too complete to be influenced, people who have been totally hardened by life (Marcel, 1962). In simple terms, we should never give up on
anyone. There is always hope that the journey terminated can be exchanged for the adventure going forward. In some cases, however, the
journey this side of death may be frozen. And, in the final analysis, each of
us has a right to that sort of itinerary as well.

CLOCK TIME, STORY TIME, AND JOURNEY TIME: INNER AND OUTER AGING

As we considered in Chapter 3, at first glance time appears to be just
what it is: a series of clock movements or calendar units that encompass a
past, a present, and a future. These three elements of time are thought to be
discrete, linear, and unidirectional. The past refers to things that have happened and are irretrievable, the present is now, and the future is something that is unknown and yet to come. However, echoing the thoughts of
St. Augustine (1961), "I am quite clear about the nature of time until someone asks me about it and then I am not sure." Just think of how differently
we live time in the following two situations. First, when we are falling in
love, we may find that the hours fly by like minutes and that there is a
timeless quality to the whole experience. In contrast, when we are fearful,
in pain, or awaiting a decision from our doctor or employer, each minute
can take an eternity to pass. When we look at modern physics, the wisdom
traditions we have discussed in this book, the emerging literature in ger-

ontology, and the metaphors of story and journey, we find indeed that the definition of time with which we began refers to one kind of time alone.

In Chapter 3 we identified, in addition to clock time, something called story time, and what we can here call journey time. Clock time refers to outer time and outer aging. Best described by biologists as the decreasing probability of survival, this kind of time records the downward slope of physical aging. With its intimate association with finitude and death, it is this form of time that engenders many attempts to "beat" time, particularly among middle-aged people, through both hyperactivity and hypoactivity (Bianchi, 1995)—the stereotypical midlife crisis.

Moreover, clock time impacts on our lives in the form of such policies as mandatory retirement as well as various forms of ageism, or in some cultures as a respect for the wisdom of age and its associated status. We live much of our lives according to this form of time. In fact, for many of us, at least in the West, it is the only kind of time of which we are aware, as it gets translated into the three main boxes of life, namely, education, work, and retirement. From this point of view, our life becomes a straight line. We feel that we are determined by a static, rigid past and a future that grows shorter by the day.

It is possible, however, that living exclusively according to clock time may be partly our own creation or even a cohort phenomenon. What we mean by this is that the three boxes are being completely altered, both in their order and in their meaning. In a postmodern world, education is no longer the sole territory of youth, nor is it for career preparation alone. Work and family are now less and less age relevant, and retirement and leisure have, at least for some people, changed into a matter of either being employed or not being employed.

While it is necessary for us to develop a relationship to outer time, since it is an integral part of the journey, there is also journey time, which is associated with *inner* aging. As the philosopher Martin Heidegger (1962) says, we are being-*in*-time. In an important sense, however, we are also *not* being-*of*-time. What we mean by this is that, in journey time, the past, present, and future are intimately connected. Following Heidegger again, in a statement attributed to him by Frankl (1962): What has passed is gone, but what is past is yet to come. This paradox refers to the idea that although a historical event, personal or societal has occurred and is gone, the meaning of that event is still alive in the present. In other words, the past is not composed of objective events but of remembered interpretations or stories of those events—once again, the hermeneutic circle that we have already discussed. Echoing the views of Jean-Paul Sartre, the meaning of the past is thus "something that develops throughout life" (Charmé, 1984, p. 40). And, to complete the equation, depending on how the past can be restoried in the present, this gives rise to different future possibilities that follow from a particular past and a particular present.

To take the example that we considered earlier concerning authority figures, if I am treated nastily by my boss and I continue to harbor anger and resentment toward him, this may lead to my leaving the institution, as well as to physical and emotional distress and even illness. It will also probably lead to problems for my family and others around me. But if I can somehow discover some ordinary wisdom and let go and move on, I *may* experience a healthier present, whether I leave the job or not, and my possible future story may also be different. In this way, journey time is open and subject to personal meaning. Time is not totally locked in as part of my facticity.

The Buddhist wisdom tradition takes journey time seriously. For Buddhists, the past that can be restoried in the present toward a better future includes our past and future lives as well. Our lives as journeys come from somewhere, are something now, and are going somewhere too. The trick is to become aware that we can live according to journey time. Such awareness permits a visit to the travel agency to alter itineraries that might be very old and might inhibit the expression of our ordinary wisdom. As Yeshe and Rinpoche (1982, p. 30) note, "When you become more conscious of your actions, you develop more and more wisdom. Then you are really able to control cause and effect. In other words, you can exert a conscious influence on your karma." The term *karma* here refers both to the journey that we are on now as the result of past circumstances and choices, and to the destination to which that track leads. We shall take up the idea of conscious aging in Chapter 5.

Although the future cannot be predicted exactly, our life is predisposed to go in certain directions, as is a piece of music or a novel. What this means is that, while we of course cannot arbitrarily change the itinerary of our journey, since it is subject to our facticity, our journey is nonetheless open to our sense of possibility. The past and the present alike are open to a destination different from that which we might otherwise envision. As we alluded to earlier, this state of affairs applies even at the level of our genes. Contrary to earlier thinking, that we are locked in by our hereditary programming, geneticists today believe that, although we are predisposed to certain tendencies, our genes turn on, turn off, and both turn on and turn off depending on our environment and on the choices that we make in our life.

The idea of journey time opens up interesting possibilities for gerontological research (see also Kenyon, Ruth, & Mader, 1999). For example, it would be interesting to know more about the ways in which different people order their lifestories, that is, the ways in which they *live* time. It would also be interesting to analyze the influences that cause a specific person to find meaning in a specific version of journey time and how that may have changed over time. For example, do people move from outer time to inner time and perhaps back again as they age? If so, how and why? To what extent is our story of time influenced by social and cultural themes— that is, those of the larger stories we live within?

JOURNEY TIME AND DEATH

We have just considered how the meaning of time changes when we view it from a journey perspective. Time experienced from the inside is not the same as time experienced from the outside. Similar points can be made about the meaning of death. While there are clinical and legal definitions of death, its meaning becomes less clear when we look at it in terms of characteristics of the journey such as its opacity and indefinite duration.

From a clock time point of view, the expectation is that everyone who gets older will be anticipating, if not fearing, death. At least in the developed world, death is not seen as a younger person's problem. Relatively speaking, we do not often see death early in life. For that reason, it is seen as all the more tragic when a young person dies. Furthermore, it has been argued (see Schroots & Birren, 1988) that the awareness of approaching death among older adults makes them lose a sense of the future and become desirous to review their life before that eventuality arrives. However, these arguments are not well supported when we look at what people actually *say* about death.

In addition to knowledge derived from wisdom traditions, a powerful source of evidence that people live life as a journey, a journey that includes death, is a lengthening list of narrative studies of older people, terminally ill people, and people who have undergone near death experiences. The common observation, and, we would add, the lesson about ordinary wisdom, to be derived from these stories is that just because someone is older or seriously ill does not necessarily mean that they view life as over or that they lose a future-time perspective (although most of us do at certain times when things are acute). Conversely, both the experience of death and the awareness of it are very much a part of many younger persons' journeys.

Besides the sources we mentioned in the earlier section on loss and despair, a number of recent studies have shown, for example, that age does not tell us much about the desire for life review (see Webster, 1999). As Peter Coleman (1986) has also discovered, it is very difficult to predict who will or will not want to engage in this process and at what point in their life. Moreover, life review is best considered a life span phenomenon, since both death and aging are of this character as well.

We can clarify even further the relationship between time, aging, and death by looking at the work of researchers such as Ågren (1992). Ågren found that even the oldest old, although they must adjust to the limited number of years that they have remaining to them, experience a past, present, and future that is active and dynamically related. In a more recent study, she found the same to be the case with people who are well into their nineties (Ågren, 1997). A further fascinating finding, which may suggest ordinary wisdom, is that many of these people say that this is the best time of their life. Joyce Horner (1982, p. 16) reflects these sentiments in referring to her fellow nursing home resident: "I don't think anyone old is afraid of death, though many, including Mrs. B., who will be 108 on Monday, may want life to go on."

Finally, Jaber Gubrium (1993, p. 188) captures the essence of this argument in a statement he makes in reporting the findings of his longitudinal study of nursing home residents:

[T]he very idea of a course of adjustment at the end of life shortchanges its variety, complexity, improvisations. There is little overall evidence that affairs are ultimately settled, sundered ties finally repaired, transgressions at last righted or accounted for, or preparations for the future or afterlife completed. While some residents, of course, do speak of waiting for heaven, buying cemetery plots, and making funeral arrangements—points of information that indeed may hold considerable value for them—these do not necessarily signify terminal horizons.

The first important point about death, then, is that it must be distinguished from the aging process, from the way people live journey time. Furthermore, in terms of its existential meaning (Kenyon, 2000), death is not something solid, like an object that we can face directly or that we face automatically once we reach a particular age. Death is the quintessential narrative phenomenon, since all we can know about death are images, interpretations, and stories. We may know something about dying by being seriously ill ourselves or by being close to someone who dies, but we are ultimately survivors. As with a journey, the meaning of death is opaque.

In Heideggerian terms, death is a possibility. In a sense, it is a concept with no specific meaning content. And yet it is very real (Heidegger, 1962). As expressed by Pablo, who is sentenced to die in Sartre's (1969, p. 8) play, *The Wall*: "I can feel the wounds already; I've had pains in my head and in my neck for the past hour. Not real pains. Worse. That is what I'm going to feel tomorrow morning. And then what?" The other character, Tom, responds: "We aren't made to think that Pablo. Believe me; I've already stayed up a whole night waiting for something. But this isn't the same; this will creep up behind us, Pablo, and we won't be able to prepare for it."

Death is journeylike in another way. I cannot represent my death to myself, since I am not an object to myself. With respect to the basic characteristics of the journey that we outlined earlier, we are interpersonal beings, not self-enclosed individuals. In one way, not even my body belongs completely to me, since it is not only a physical object but also a social object upon which other people place meaning as well. Moreover, this meaning from others is part of who I am. In addition, I am not only a body but also a mind and, many would say, a soul. As a result of this situation, I cannot say exactly who I am and, therefore, I cannot say exactly what it is that my death is the death of. From such a perspective, death has the dual character of immediacy and indefiniteness: I know I will die and yet I can neither predict when my death will happen nor know what it will be like. However, these same characteristics of death make it possible for us to see it as part of the journey. As with time, death is open-ended. We have choices that we can make concerning it, whether we think we have or not. And further, since we co-author each other's lives, or travel with other pilgrims as interpersonal beings, we can help one another "to trade in and trade up our personal metaphors" (Birren, 1987)—in this case, our metaphors about death.

From a journey perspective, I have the choice, then, of viewing death as the annihilation of my being. Indeed, this follows from my view of myself as a body only and as an egoistic being. I can *choose* to think of myself and my death in this manner. Along with denial, this is in fact the most common North American story of death. As Marcel (1952, p. 202) notes, from the standpoint of such a story, "death at first sight looks like a permanent invitation to despair." Moreover, as we considered earlier, it is possible for my despair to be virtually complete, in that I may see nothing else. For authors like Marcel (1964), such despair is manifested in suicide, as the ultimate negation of, or closing in on, myself. It is this characteristic of suicide that of course makes it so difficult for those whom the victim leaves behind, for the survivors. They are left to wonder how to end that person's story in a way that is different from how they would end the story of a person who has died some other sort of death.

The contemplation of human death can provide an excellent opportunity to experience despair or existential meaninglessness, as we have just outlined. However, the very qualities of our humanness that provide this opportunity also make possible a rather different story of death, one that is imbued with ordinary wisdom.

The fact of death is a fundamental aspect of the human journey. Human life is not complete without its inclusion (Frankl, 1962). Yet, since it is part of the opaqueness or indeterminacy of our journey that the nature of death is unknown to us, at least experientially, it is possible to view death as part of the voyage.

A specific approach that considers death an integral part of our journey is what can be called the floating perspective (Kenyon, 1990). From this perspective, since we cannot know death, we can allow our personal story of it to change and grow with us throughout the span of our journey. The floating perspective suggests that it is possible to deal with death by leaving it as an open question and, therefore, not taking an ultimate position on it. This view might appeal to people who have trouble accepting what can be considered as remedies for death, whether these be denial, running at death, orthodox religious views, or even extreme, cultlike remedies for death that can be increasingly observed. In this important sense, human life can be viewed both as a journey and as a journey that does not necessarily end as a fait accompli. This discussion calls to mind the often cited line from the poetry of Dylan Thomas (cited in Cole & Winkler, 1994): "Rage, rage against the dying of the light." When it comes to death, while resignation may not be the healthiest attitude, given the circumstances, yielding to it and following wherever the journey leads us can perhaps be a wiser route to go. As the saying runs, "Let life ripen and let it fall."

The floating perspective advocates working both with and through our personal story of death and giving death neither too little nor too much importance in our journey. Thus, we are open to changing our attitudes and feelings toward it, depending on the circumstances. Consequently, depending on how a person is viewing death at a particular time, by adopting the floating perspective, he "is not contradicting himself if death seems to make him despair and at the same time to make him conscious of his inmost being: if he fails to understand and feels trustful all the same" (Jaspers, 1970, p. 201).

Furthermore, the floating perspective does not preclude us from finding refuge in a previously held remedy, or story, of death. For example, during times of crisis we might find comfort and solace in attending church again or in returning with a sense of renewed relevance to the views of death and God that we held as a child. Then, when we find our strength coming back, these views may or may not recede again to the background of our ongoing inquiry into death. There is no contradiction involved in the lack of consistency in our personal story of death, just as there is no problem with the fact that we might experience periods of anxiety and conflicting emotions, and even peace, in contemplating death.

One feature of ordinary wisdom that is highlighted by such a perspective is that it is not necessary to fear this life or to hope for an afterlife. Whether the outcome of the human journey is annihilation, immortality, or something else, we are not thereby precluded from finding meaning in our present life, and even joy. Indeed, this is the wisdom contained in our discussion earlier about the Zen master's attitude toward death.

Death also becomes a powerful source of meaning, hope, and comfort, in so far as it enables us to live a more interpersonal journey. What we mean here is that while death may end a life, it does not necessarily end a relationship (Birren, 1988). The death of someone may provide one of the most potent catalysts for wonder, openness, or a search for meaning (Frankl, 1962) on the part of the survivor. Moreover, the loss of a loved one, or of a fellow traveler, does not remove the experience of what that person meant to the one who is left behind. In an important way, the former may still be present to, and may continue to share the journey of, the latter. Gabriel Marcel (1956, 1973) provides a sensitive treatment of this notion in his discussion of the phenomenon of presence. Beginning with the fact that we are larger than our individual selves, or that participation founds subjectivity, he argues that we can be present and open to each other in both life and love. Thus, there is no reason why the relationship cannot continue after a loved one has died.

The phenomenon of presence is a mystery for Marcel and does not refer to the survival of a person after death in some sort of parapsychological manner. Rather, presence is grounded in the fundamental fact that we are part of each other. As such, it is something that can be spoken about. It is meaningful but it cannot be known exhaustively. In Marcel's (1956, p. 39) own words to a deceased loved one, "Even if I cannot see you, if I cannot touch you, I feel that you are with me." Whatever we want to make of this phenomenon, it is a very common and a very real one for many people, and it cannot be easily dismissed as either wishful thinking or hallucination.

From the point of view of journey time, aging and death are not related in the way we often take them to be when we look at clock time. Furthermore, many older people, and many people who have been through the sorts of losses and traumas that we have been considering, do have a journey relationship with death and time. While we cannot say how this ordinary wisdom comes to be, we can discuss its features. For example, Ruth and Coleman (1996) review a number of studies that indicate that in older age, people come to live more in an active present, or in what has been called the eternal now, which involves both a connection with past generations and an affinity with the unknown. This description sounds very much like the characteristics of wisdom that we discussed in Chapter 2. In another study, Munnichs (1966) found that most of the older people whom he studied who were dwelling in the community neither were preoccupied with death nor feared it. They had an awareness of finitude, which means they realized that time was limited. Yet this realization issued in a situation in which "there [was] a renewed engagement at a distance, allowing a renewed sense of significance in old age" (Munnichs, 1966, p. 125).

These studies, as well as the many other examples we have been considering throughout this book, suggest that we can indeed discover our ordinary wisdom and thus can find some insight and peace in the human condition, as unknowable as that condition is. As we did with our discussion of time, the journey metaphor, and its close associate the story metaphor, can be employed in gerontology to further our understanding of death from the inside. For example, since we have only stories of death to go on, we could look more at the potential ordinary wisdom concerning death that is expressed in the narratives of both older and younger persons, of both women and men, and of different ethnic communities.

We might also learn more about the relationship between personal stories of death and cultural ones, and about how they interact. There are three interesting questions here: First, what is the relationship between a person's story of their aging and the story of their death, and how does the one affect the other? Second, in what ways does a person's story of death remain the same throughout life and in what ways does it change, and why? Third and finally, can we understand more about the phenomenon of presence and of shared journeys *after* death?

THE FACES OF ORDINARY WISDOM

The human journey is creative, dynamic, and idiosyncratic. It is true, of course, that we can and should discuss lives from aggregate points of view, such as those of a whole culture and society (Ruth & Kenyon, 1996a), since the station stops for human beings are similar. However, we should not forget that the source of ordinary wisdom is, in the end, our inside story, our particular existential-spiritual center. Thus, while we can learn a great deal from sharing with each other the stories of our respective journeys, each of our itineraries is, in the final analysis, unique. This is the case from genes to soul. But how are we to see and understand the ordinary wisdom that is associated with either our own adventure or another's? As Kekes (1983, p. 281) argues, "Wisdom ought also to show in the behavior of the man who has it. But it is not clear that it shows, or, if it does, how it shows." The key to understanding the idiosyncratic expression dimension of ordinary wisdom is the intimate link between a life viewed as a story and a life viewed as a journey. Still, though, what should we expect to see in this way? Continuing with our discussion in Chapter 2, traditionally, wisdom may not necessarily be expressed in articulated ideas or, as Kekes has just indicated, in manifest behavior. The following three points will help to clarify this insight.

Autobiography

Ordinary wisdom might be expressed in an autobiography. At one extreme, there is the view, sometimes mistakenly attributed to Erikson, that a meaningful life must conform to a well-written story with a good beginning, middle, and end. At the other extreme, there is the view that sees only chaos and complete unintelligibility, or perhaps the view we discussed earlier of the postmodern self as consisting of ever changing images with no center. What is at issue with these views is the degree of coherence and/or continuity that one should expect in a life and a lifestory. From the perspective we are developing here, a human life is lived somewhere between these two extremes.

Life viewed as the story of a journey precludes the possibility of gaining a complete diary of the voyage (see also Kenyon & Randall, 1997; Kenyon, 1996a; 1996b). There are several reasons for this. First, we are in the middle of our journey; we are living it from moment to moment. Thus, what we reflect on is the most recent station stop. However, as we look back on that destination, we are already en route to the next one. Furthermore, as we said earlier, there are aspects of my personal journey that are accessible only to other people, since that journey is simultaneously interpersonal and co-authored.

Finally, as we considered in Chapter 3, there may be no such thing as the story of my life, or only one story of my journey. We seem to be many stories at once. Although we can say that all of these stories belong to me, they do not necessarily add up to one recognizable and integrated volume. Among other things, we are social stories, ethnic stories, biological stories, sexual stories, and spiritual stories. This situation has prompted the observation that a detailed biography does not necessarily make a good story (Carr, 1986), and moreover, that the biographical unit is larger than the biological body.

We are many stories in another sense, too. Over time, we may live stories, or take parallel voyages, that do not blend easily together into an overall, coherent travel theme. For example, we may experience a divorce or the loss of a loved one, which may be followed by remarriage. Or we may experience a basic career change. As we indicated earlier, we may be living several genres of story at one and the same time.

A further powerful source of discontinuity in our journeys is the realization that we are finite, that, in terms of outer time, we are getting older, and cannot do everything we may have previously thought we could. New and deeper continuity may result from this process of switching tracks, but it does not readily go with our former views, that is, as an easily written, coherent story.

Further insight into the complexity and lack of complete coherence of our lives, as both journeys and stories, comes from research in narrative gerontology, as well as from other disciplines. Such research increasingly indicates that we do not have ready-made versions of our stories that we express whenever we are asked to "just tell your story." Rather, the stories we tell are a function of, among other things, who we tell them to (a best friend or a complete stranger), our purpose in telling them (an interview or a formal biography), and even our state of health (depressed or healthy). Nevertheless, this does not mean that all these different versions of our journeys are discrete or even that they are fabricated on demand. It indicates that we are creating meaning in a particular situation, a situation that is already larger than we are as individuals.

The life of each of us is complex and ever changing. Yet, it is also bounded dynamically by our facticity. It is not just an anthology of unrelated stories or a set of confused and chaotic wanderings. On the one hand, a life that has lost its story, or whose journey has been derailed, is probably going to reflect a person who is experiencing existential meaninglessness. On the other hand, as we have already discussed, it does not matter what has happened in a life. Often ordinary wisdom is expressed in letting something go rather than in making sense of it or in completely understanding what has occurred.

Sometimes the letting go might allow new understanding to make itself known, and sometimes letting go is just that; things don't need to add up any more. In any case, a good journey does not mean that everything must fit together in a life. In fact, as Manheimer (1992, p. 432) explains, "The coherent life story may be too coherent, suppressing the diversity of life events and simultaneous levels of experience because of a preoccupation with continuity." As we discussed in Chapter 2, the question concerns how intelligent we need to be in order to be wise, or how much cognition is required for us to be considered ordinarily wise.

The argument that a good journey and ordinary wisdom do not presuppose the truth, the whole truth, and nothing but the truth is also supported by a cursory look at the process of spirituality. It may be quite natural for people not to find coherence between their present inside story and an earlier version of themselves. In following spiritual traditions, we may find that through meditation and reconciliation, we become less fond of the person that we have been in the past (Tornstam, 1989). We may find that the earlier version of ourselves was egotistical or narrow-minded, perhaps lacking in compassion as well. In Eriksonian terms, a degree of integrity may lead us to a desire for "generativity" (McAdams, 1996), meaning that we see ourselves as a larger being with desires for things such as communion and participation rather than for achievement and competition. Whatever initiates this transition, it involves, in Bianchi's (1995, p. 71) words, "a new inwardness, a search for depths in the face of personal finitude and the brokenness of human society," which "leads to nonviolent commitment toward nature and humankind." Paradoxically, it is by going through the story of our own journey that we arrive at more universal insights into the world and other people.

This going in, in order to go out, is what we mean by our earlier discussion about the hermits and about how, eventually, the Tao comes to town. Such sentiments are also found in the Western monastic tradition in the following statement: "A man or woman goes apart to embrace the monastic life because he or she wants to find freedom and the support to enter a very complete union with God. They may or may not immediately perceive the fact that it is by such a union with God that they can make the greatest contribution to the well-being of all, that they can be most fully an instrument of God's creative and redeeming love, the source of all good" (Pennington, 1983, p. 53).

Aside from intentional restorying, or conscious aging (Moody, 1994), such an experience of new meaning can occur, as we discussed earlier, as a result of widowhood, illness, near-death experiences, career loss, or divorce. From processes like these, we can emerge a new person, both to ourselves and to others. Nevertheless, it is ironically sometimes the case that we can see the significance of this result only when we meet a person from the past who continues to see us in our old story. Often in vain, we try to convince such a person that we not only *have* a new story but *are* one as well, in terms of the new sources of meaning with which we identify and in terms of our feelings, actions, and thoughts.

Behavior

In contrast to the cognitively focused expression of it that we just discussed, ordinary wisdom might be expressed in Erikson's (1979, p. 32) description of Dr. Borg's last stage of life, as "transcendent simplicity, rather than mystical rapture or intellectual reconstruction." Even this simplicity, though, might take a variety of forms. For example, a later life insight into the journey of life might be expressed in deep contemplation or meditation or in the cross-legged immobility that we referred to before. However, as an indication of the subtlety of wisdom, behavioral quietude may also not reflect wisdom at all. From his experiences as a Trappist monk, George Fowler (1995, p. 149) explains that "the problem is that external peace is too often, too easily, taken to be proof of inner wholeness, or even as authentic spirituality itself." In many walks of life, what looks like wisdom may merely mask socially accepted forms of neurosis, which have not yet begun to be experienced as part of a person's journey because they have not yet been challenged by an inner or outer experience. Thus, the before and after of wisdom may look the same, yet be worlds apart.

Or wisdom might be expressed in intense political activity or service. It could also involve combinations of the two, as we might attribute to persons who are well known and generally perceived to be wise, such as Pope Paul II, Mother Theresa, Ghandi, and the Dalai Lama.

Wisdom might also be expressed in some forms of eccentric behavior, as is said about the Zen Lunatics. Accompanying the experience of having seen through the absurdity of life can be humor and apparent foolishness as well. A good example of this is the movie *The Seven Samurai*. In it we see the wisdom of quiet and age in one character, the wisdom of serious activity in another, and wisdom masked as outrageous behavior in one of the bravest characters. As Manheimer (1994, p. 9) explains, "not to deny one's finitude, but to acknowledge the paradox that one is acting as though he or she would endure forever, yet in full awareness that tomorrow may not arrive, is the basis for humor's unique perspective. Except, instead of bemoaning this fact, despairing over it until we become immobilized, the shift of humor liberates us to see our lives as a tiny part of a vast, perhaps unfathomable cosmos." Humor may very well be an important part of wisdom, but as with everything else about this phenomenon, we need to look at it carefully. For example, Birren (1987) notes that humor indicates a mastery of a problem. While this may be true in some cases, humor may not only indicate wisdom and transcendence. It may also mask denial, cynicism, and pain.

Nevertheless, humor does often indicate joy, happiness, and wellbeing, and these are potential aspects of the discovery of ordinary wisdom through one's journey. As George Fowler (1995, p. xiii) notes in his autobiography *Dance of a Fallen Monk*, "I've learned that healing and wholeness mean more than just getting by. They mean getting by securely, confidently. They mean freedom not only from feelings of guilt for what we've done amiss, but even more from the psychological guilt of feeling bad about ourselves." Furthermore, as Joyce Horner (1982, p. 184) notes in her nursing home writings, "When happiness comes to one so, in old age, it leaves one with the feeling that it may never come back. And it is not ecstacy. One is inside oneself, not beside. (Another thing I forgot about today was that it began, after the creature-comfort of my bath, with Beethoven's 3rd Piano Concerto, my favorite. And then went on to more Beethoven, including a sonata I like, remade as a quartet.) But it comes on one like other unexpected, unrepeated things—the bird seen once." Or, in the words of Rebecca Latimer (1997, p. 20) in her book entitled *You're Not Old Until You're Ninety*, "It is more than peripheral, it is vitally important: You must keep your mind open, listen to new ideas, keep that marvelous childhood attitude of wonderment, half believing, not quite disbelieving."

Hidden Wisdom

Less obvious expressions of ordinary wisdom are captured in statements such as "survival with grace." Jylha (1997) found this to be a common theme in her study of oldest-old persons in Finland. Wisdom was expressed not necessarily as happiness but as dignity, independence, and acceptance of an often extremely difficult journey that included abject poverty and illness. For Jylha, these people experienced meaning in the sheer fact that they did survive. (Again, they had to be good travelers to have gotten this far.) Moreover, they presently expressed both an interest in life and a readiness to die. There was little evidence of bitterness, anger, or regret. Similar insights are found in the Swedish studies of people in their eighties and nineties that we discussed earlier (Ågren, 1992; 1997), as well as in a second Finnish study by Ruth and Öberg (1996).

Still more subtle but commonly observed examples of ordinary wisdom are expressed by those who know and/or work with people who are frail or dementing. It comes in the form of a look—for instance, of serenity or acceptance—or even of a touch. Over the years, as the two of us teach courses in gerontology and conduct workshops in the community, such sentiments are relayed to us on a regular basis. A frail person may not have health, family, money, or even cognitive competence, nevertheless, that person may *be*, in the sense of experiencing hopefulness, acceptance, transcendence, and wisdom. As Joseph Foley notes in discussing dementing persons, "We too often assume that the absence of emotional display means that no emotion is being experienced. We too often assume that because communication is absent, internal mental process has stopped" (cited in Callahan, 1995, p. 26). As we indicated earlier, researchers and practitioners are finding interesting features of dementia as they look more closely at it. For example, in severely dementing people there are episodes of a clear mind, in which they act in a way that demonstrates wisdom in understanding a nurse. There are also many cases in which they express empathy toward the staff by caressing them or by touching their shins or even by words (Holst, Edberg, & Hallberg, 1999; Hallberg, in press).

Finally, when such people respond angrily or sarcastically to tests of competency with statements such as "Who cares what day it is today" or "I am not interested in whether it is morning or evening," is it because they are attempting to protect the dignity of their personhood? In other words, is it not possible that they may be struggling from deep within themselves to express their wisdom story as they feel their very being, the part of their journey that is self-aware, slipping steadily away?

We are only at the beginning of learning how to understand the journey of the story of dementing persons. The key point, in our view however, is that they are still on a journey and they are still telling a story. Dementing persons may be phasing in and out of *our* reality, at least as far as we can tell. Yet, as authors such as Crisp (1995, p. 137) explain, "At a time when memory is being eroded and one's sense of who and where one is [sic] falling apart, narrative provides a means of bringing the fragments together and constructing an active identity for the narrator. And the very environment around oneself, by becoming the setting for these life events, becomes invested with personal meanings that support that sense of identity, of belonging." We should also keep in mind that in a biographical encounter (Kenyon & Randall, 1997) not only is the storyteller's journey changed but so is the storylistener's. Thus, it is not only a case of allowing the dementing person to experience whatever ordinary wisdom is available to them, it is a case of letting them share that experience with us by telling us, in whatever way they can, what their journey is like. Perhaps, then, a focus on ordinary wisdom, with its agenda that extends "beyond cognition," can help further our understanding of the journeys such people are on.

SPIRITUAL AGING

The perspective reflected in our discussion so far flies in the face of stereotypes of aging and of a view of aging that sees it from the outside alone. However, it supports the importance of looking at the inside of aging as well. We are reminded here of a quote by Simone de Beauvoir (1973, p. 420): "Our private inward experience does not tell us the number of our years; no fresh perception comes into being to show us the decline of age." Because we live journey time as well as clock time, we are not necessarily in denial, or in what Sartre would call bad faith, when we assume that *the old* is always someone else, regardless of our own age. In this context, we have been informed by ninety-year-old nuns that they care for the old sisters in their convent. There is no light switch that goes on at a particular calendar marker to tell us that now we are old. However, illness and frailty will, rather effectively, accomplish that end.

Despite the potential difficulties in identifying and categorizing instances of ordinary wisdom, a common feature of this phenomenon is that a person is able to view his or her life as the story of a journey. This presupposes a degree of self-transcendence, a space between my life and my self. In journey terms, a person is able to watch the scenery of life, as if from the window of a train. It also presupposes that a person has seen through certain things about him or herself, has read his or her story, and is available or present to other journeys.

Ordinary wisdom presents itself, paradoxically, as both detachment from life and active concern for it. As Sherman and Webb (1994, pp. 259–260) found in studying themes of spirituality in older persons' stories, most people "most certainly did display a 'letting-go' quality and an acceptance of their inevitable losses, but they definitely cannot be described as 'resigned.' They appeared to be in a state of being that was quite alive, but that was also more contemplative than they described themselves as being in earlier life stages." Ordinary wisdom also involves a capacity to value what we have, rather than long for that which we have not. It involves the realization that life cannot be guaranteed against the unknown (Bianchi, 1995). It involves giving up the expectation that something will make it right. In terms of time, the present becomes valuable in itself; life is not postponed for the future.

An important aspect of ordinary wisdom involves the distinction between solitude, loneliness, and aloneness. As we have emphasized, the journey is personal; we can learn from all that is around us. But we discover our wisdom through our own inside story. There is a Zen Buddhist saying that "you are on your own, together with everything." The journey can sometimes initiate intense feelings of loneliness, or what has been called the dark night of the soul. This loneliness is a part of the journey. As Mary Morrison (1998, p. 62) expresses it in her autobiography, *Let Evening Come*, "solitude does not arise out of loneliness automatically, . . . even for those who consciously seek it." Furthermore, when serious illness or other traumas strike, periods of loneliness and isolation seem to follow. However, this latter experience is not equivalent to a healthy need for solitude and meditation.

As is exemplified in Florida Scott-Maxwell's (1968) autobiography, many older persons treasure quiet times alone, and many live alone by choice. It is often a problem for well-meaning younger people to recognize the value of the inner life of an older person and not assume that the solitary journey is an indication of depression, isolation, and dysfunction. As Moody (1991, p. 64) points out, "We can easily feel a sentimental pity toward the old when they are unable or unwilling to share those reflexes of haste and superficiality that have become our daily habits. In our common desire to help the elderly, what we secretly wish is to prolong the haste that excludes us from even a moment of quietness and contemplation. We find the quietness of the old, even their very presence, disturbing, as if it were a repudiation of all that we hold dear."

Viewing our lives as journeys suggests that there may be, in one sense, no final destination to the human adventure. In essence, the real purpose of human life and human aging becomes the journey itself. More precisely, it becomes the *quality* of the journey and not the destination. It is less a case of where we are going than of how we get there. As a gerontologist might put it, it is not how long we make it, but how we make it long. Hence, the saying that a good traveler has no fixed plans and is not particularly intent on arriving. It is possible that there are no better or worse paths in life, although there may be a high price to pay for self-destructive and evil itineraries.

Nevertheless, the real significance lies in what we do with our path and in whether we can keep the journey going and not cut it off. Furthermore, the best that we can hope for and work for is that the quality of our voyage will be informed by ordinary wisdom, with its qualities of wonder, love, curiosity, openness, and even enthusiasm in the face of suffering, loss, and disillusionment. As Rosenmayr (1996, p. 9) notes, "Consent to one's finiteness—to incompleteness—is a condition to elaborate hopeful faith in a new birth, in an ever 'new being' within oneself. In the future, old people will have to generate such an orientation toward accepting their finiteness and 'new birth' if they are willing to resist mere adaptation to social fashions and set up their own life wisdom, together with conditions for 'faith,' trust, resilience, venturesomeness and the ability to take their inevitable leave."

In the next chapter, we take our thinking about wisdom one step further by exploring the intriguing possibility that we can learn to live the profoundly existential journey of our lives as an adventure. This means that we can learn to direct that journey and can therefore age consciously.

5
Conscious Aging: Life as Adventure

In your own life story is where you will find your truth.

—Robert Atkinson (1995)

You need only claim the events of your life to make yourself yours. When you truly possess all you have been and done, which may take some time, you are fierce with reality.

—Florida Scott-Maxwell (1968)

THE ADVENTURE METAPHOR

At its heart, this book is a meditation on a trio of metaphors by which to understand both wisdom and life. In Chapter 3, we looked at life as story. This led us to explore such things as biographical aging, narrative intelligence, and the novelty of our lives. By the end of the chapter, we were developing the idea that wisdom pervades lives like meaning pervades literature, that lives are inherently and cumulatively wise in the way that great works of fiction are inherently and cumulatively meaningful, and that, ultimately, they are meant to be "read." In the last chapter, we explored the entailments of an equally venerable metaphor: life as journey. In this chapter, we pick up where we left off with story and blend both of these explorations in terms of a metaphor that possesses a similar legacy and a comparable conceptual potential. It is life as adventure.

As we have been saying all along, story and journey beg to be joined. Inasmuch as its plot must "go somewhere," every story is about some sort of journey. At the very least it involves movement from one set of circumstances to another: from problem to solution, from chaos to order, from question to answer, from conflict to calm. But just as stories recount journeys, so, sooner or later, do journeys result in stories. A journey is made, whether outer or inner, physical or spiritual, and a tale demands to be told. Travels tend toward tellings, and treks, toward text and talk. What, then, is an adventure? It is an extension of both of these tropes.

On the one hand, an adventure is a special kind of journey: a journey with a goal, a purpose, an aim. It is more than mere movement, and more than relocation from A to B. It is movement with a mission. Among its elements are suspense and sacrifice, challenge and choice. Among its dynamics are discovery and danger, curiosity and courage, vision and hope. On the other hand, an adventure is a special kind of story. Indeed, it is one of the traditional genres of story, whose hero overcomes odds, struggles with foes, or races with time to attain a particular end. Not only is adventure a type of story, however; it is essential to story as well. Plots turn on events that break the routine, on crises that contradict expectations, on occurrences that conflict with the norm. In essence, no trouble (Bruner, 1987), no tale. Such turning-points or nuclear episodes (McAdams, 1988) are critical to narrative emplotment in both literature and life.

As far as life narratives are concerned, these sorts of episodes are the core of many of the signature stories that can be central to our identity. In the words of one psychologist: "People require adventures in order for satisfactory life stories to be constructed and maintained" (Schiebe, 1986, p. 131). As we saw with memory in general, what we remember and recount is what we *need* to remember and recount, or what we cannot forget (Linde, 1993). The stories we like to tell tend to be about what goes against the grain, what stands out, what is different or surprising or wrong, unusual, exciting, or odd. "[T]his, we say somewhere deep within us, is something I'm hanging on to" (Hampl, 1996, p. 207). Eventually, we come to equate these memories with who we are. Thus, one writer says, "We are what we remember ourselves to be" (Casey, 1987), while another insists, "We are the stories we like to tell" (Schank, 1990, p. 137). In short, then, no adventure, no story, and no story, no life.

The technical term for adventure in literary theory is *romance* (Frye, 1966), which is fitting since it has a romantic dimension. It is from adventure that myths are made, epics compiled, and legends laid down. And it is arguably the heart of history as well (Hook, 1943). It is certainly the core of the news, whose top stories commonly revolve around adventures major or minor, successful or failed: from scaling Mt. Everest to tackling inflation to battling cancer or crime. Adventure injects news with excitement and keeps us hungry for more. Because adventure lies on every side, then, it is no great stretch to think of our own living—and aging—in terms of it. In any case, exploring the connotations of such thinking is our agenda in this chapter, as is elaborating the positive approach that we believe it inspires. Viewing life as adventure invites us to face the vicissitudes of existence with excitement and expectation, to tackle the challenges of life with heads up and eyes open. Thus the phrase that is part of our title: *conscious* aging.

Besides those of life as story and life as journey, life as adventure accommodates elements of other metaphors with which we could conceptualize our lives, such as life as battle, life as puzzle, and life as game of chance. This ability of life as adventure to absorb entailments from a variety of metaphors at once is evident when we contemplate the terms it brings to mind, terms that indeed sprinkle our everyday speech and lurk behind our most cherished conceptions of creativity and development, learning and faith. We mean terms such as commitment and conviction, struggle and survival, guide and goal. We mean references to situations as risky or uncertain. We mean talk of projects and purposes, obstacles and objectives, decisions and dreams, of wondering what something might lead to or how it will turn out. We mean words such as "advance" and "advantage," "venture," and even "event" itself. *That was quite an event*, we may say of some occurrence, thereby betraying the view that events are implicit adventures, parts of adventures, or adventures-to-be.

The etymological evidence alone, we believe, qualifies adventure as a root metaphor, on a par with story and journey alike. References to the adventure of living (Tournier, 1965) are thus more than mere rhetoric. They reflect a fundamental picture of what life is about. We enter tricky intellectual territory, however, when we suggest that aging itself is an adventure, that what Eva and Boaz Kohana call adventurous aging is a real possibility (cited in Friedan, 1993, p. 582). Although such a suggestion is implicit in notions of creative or successful aging, it flies in the face of popular perception. "The vast majority of mankind looks upon the coming of old age with sorrow or rebellion," writes Simone de Beauvoir (1973, p. 77). "It fills them with more aversion than death itself." Even though we shall be thinking of adventure, here, in a broad and open-ended sense, the stereotype of a tidily composed tale with a thrilling climax and happy ending means, then, that this chapter may be our most contentious yet. It is certainly our most adventurous, not to mention our most playful, most prescriptive, and, for all of these reasons, most tentative too.

While not all of us may experience our life as an adventure, we shall be suggesting here that it is at least possible to do so and that it is, potentially, a way to *try* to live. Moreover, life as adventure, like wisdom itself, is not an extraordinary concept but an ordinary one, insofar as everyone's life is in fact filled with adventure. Concerning the six dimensions of wisdom we have been identifying throughout, these too will weave back and forth in all that ensues.

The dimension of idiosyncratic expression will be evident as we consider that the adventure of life is *my* adventure and is thus different from that of anyone else. The cognitive dimension we will see in the section on reading ourselves, as well as in our references to the stages of adventure through which, more or less consciously, we move. The moral-ethical dimension lies in the idea that we engage in the adventure of living with, on some level, a goal in mind that represents, in some manner, an improvement on our present condition. It also lies in the notion of pursuing an adventure that is positive, hopeful, and life affirming. The spiritual- mystical dimension will be seen when we argue, particularly in discussing what we call "literary self-literacy," that life viewed as adventure has an inherent purposefulness, meaningfulness, and openness about it. The practical-experiential dimension will be apparent in the idea that living life as adventure is a proactive process that is grounded in everyday life, moment by moment. Moreover, thinking of our lives as adventures is implicitly empowering and enables us to feel that our lives do indeed make a difference. Finally, the interpersonal dimension of wisdom will be acknowledged in terms of the fact that, both potentially and ultimately, our adventures are entwined.

TYPES OF ADVENTURE

To illustrate the ubiquity of adventure in everyday life, we can catalog a number of areas in which it is arguably at work. Before we do so, however, some attempt at defining adventure is clearly in order. *The Concise Oxford English Dictionary* lists the following equivalents: "1. an unusual and exciting experience. 2. a daring experience; a hazardous activity. 3. enterprise. 4. a commercial speculation." Following this lead, let us say that, in the most basic sense, an adventure is any activity we could describe as, or that issues in an outcome we deem to be, exciting or different or odd. It is in this sense that there can be no story at all unless there are adventures to build it around: unexpected or unusual occurrences that, sequenced together, can constitute a plot. But our use of the term *adventure* generally reflects an evaluative sense as well. Let us extend our definition, then, to say that an adventure is any endeavor on which we embark to achieve a goal, arrive at a destination, or attain a state of affairs that is not merely different from, but somehow an improvement on, where we are at present. In this way, we hope the endeavor will prove to be worth our while. While the former or basic sense of adventure is in the background of what ensues, it is this latter evaluative sense that is central to the view we shall be developing here.

Embarking on an adventure is of course no guarantee of succeeding at it, and it may well come to a tragic end—as a misadventure. Furthermore, the end toward which we strive may not necessarily be better than before, let alone good for either us or our world—however we reckon "better" and "good." Nonetheless, it is ultimately because we humans are peculiarly adventurous creatures that human society (versus, say, sparrow society or cabbage society) has progressed to the degree that it has. In other words, it has moved from naive immersion in the rhythms of the natural world and sought continuously to expand its knowledge of nature and, for better or worse, to design its relationship to it. Armed with such a definition, then, we immediately recognize numerous endeavors as types of adventure.

For starters, there are social or interpersonal adventures. These include everything from going out on the town to joining a club to chatting with friends. All are motivated by the longing for adventure: the adventure of other people, of exploring the intricacies and puzzles of their worlds, of getting to know them—and of getting to know ourselves in the process. Two subsets of social adventures, then, are romantic adventures, which may be fraught with agony and ecstasy, the risk of rejection, and numerous ups and downs; and sexual adventures, in which the goal is connection with other people but not necessarily relationship. The apex of all such adventures, we might say, is the adventure of intimacy, of commitment to one person alone: a journey in which the risks can be great, but so can the rewards: happy marriage, happy family, happy ever after.

Another type, professional adventures, includes pursuing a particular career. Such adventures are not quite the same as social adventures, though there are links between the two. The goal, however, is distinctive, and so are the risks. The goal is either success for ourselves—be it fortune or fame, power or prestige—or service to others, or some combination of the two. In financial adventures, which are often combined with professional ones, the goal is making money. Such adventures include playing the stock market, buying a lottery ticket, or starting a business: any venture in which the bottom line is profit: getting more out of something than we put into it at the start.

Then there are physical adventures, where our purpose is to extend our strength, expand our skill, or test our limits, whether by surfing or skiing or simply getting in shape. Vehicles for this type of adventure include many of the hobbies we pursue, all of the thrill-seeking, and most of the sports. In his analysis of the enduring importance of sports in our lives, psychologist Karl Schiebe (1986) argues that games of sport, along with gambling in general, "are but stripped down, stylized and abbreviated dramas, inviting the direct or vicarious participation of masses of people seeking for some adventure, no matter how minuscule, to provide story matter for their lives" (p. 134).

Cultural adventures, or aesthetic adventures, are another type. One example is going to a gallery, exposing ourselves to art, and discovering in the process that our entire perception of reality has been oddly revised. Another is being transported by a symphony or poem. Still another is reading, which we will consider later on. Whether or not we seek them intentionally, such cultural-aesthetic adventures abound, of course, whenever we travel and open ourselves to the kind of culture shock that can forever unsettle our world.

Creativity is an adventure of this type. In a sense, it is the most basic adventure of all. Like others, it entails a special kind of journey, a forsaking of the familiar and a forging of the new. Self-creation (Randall, 1995) is perhaps the supreme example. Any specific creative activity, be it doing a painting, composing a ballad, or writing a poem, holds the possibility of aesthetic adventure. It pushes us to relinquish old, comforting certainties and advance to new levels of awareness—of ourselves, of others, of our world. This is the difference between art and craft. Accordingly, artists are often viewed as mavericks, composers, as visionaries, poets, as rebels. In general, insists Anais Nin (1976, p. 56), the artist is the one who "sacrifices a great deal of security, peace of mind, for the perpetual adventure, for the discovery of new colors, new words, new horizons, new territories of experience."

As we began to see in Chapter 4, spiritual adventures are another type. A spiritual adventure, we could say, is any endeavor in which our central if unstated purpose is the enlivening of our sense of connection with the ultimate context of our lives, whatever we understand that to be: God, The Good, The Beautiful, The True, The Tao, or simply our True Self, a phrase that suggests that spiritual adventures are frequently linked to autobiographical ones. We shall return to this connection later.

For some, membership in an organized religion constitutes a spiritual adventure, though it may be the social side of their affiliation and not the spiritual side that attracts them the most. For others, the adventure goes deeper. For the Christian, for example, "the Christian life [itself] is an adventure, a voyage of discovery, a journey, sustained by faith and hope, towards a final and complete communion with the Love at the heart of all things," or at least so says the Doctrine Commission (1976, p. 3) of the Church of England. No doubt comparable statements can be found in other traditions too. Whatever form a given spiritual adventure may take, however, the sense of movement is inevitably involved. Monastics, mystics, and seekers of every sort refer routinely to being on a path. They see themselves not just as travelers, certainly not as tourists, but as followers, as pilgrims in search of a Promised Land. As theologian Monica Furlong (1984, p. 14) writes, "the religious man is the one who believes that life is about making some sort of journey."

Obviously, a spiritual adventure can involve a physical adventure as well: journeying to Mecca, for example, or mounting the steps of the temple on our hands and knees. By the same token, the activity entailed may be nothing more dramatic than writing in our journal or going for a walk or going to bed and entering the dreamworld—an adventure in itself—or, beforehand, simply kneeling to pray. Note the sense of adventure, and purpose, that is touchingly described in this excerpt from a story by Alice Munro (1986, p. 2):

My mother prayed on her knees at midday, at night, and first thing in the morning. Every day opened up to her to have God's will done in it. Every night she totted up what she'd done and said and thought, to see how it squared with Him. That kind of life is dreary, people think, but they're missing the point. For one thing, such a life can never be boring. And nothing can happen to you that you can't make use of. Even if you're racked by troubles, and sick and poor and ugly, you've got your soul to carry through life like a treasure on a platter.

Another in the list are intellectual adventures. Often linked to spiritual adventures, these are central to what educators call learning. Learning constitutes adventure par excellence: adventure that is lifelong and continually transformative (Daloz, 1986). To some, this type of adventure is the heart of civilization. To Alfred North Whitehead "the Adventure of Ideas might be taken as a synonym for The History of the Human Race" (1957, p. 11). To Freidrich Nietszche, a philosopher should "live dangerously" (cited in Zweig, 1974, p. 204). Science itself can be seen as one grand adventure of pushing back the frontiers of human understanding. Indeed, histories of science are commonly composed as romantic tales whose unfolding depends on courageous explorations and eleventh-hour discoveries, and hinges on the intellectual heroism of a Galileo, a Darwin, or an Einstein. As Theodore Plantinga (1992, p. 81) has observed, history books, period, tend to be written by the victors of whatever adventure they set out to record. At the very least, they are written from a present that is implicitly portrayed as more enlightened than the past, for which the latter has paved the way. At the same time, though bias inevitably infects it, the study of history is, in general, an adventure: an exploration of the mystery of the past, an endless inquiring into what really occurred, and why.

We can embark on intellectual adventures by many means, whether reading a book, recording our thoughts, or completing a degree. In each, the goal will vary, be it to pursue an idea, fathom how something works, or inspect some unexplored corner of the mystery of life. For the scientist or scholar, the goal could be to scout out a fresh frontier and invite one's colleagues to a deeper understanding of the issues with which their field is concerned. Each such undertaking is a form of research. At the center of research is simply *search*, and the key to a successful search is a good question to guide us along. To ask a question, furthermore, is to set out on a quest. So it is that many of us become academics, because we are adventurers at heart.

Writing this book has itself been an adventure: an adventure of collaboration in an adventure of thought—one fraught with challenges, riddled with risks, and guided by a question that is both simple and grand: *What is wisdom?* In each section of it, moreover, we are attempting to assign logic and flow to what are frequently elusive ideas. Indeed, any attempt to use words to convey ideas is, at bottom, a leap in the dark. Language itself is an adventure. And what can be seen as the heart of language—metaphor—is a further adventure as well: a reaching from the known to the unknown. Ironically, then, not only is adventure a metaphor, but the metaphor of adventure is an adventure in itself. Accordingly, there are intellectual adventures inside of intellectual adventures inside of intellectual adventures, and so on.

Stepping back from this list, we see, first of all, that however quiet our lives may seem on the surface, they are in fact filled with adventure. The possibility of it, the allure of it, the hunger for it, the attempt to articulate it, and the savoring of it after the fact . . . adventure pervades our lives. To be human is to be an adventurer. If we are not in the middle of one adventure, we are on the edge of another. Moreover, there are types of adventure besides those we have noted here. There are technological adventures, for example, such as buying a new computer and figuring out how to use it; or, on a grander scale, the whole, vast adventure of modern civilization, in its headlong race toward technological nirvana. And there are corporate adventures too. Certainly, there are military adventures, as well as political or ideological adventures, where we commit ourselves to a cause that is larger than our immediate agenda and is potentially so all-consuming as to become, at bottom, a spiritual adventure as well. Closer to home are culinary adventures, whether trying a new restaurant, testing a new recipe, or combining yesterday's leftovers with a dash of this and a pinch of that, not knowing what taste will result. And so the list might go.

Second, various adventures are entwined in various ways. Going off to the university, for instance, is at once an intellectual adventure, a social adventure, a personal-spiritual adventure, and, in a preparatory sense, a professional adventure too. And inasmuch as it is an investment from which we hope, eventually, to profit, it is a financial adventure as well. Similarly, a major trip can entail the physical adventure of sheer movement, the social adventure of meeting new people, and the cultural-intellectual-spiritual adventure of opening ourselves to a different worldview. Being entwined also means being interconnected. For example, one adventure often leads to another. The adventure of attending a university can lead to the adventure of love and in turn to the adventure of sex. Like the larger stories we pursue them within, adventures are often not isolated but, as it were, ecologically related, with one adventure nested inside another inside another, with the ashes of one adventure containing the seeds of the next.

By the same token, in the third case, adventures can also contradict one another. In playing tennis with friends, an activity that is part physical adventure and part social, tension may develop when one of us is in it for the workout, another for the social time, and another to win, while another for the Tao of tennis. Also, some adventures are more exclusive than others, demanding more of our energy and time. Thus, my all-consuming intellectual-professional adventure to obtain my Ph.D. may be at odds with my incipient spiritual adventure to be in touch with my true self, an adventure that would require less filling of my brain and more feeding of my soul. Each adventure takes me in a distinct direction. Similarly, the entire adventure of pursuing my degree may be in direct competition with my partner's postponed adventure to attain greater autonomy from me. Along the same lines, I may be a veritable superhero in my professional adventures yet, as a workholic, a dismal disappointment in my interpersonal ones. One way to account for such discrepancies, of course, is to suggest that just as people can be considered intelligent in differing ways, so they can be adventurous in differing ways too. Thus, some may be utterly unadventurous in physical respects yet repeatedly take breathtaking risks in the realm of ideas and words.

Fourth, adventures can be placed between the poles of a variety of spectra, such as chosen-unchosen, inner-outer, real-contrived or real-vicarious, major-minor, and individual-collective. Obviously, a chosen adventure is one that we choose on our own, perhaps to prove a point to ourselves or to make an impression on others—or simply to make memories from which we can derive pleasure as we age. An unchosen adventure is one into which we are thrown by circumstance or chance. In an outer adventure, the goal is clear, concrete, even public—like climbing a mountain, making a million, or finding a mate. In an inner adventure, the goal is more elusive, more difficult to define, less tangible and visible. It is a state of mind or a quality of emotion, such as might be achieved in completing a poem, mastering a concept, or discovering true love. The point is: We cannot tell simply from looking at someone in what internal adventure they might at that moment be immersed. To be fair, many outer adventures are inner ones as well, and vice versa. Topping Mt. Everest is a triumph not just of the body but of the spirit as well, while finding inner peace may entail an arduous hike to an alpine shrine. By the same token, the pursuit of "the soul's high adventure" (Campbell & Moyers, 1988, p. 148) may have little to do with undertaking a physical adventure at all. Witness the scholars and writers whose grand explorations have happened entirely in one tiny room.

A real adventure is one in which we actively engage, taking definite risks in pursuit of actual goals toward uncertain results. In a contrived, or planned, adventure, the experience is similar to a real adventure, yet the rules are determined, the limits are clear, and the overall ending (if not the precise outcome) is set in advance. Games and sports are of this type, as are things such as the weekend wilderness adventures that are a key commodity in the exploding field of ecotourism. Contrived adventures, such as bungee cord jumping, skydiving, or white-water rafting, are the type we engage in intentionally, in order to provide ourselves material for stories with which both to enrich our sense of self and to entertain others. A vicarious adventure is someone else's adventure that we experience second-hand, by watching a movie or sports event on television, by losing ourselves in a novel, by listening to the news about our world or the gossip about our neighbours, or, on a larger scale, by living through our children. While vicarious adventures provide some sample of the suspense and satisfaction of real adventures, the emotions they inspire are comparatively contained. We get caught up, alright; we feel the thrill and taste the risks, but the rewards will be others' to reap.

Major adventures are distinguished as such because of the time and energy required to pursue them, whereas minor adventures can be lived between them, sometimes during them, like subplots in a larger tale. In many cases, because it seems safer or less unsettling, a life of many minor adventures may substitute for a life constructed around one or two major ones. Thus, amid the routine of what is otherwise a tranquil life, we occasionally crave a little adventure—little in the sense of either a manageable amount or simply one we are able to afford: a minivacation or a minor affair. By the same token, what seems a major adventure to us who are immersed in it may seem only minor to someone viewing our lives from outside-in, and of course, vice versa. Not only that, but, over time, the same adventure can change rather dramatically in our own imagination. The war we went off to so vigorously as a youth is, in hindsight, far less *le grand aventure* it seemed at the time than the backdrop, however horrific, to one stage of a still more major adventure in which we see ourselves involved, that of seeking our "true self." Whether an adventure is major or minor is ultimately determined by the memory of the person involved.

A collective adventure is one we pursue in the company of others, such as when we are playing a sport, raising a family, or fighting a war. These adventures can be either small-scale or large. A religion is an example of the latter, as is a political party: Each involves a large group of people who, supposedly, share a common mission. Of course, not all such adventures are especially benevolent. The vast financial adventure of which we are part, as an employee of a huge corporation, where the goal is profit for profit's sake, may be violently at odds with the natural environment or with the dream of a local community for greater self-determination—or with the dream that we harbor within ourselves to become our own person and chart our own course.

In not all adventures, however, do we receive or even require the support that is afforded by a collective one. Some adventures, like some adventurers, are solitary. An individual adventure is one we pursue primarily on our own. Though we may consult with others, it is by ourselves that we must "walk that lonesome valley." Yet even the most solitary adventurer can appreciate some company along the way. It is gratifying, for example, to know that others are involved with us in the exciting adventure of narrative gerontology. Even if we are wrestling with the relevant issues from our respective angles, we find comfort in knowing we are not alone in our quest.

Few adventures will be exclusively at one pole or the other of these various spectra. Few will be solely outer or inner, individual or collective, real or vicarious. Besides, there can be movement from pole to pole. Thus, an exploit that has auspicious beginnings, with all the appearance of a major adventure, can fade into a fool's errand that we eventually abort and conveniently forget. Conversely, the minor affair we figured we could easily afford becomes a painful turning point in the major adventure of salvaging our relationship with the person we wed. In the same vein, an endeavor that is primarily outer can become steadily more inner. One that is primarily collective can become progressively more personal. One that is thrust at us by circumstances can become one we increasingly embrace as our own. And so it goes.

STAGES OF ADVENTURE

Having surveyed the types of adventures that can be central to our lives, we shall now try to sketch the principal stages in the unfolding of a given adventure, regardless of its type. We see at least eight of these stages, though eight is admittedly an arbitrary number. There may be far fewer and there may be many more, depending on how detailed we feel the need to be. The legendary Joseph Campbell distilled what he saw as the hero's adventure to three archetypal phases: departure, fulfillment, and return. The same pattern is echoed by Robert Atkinson (1995) and Laurent Daloz (1986) in their respective analyses of what Campbell (Campbell & Moyers, 1988) calls the monomyth, whose stages of separation, initiation, and return appear in hundreds of legends from numberless lands. Our list here, we believe, incorporates all of these stages but at the same time expands them. For the sake of discussion (and the love of alliteration), they are call, calculation, commitment, consolidation, conflict (or confusion), crisis (or climax), conclusion (or consummation), and communication.

Call

All adventures begin with some kind of call. The call may come from within or without: from our deep inner restlessness, from a dip in the economy, from a disaster in our community, from a dare by a friend. It is the challenge to action. It may build in us gradually and quietly or burst like a bomb above a sleeping town. It is the invitation to set out, issued amid the sense that something is not right and needs to be fixed, that there is an enemy that we need to confront, a problem we need to resolve, a question to answer, an issue to settle, a goal to achieve. The call can be felt in curiosity, in concern, or in ordinary boredom. It can come as a vague longing for something different, for something other than the status quo. Or it can come as a revelation from out of the blue, a sudden vision of a far off frontier or a glimpse of an undiscovered territory that seemed previously beyond our reach. Finally, it can be responded to vigorously or it can be quietly ignored, dismissed immediately or eventually with a "what's the point" or "what's the use."

Calculation

Once the call has been heard, however, once there has been an unsettling of our natural calm, comes some critical questions: What will be entailed in tackling this problem, exploring this issue, attaining this goal, pursuing this dream? What are the pros and cons, the possible payoffs and losses? What must I sacrifice? What security will I have to forego? How long will the ordeal last? Who might be my mentors, my competitors, my allies, my foes? Who will be for me and who against me? Can I manage it at all? Finally, will it be worth my while? Calculation involves counting the cost. The cost may be a few dollars or a few days, or it may be a matter of our marriage, our health, or our life.

Commitment

Once we have made our calculations, counted the cost, weighed the pros in favor of the cons, we throw ourselves into the adventure, however half-hearted our throwing may be. The point is: We decide, we say yes, and so we set out. We take the initial risk: *I'm returning to school; I'm asking her out; I'm taking the plunge.*

Consolidation

This stage involves the serious contemplation of what must be done, step by step. A kind of postcommitment calculation, it is fully digesting what will be expected of us. It is a period of preparation: of laying in supplies, of stocking up on resources, perhaps of building an ark; of bidding adieu to those who will stay behind; of acquiring the necessary information or training or advice. We are heading toward the goal, but we are continuing to tally what will be needed for the challenges to be met, the hurdles to be jumped, the struggles to be endured, the enemies to be fought, the demons to be subdued.

Conflict/Confusion

This stage is where the trouble begins in earnest. We have gathered our supplies and forsaken the security of home. With the path ahead uncertain, we must buckle down and plod along. At times there are setbacks; at times, success. Now the suffering and the struggling, and now the flashes of victory, the periodic glimpses of our goal at last achieved. During this often protracted stage, infusions of hope, of commitment, of vision must be regularly supplied, for it can become unclear why we are doing this in the first place; what, after all, is our goal. To continue or not to continue: This is the continual question. Should we cut our losses and run? Should we quit while we are ahead? Or should we throw caution to the wind and persevere? Turning back becomes less and less possible, however, the closer we get to the end. Whether closer or farther away, this is the stage of change, of discovering both our limits and our strengths, both our restrictions and our resources. The conflict we face may be external primarily, or internal. Along the way, there may be much support from others (especially in a collective adventure) or comparatively little. Amid the conflict and the movement from periodic setback to provisional success, there may be much self-discovery stimulated or very little—depending on where we perceive our enemy to lie: without or within.

Crisis/Climax

At this stage the conflict becomes intense. In an adventure movie, a chase scene commonly precedes it. The point of no return has long been passed. We have given our all and at last we discover of what sort of substance we are made. It is the stage of the final push, come hell or high water. Our energies are at their peak, but so are our enemies' too. It is now or never.

Conclusion/Consummation

At last, the goal is achieved, the problem solved, the issue settled, the question answered, the grail secured. This is the stage of satisfaction, of (relative) peace, of self-congratulation even: We did it, we made it, we followed through. It may be followed, however, by a letdown as well, by a wondering "Is that all there is?" It may be followed by both an emptiness and a beginning boredom that barely quiets the call to another adventure still, like the clue that is dropped in the last chapter of a child's mystery book to assure us that in the next volume of the series, further adventures await.

Communication

This final stage is, conceivably, the most important of all. If an adventure is not recounted, can it be called an adventure at all? To complete the cycle, the hero must return to tell the tale. In this way, whatever learning or insight has been gained can be of benefit to those who remained behind—or, more likely, were busy pursuing adventures of their own.

As grossly as we have sketched them here, these stages seldom succeed each other in lock-step fashion. For instance, we often go back and forth between commitment and confusion, to-ing and fro-ing between consolidation and conflict, recommiting ourselves, again and again, to the original goal (which itself might get revised in the process), and reentering the conflict afresh. Furthermore, though in major adventures, these stages can be clearly marked, there can be wide variation in their respective duration and in the balancing of elements within them—not to mention in the experience of the adventurer amid them.

In the mini-adventure of playing bingo on Friday night, the stages of calculation and crisis are neither terribly protracted nor easily distinguished. The adventurer goes straight from call to commitment, endures much conflict (periodic successes and losses), and may or may not attain a satisfactory result. In this respect, adventure is commonly entwined with addiction. In other adventures, although we may spend a long time hearing it, once the call is clear, we move quickly through calculation and commitment. By the same token, the conflict may be long and drawn out, while the crisis is furious and fast. Furthermore, the time and energy spent on each of these stages will vary according to the temperament of the adventurer and to the circumstances and pressures that impinge on the adventure itself.

In some adventures, or for some adventurers, the call comes clearly, such that we can visualize ourselves attaining it, while in others, it is ill-defined and requires meditation to discern. In some, we are intentional about answering the call. In others, the call comes despite us; we are reluctant adventurers who get dragged kicking and screaming into a conflict and a mission that we did not choose. This theme of the reluctant hero is one around which, curiously, moviemakers have composed the plots of numerous thrillers. Many films starring Harrison Ford are of this genre, for example. In short, some people look for adventures, while some stumble into them, unwittingly and unwillingly. Others resist them, while others simply ignore the call.

In some adventures, the calculation stage is passed through so speedily that the commitment, however decisively made, is founded on uncertainty. The consolidation stage may thus be more complicated than necessary because the possible problems and costs are not sufficiently envisioned. In the adventure of Olympic athletics, for example, the stage of consolidation—the training, the getting in shape, the practice—may last for months, while the stages of conflict in the competition itself, as of crisis and completion, are mere minutes or seconds apart. In some adventures, the cost is mighty—leaving home, investing much money and time, putting oneself at physical risk—while in others, it is small: the purchase of a ticket, the price of admission.

Then there are differences in the sweetness of the consummation achieved. The sense of completion that comes with certain adventures is of short duration, and so the emptiness that soon ensues holds the seeds of a call to another adventure still—often of the same kind, in which case, whether negative or positive, we are in the realm of addiction. Other adventures take so long to complete and take so much out of the adventurer in the process that the satisfaction of completion (if completion there be) must be made to last, for there is no way that another, similar adventure can be embarked upon soon. Adventurers themselves obviously differ, therefore, in terms of the energy, freedom, and opportunity they have to embark on a series of adventures—whether of the same type or different. In other words, people conceivably vary in terms of their adventure threshold, of their tolerance for adventure and their requirement of it.

ADVENTURE—PRO AND CON

With this look at the overall stages of adventure, we are getting ready to consider the adventures of both living and aging. Before we proceed, however, we need to examine the possibility that the metaphor of adventure is less helpful than we imagine. The very prevalence of adventure-thinking makes the metaphor a candidate for critique. Indeed, from a variety of corners, such critique is frequently heard.

The most compelling critique comes from common sense. Not all journeys are necessarily adventures, nor are all stories automatically adventure stories. Adventure is not the only story in town. Literary theory corroborates this view. In Northrop Frye's (1966) list of the five main modes of fiction, romance (or adventure) is only one. Nor is it the most prestigious. Among literary critics, adventure stories are judged of comparatively low status for inspiring escapism rather than inviting a responsible wrestling with the complexities of the text. They are dismissed from serious analysis for appealing to our narrative lust, for encouraging us to read for the plot (Brooks, 1985), and little more. Satire or irony, on the other hand, is deemed more true to life insofar as life presents us with the full range of generic possibilities. As in better literature, the genres are continually blurred.

This leads to a critique from developmental psychology. Insofar as "literary conventions serve to fashion the theories of science" (Gergen & Gergen, 1986, p. 22), the convention of adventure can be seen to underlie our most popular theories of human development, which are of the "happy ever after" variety (pp. 32ff). For instance, in Gail Sheehy's best-selling book *Passages*, one scholar "identifies the underlying narrative structure as romance, where the hero engages in adventures of self-discovery filled with hope" (Sarbin, 1986a, p. xviii). In an analysis of the hero archetypes by which she sees her clients living, psychotherapist Carol Pearson (1989) says people can be heroes within a variety of stories, and not just adventure as such. While there is certainly the warrior hero, there is also the martyr, the wanderer, the orphan, and the magician—each of whom lives out a plot line of a particular mode, whether irony, in the case of the wanderer, or tragedy, in that of the martyr, and so on.

The critique of the adventure motif in developmental theory, however, is an implicit critique of American culture, in which it could be said to be rooted, a culture still characterized by a confident, optimistic view of human history—indeed, as reflected in its foreign policy, its capitalist ethos, and certainly its cinema, by a thirst for adventure (Schiebe, 1986). In cultures shaped by different geographical-historical conditions, such a raw, adventurist spirit seems utterly out of place, particularly when they are faced with the stark realities of starvation, depression, and drought or the horrors of concentration camps and killing fields. "Life is not a happy event," writes holocaust survivor, Elie Wiesel (1988, p. 259), "It's always a tragedy, by definition. It's short. We come from nowhere; we go nowhere." Ironically, however, American adventure-thinking in turn has roots in Judeo-Christian thought, the grand story behind which, as traced in the Bible, is a vast, sprawling, narrative collage featuring the exploits of spiritual heroes such as a Moses or an Abraham, who ventured from the land of Ur "not knowing where he was to go" (Hebrews 11:8, RSV). Through the lens of this master narrative, time is seen as finite and purposeful, history as the record of divine activity in human affairs, and the future as the final frontier, at whose edge lies the Kingdom of God.

Religious adventures generally take one of two forms: outer and inner. Inner adventure, or the adventure inward (Kelsey, 1980), is one which all traditions, in their own ways and own terms, prescribe for their adherents. Outer adventure usually entails taking something over, generally territory held by the infidels, and claiming it as the Promised Land. Unfortunately, the concept of an outer adventure—at least in Christianity—has enchanted the collective imagination more powerfully than has that of an inner one, perhaps because, compared with most versions of heaven, its goals are more tangibly envisioned. It has, in any case, received widespread secular adoption in cultures and economies that have been shaped only marginally or originally by it, from socialism and communism to the whole horrific misadventure of the Third Reich. It has also encouraged the belief that not only must the infidels be defeated but so must nature itself: dominated, subdued, made a servant to human wants. So-called nature religions are therefore somewhat suspect because they refuse to view nature as an obstacle, an enemy. And an adventure without an obstacle or enemy is in some ways not much of an adventure. By the same token, a nature abused for centuries as obstacle or enemy is eventually not much of a nature.

While our relationship with the natural world has borne much of the brunt of our more destructive expressions of the adventure mentality, our relationships with each other have fared little better. Such a mentality informs our preoccupation with getting ahead, with keeping up with the Joneses, with the proverbial rat race in which our neighbors are not neighbors but competitors. Such a mentality is central to the adventure of modernity, driving us onward and upward to an ever more exotic technological paradise and to progress at any price. Fortunately, much of the postmodern mentality is attuned to the tragedy of this trend and seeks a more harmonious relationship with the natural world, one that accords humans a humbler place in a dynamic web where no species has special rank, or divine right, in relation to the rest. As we indicated in Chapter 1 in discussing the reasons for revisiting wisdom in a postmodern age, the vision that guides such a mentality sees nature as essentially alive (Lovelock, 1979), as a forward-moving, open-ended, intelligent entity involved in an adventure of its own. In the totality of this whole, unfolding process we are but one life form among many. John Haught (1984) expresses it in a book called *The Cosmic Adventure*:

According to modern science our universe appears to be, by all accounts, an adventure. By adventure is meant the universe's search for continually more intense forms of ordered novelty. . . . Because of the adventurous nature of the cosmos, eventually life appeared, then consciousness, then civilization. Whatever else this cosmic adventure leads to (further expansion of consciousness? planetary unification? inter-galactic communication?), we can safely say that it would take the form of a heightening of the intensity of ordered novelty. It would continue the trend of intensifying cosmic Beauty.

Such a vision of the universe story (Swimme & Berry, 1992), or of the ultimate larger story within which we live, places the adventures of our particular lives in a grand and essentially supportive context. It lends meaning to our individual searches for meaning and thus credibility to the very notion of the adventure of living.

At the same time, adventure also operates in cultures that we might otherwise romanticize—aboriginal ones, for instance. From the perspective of such cultures, it can seem that Westerners are "addicted to novelty" and that "man . . . is by definition a restless soul always in search of new frontiers, new challenges" (Ross, 1992, p. 91; see also Abrahams,

1986). Nonetheless, though the adventure such cultures call us to live may not, fortunately, be an adventure against nature or against other people, there is still a goal to be sought—on one's vision quest, for example—and there are still enemies to be fought, inner though they be.

Some feminist writers have expressed suspicion of adventure-thinking, seeing its origins in a mindset that is decidedly male. The traditional pattern of adventure has been one of men going off "a-questing" (Schiebe, 1986, p. 147) while women remain at home tending the fire and awaiting their hero's return. One reason for this suspicion arises in relation to the very concept of hero. Joseph Campbell talks openly of the hero's adventure and urges us to see ourselves as heroes in the context of our own lives, to find "the thread of the hero path," and to follow our bliss (Campbell & Moyers, 1988). Campbell's view parallels that of Carol Pearson (1989) in *The Hero Within*. Heroes, Pearson says, "take journeys, confront dangers, and *discover the treasure of their true selves*" (p. 1; emphasis ours).

But "hero" carries connotations that can be problematic from a gender perspective: those of a self-contained individual charting a course toward a destiny that takes "him" not closer to others but farther away. Such connotations are noted by Bateson (1989) in her acknowledgment of the demise of the dominant model of "single-track ambition" (p. 15) against which both women and men have believed their lives to be judged. Such a model, which she sees as fundamentally male, is built "around the image of a quest, a journey through a timeless landscape toward an end that is specific, even though it is not fully known" (p. 6). Arguing in favor of "the creative potential of interrupted and conflicted lives"—which she says most women's are—Bateson makes the case that "the knight errant, who finds his challenges along the way, may be a better model for our times than the knight who is questing for the Grail" (pp. 9ff).

Frieda Forman (1989) goes still further and strikes at the very ways in which she believes each gender is geared toward time as a whole. Insisting on the male domination of our notions of time in Western philosophy, religion, and civilization, she argues that "a critical component of masculine time consciousness" is "awareness of the future," awareness "that one is not-going-to-be," awareness of death (p. 6). For truly authentic being in the existentialist sense, such an awareness is of course central. It is also, we could agree, central to the dynamics of both story in general and adventure in particular, whose sense of an ending (Kermode, 1980) in effect drives things on, supplying the tale with the forward momentum that it needs to exist. However, in Forman's analysis, women experience time in fundamentally different ways, or, so to speak, live a significantly different version of story time. "[F]or women," she says, "the giving of time, i.e., birth, is prior to and takes both ontological and temporal priority over the taking away of time, i.e., death" (1989, p. 7).

It is difficult to know how to address Forman's point. If valid, it is profound. But it may also be tangential, for surely feminism is itself a movement. And like all movements, it is an adventure with an overriding goal: to identify and undo male domination wherever it exists—in politics and business, in industry and education, in relationships and religion. Indeed, inspired by the progress of the movement as a whole, countless individual women have been empowered to embark on their own unique journeys and to tackle obstacles, within and without, that have hitherto limited their lives.

Perhaps the most serious critique of adventure-thinking comes not from a spiritual, socioeconomic, or even gender perspective but a philosophical one, carrying with it important implications for both our experience of time and our very concept of reality and our relationship to it. The philosopher who has best articulated this critique is, ironically, Jean-Paul Sartre. We say ironically because the philosophy of existentialism, behind which he is a principal figure, has done more than most philosophies to inspire adventure-thinking, through its stress on the radical reality of human freedom, on the necessity of choice and the courage to be (Tillich, 1952), and on the responsibility to create ourselves that each of us bears (Charmé, 1984).

In his novel entitled *Nausea*, Sartre's (1965) main character, Roquentin, is attempting to compose the biography of an obscure statesman, long since deceased. The incredible difficulty, however, of reconstructing a life in the present from scraps of information about the past predisposes Roquentin to periodic spells of a kind of psychological-philosophical vertigo. He calls such spells *la nausée*, or "nausea." In the midst of them, he becomes aware of the stark reality of things and events as they are, stripped of any interpretative context, of any story. Reflecting on these spells, the insight dawns on him that there are ultimately no adventures at all, in the sense of stories that are somehow inherent in events as they happen. "I haven't had any adventures," he confesses to his journal. "Things have happened to me, events, incidents, anything you like. But not adventures. . . . Adventures are in books." Nonetheless, "for the most commonplace event to become an adventure, you must—and this is all that is necessary—start *recounting* it" (p. 58; emphasis ours).

It is hard to counter Sartre's point, one that Northrop Frye has made as well: "Real life does not stop or start," he says; "it never ties up loose ends; it never manifests meaning and purpose except by blind accident; it is never comic or tragic, ironic or romantic, or anything else that has a shape." It is impossible to disagree with such an analysis. True: Events in themselves are not adventures. But then, it is hard to know what events in themselves would be. Indeed, from a narrative perspective, as we have argued both here and elsewhere (Kenyon & Randall, 1997), there is no such thing as an event in itself. Adventures—narratives, stories of any kind, including comedies and tragedies—are creations of our imagination, poetic compositions we impose after the fact upon the data we receive through our senses and filter through our minds. The story in events is truly in the telling. But in a real sense there are no events without telling. By virtue of our very humanness, we are inveterate storiers. As Roquentin himself puts it, "A man is always a teller of tales, he lives surrounded by his stories and the stories of others, he sees everything that happens to him through them; and he tries to live his life as if he were recounting it" (Sartre, 1965, p. 61).

To story or not to story: that, then, is not the question, and it never has been. Our lives are structured *by* narrative and *in* narrative whether we like it or not. Storying our life's events—past and future, experienced and expected—is something we inevitably do. What Bruner (1996) calls the narrative construal of reality is a process in which we habitually engage. While there may be wide variations in how—in different cultures, eras, languages, and genders—we each construe our reality, and in how we experience and express our narrative intelligence, the fact *that* we story is uncontestable. And if that is uncontestable, then so is our tendency to genre-ate our reality as well (Bruner, 1996). Certainly, newspapers commonly incorporate references to genre in their construal of events, especially in their headlines: *Weekend Adventure Turns to Tragedy.* As we have seen in Chapter 3, our lives as a whole may be seen to take a generic shape as well, at certain times and in certain ways, whether in our own eyes or in those of others. We routinely refer to people as having had, for example, a tragic life. When we do, it is more than mere rhetoric we are employing; we believe we are making a statement about what is real. This raises the question of whether there may be a general type of wisdom that accompanies each genre of life plot—tragic wisdom versus comic wisdom, and so on. In any case, whether we are thinking in terms of individual events or of entire lives, the question is not *why story?* We are going to assign story to life regardless. The real question is *why adventure?*

It may clarify our line of thinking here to introduce a further spectrum in terms of which adventures can be distinguished, with "high" at one end and "low" at the other. High adventure is the convention around which popular novels and movies tend to be composed. In it, the constituent components are heightened to the point where the story becomes almost a caricature of the convention itself. The various stages are so recognizable, their presentation so unmistakable and their pacing so predictable, the good guys and bad guys so easy to pick out and their introduction and interaction so intricately timed, and the ultimate conclusion so tidy that, after experiencing only a few examples, we know at the outset what sort of story we are going to get. High adventure is highly contrived. For that reason it is, storywise, craft, not art. It is, we could say, canned. Packaged to appeal to our narrative lust and, as some feminist theorists have argued, to emulate the cycle of arousal, climax, and collapse that is central to sex itself (see Bogdan, 1990), it is what readily sells.

In low adventure, though the stages we have identified still pertain, there is little that is stock about their arrangement. Permutations and combinations abound. The forward direction, the pursuit of goals, the intentional journeying from one state of affairs to another—such elements are present, but there is greater complexity in how they play out and more subtlety in how they are portrayed. Similarly, the ending is far from a foregone conclusion and is not automatically happy. It is open, ambiguous, yet to be seen. We cannot tell in advance how things will wind up. It can be argued that low adventure is therefore real adventure or true adventure, precisely because it is not canned, not constructed to a formula, not intrinsically predictable. Nor are its central characters either clearly good or clearly bad. Rather then being stock or static, they change over time in ways that cannot be anticipated as they react to the circumstances in which they are set. Instead of the plot determining the characters, the characters determine the plot. To set out on a true adventure is to enter not a formula, therefore, but a mystery. The destination to which it leads is not a foreseeable falling into place of preprogrammed factors but a genuine discovery.

All high literature, it could be argued then, and as we were hinting in Chapter 3, is low adventure, a view that is implied by Frye (1963, pp. 20ff), for example, when he suggests that literature overall is concerned with the problem of "lost identity," the regaining of which, he says, is "the framework of all literature." By this he means "the story that's told so often, of how man once lived in a golden age or a garden of Eden or the Hesperides, or a happy island kingdom in the Atlantic, how that world was lost, and how we some day may be able to get it back again." Inside this story, he goes on, "comes the story of the hero with a thousand faces . . . whose adventures, death, disappearance and marriage or resurrection are the focal points of what later become romance and tragedy and satire and comedy." In a sense, then, all stories are ultimately adventure stories, some of which come to a tragic end, while others are comic, ironic, or picaresque. Accordingly, we could say that adventure is the genus of which each of these others is a particular species.

Having in this way further refined the definition of adventure that we are assuming in this chapter, we can start to see how, despite the foregoing critiques, adventure has its place. We offer the following points therefore to crystallize our thinking up to now.

First, while our everyday speech is sprinkled with adventure talk, it is more than the rhetoric of adventure that runs through our lives. So does its reality as well. Our lives are filled with one type of adventure or another. There is an adventure instinct that is impossible to excise from our nature, an instinct that distinguishes human nature from any other. Hence, for better or worse, we have the quest for progress to which our species has been prone.

Second, just as adventures can be categorized differently, so can they be evaluated differently. From a moral perspective, adventure, as such, is not the issue, nor are the stages of adventures suspect in themselves. However, the goals of particular adventures and the means employed to achieve them can certainly be. In short, some adventures are evil, while others are essentially good—that is, wholesome, healthy, life giving and life promoting—for us, for others, for the planet.

Third, it is true that adventure-thinking can be critiqued from a number of angles: as the product of a male mentality, as anti-nature, as fixated on the future. And it is also true that adventure is not inherent in reality per se; rather, we compose adventures (as stories) and impose them on events both after the fact, in memory, and before the fact, in imagination. However, this imposition, this storying of the stuff of our lives, is not negative so much as instinctive. Once again, the issue is not *why* story but *what* story: What genre? Adventure or something else?

Naturally, we can offer no neat conclusion as to whether adventure is a worthy genre for construing our lives, let alone a superior one. However, given that none of the critiques we have noted is entirely airtight, and given our view that genre-ation of some type is inevitable, adventure, we believe, is a viable option. Indeed, certain things about adventure-thinking, though each has its down side, deserve to be acknowledged, if not actively embraced. For one, it has the potential to generate within us a radical openness to the future, a positive uncertainty (Gelatt, 1991), a basic and liberating hopefulness that, even though knowledge of our destination eludes us, our life is worth living, that it counts for something, and that we are never too old to learn—about ourselves, about others, about our world. It can also therefore confer a sense of purpose on our many and often meandering endeavors.

Admittedly, such a sense can border on naive belief in destiny or fate, yet once we open the door to life as adventure, such notions may well have a certain validity. At bottom, life as adventure offers the possibility that otherwise random events have meaning within a lifestory that is ultimately going somewhere, elusive and invisible though its goal may be. Granted, viewing our life from such a perspective can result in an over-valuing of the future, an ignoring of the present, and an under- or devaluing of the past; a balance between these three temporal dimensions is always important to find. But the future orientation of adventure-thinking is not, in itself, a negative feature, for surely this is the thrust of the arrow of time itself.

In all, the adventure of living, to which we now turn, may be an utter illusion. But if it is, then so, we must consider, is the tragedy or comedy of it too—as is the supposedly neutral, noninterpreted, objective recounting of it, fact by raw fact. And recounting it we inevitably do. What we propose, therefore, is that, while being aware of the evident dangers of *high* adventure-thinking, we continue to see life as adventure, indeed, embrace it as such. In this manner, we open a path to appreciate and celebrate our ordinary wisdom.

THE ADVENTURE OF LIVING

We have seen how stories, including lifestories, require adventures. More important, we have seen how our otherwise ordinary lives involve several adventures at once. They can involve, for example, the interpersonal adventure of raising a family, the intellectual adventure of acquiring an education, the professional adventure of developing a career, the aesthetic adventure of reading novels and attending plays, the physical adventure of fitness or golf, and the spiritual adventure of yoga or prayer. They can also involve, as we shall discuss in a moment, the autobiographical adventure of learning about ourselves.

In relation to each type, there are, once again, numerous variations. Some adventures are major; many are minor. Some last a lifetime, others, an hour. Some are high, others low. Some are easy to manage, others incredibly hard. Some must be pursued on their own, with the exercise of one or two talents; others can be combined with other adventures and involve a range of abilities at once—physical, mental, emotional, and interpersonal. Some adventures take place on the outer level of our lives primarily; others unfold on the inner. Some are real, others merely vicarious. Some are natural and spontaneous; others planned or contrived. Some adventures are solo endeavours, while others are collective, ones we engage in with partners, colleagues, or friends—our fellow characters, as it were, in the larger story of a particular marriage, community, or firm.

What we wish to propose here, however, is that, taken together, all such adventures constitute the adventure of our life as a whole, the one grand adventure that is thrust on us whether we like it or not, that we do not choose so much as it chooses us. We speak of the adventure of living our particular life; the adventure of self-creation (Randall, 1995), of individuation (Jung, 1963), of our fundamental project (Sartre, 1956). We mean the adventure of discovering and becoming ourselves, an adventure about which all other adventures have something to teach us, though they may be ways to avoid it as well. As for the stages of this adventure, we would summarize them something like this.

Technically, the call comes with birth. It is our summons from the cosmos to get out and get going—and it is nonnegotiable. Paraphrasing Martin Heidegger (1962), we are thrown into the world. Once we exit the womb, there is no going back. In a more conscious way, the call can be heard at any time. Beginning somewhere in the period that we label our youth, it comes as an inner compulsion to declare our independence from our parents and family, to stretch our wings, to assert our will, and to set out in search of adventure in the wider world.

The goal implicit in this call to the adventure of living is not always easy to grasp. In fact, it may remain unexamined and unarticulated for much of our life. For it is nothing less, we could say, than self-actualization, self-fulfillment, self-realization. It is nothing less than the exploration and development of our unique talents for understanding and awareness, for relationship and love, and the consequent contribution of possibilities for human existence that no one before us or after us could introduce to the world. In the words of James Joyce (1916), it is "to forge in the smithy of [our] soul the uncreated conscience of [our] race." In our imagination, this goal can take a number of provisional, more visible, forms as we grope our way toward it: independence, a career of our own, a partner, a family, a home, success as conventionally prescribed in our culture or class. But these may be nothing more than substitutes we pursue for lack of the courage to be. They may only be diversionary paths that we follow for lack of imagination, in hope that the call to "the soul's high adventure," the summons "to find the inward thing that [we] basically are" (Campbell & Moyers, 1988, p. 139) will eventually fade and prove to be a fantasy born in the naïveté of youth, one we are better off ignoring in favor of "real life."

Some of us, therefore, though we hear the call and cannot discount it, are either unable or unwilling to respond to it in a full-blown way. Thus we may opt for a series of smaller, shorter, and safer adventures instead, or, for that matter, adventures that are not our own at all but those of others, parents for instance, to which, subtly or otherwise, they insist that we commit. Often, of course, we are driven to do so because the larger stories within which we live—of family, gender, class, or creed—are too powerful for us, de-storying us, as it were, by robbing us of authority and depriving us of opportunity to compose our life ourselves.

By the same token, the call to adventure may refuse to subside but continue to haunt us down the labyrinthine ways of our entire lives, coming to us amid the earthquake, wind, and fire of "normal" life—the vicissitudes of unemployment, estrangement, illness: the still, small voice that pushes us repeatedly to attend to our deepest longings, to pursue our highest aspirations. Each time it does, we must calculate afresh: Is this the time to break out and go for it, or should we continue to coast? Of course, the very vagueness of the goal at stake does not help us to discern. It is difficult to know what we will need to give up if it is unclear what we will gain if we do; in other words, whether or not the sacrifice will be worth our while.

So much for the stages of call and calculation in the adventure of living. As regards the stages of commitment, consolidation, and conflict, these can be even harder to make out, certainly harder to identify than in the high adventure that we see in the movies or in the short-term adventure of taking an exotic vacation, playing a round of golf, or getting a degree. But they are there, nonetheless. The conflicts can originate in circumstances outside us that we can neither control nor ignore. Or it can come from inside—the sort of internal, deep, lingering conflicts that psychiatrist Karen Horney (1945) considers can be part of all of our lives, so much so that we may suffer profound emotional pain as long as they remain unexamined and unresolved. As Jung (cited in Sarton, 1977, p. 101) has suggested, however, such conflicts may ultimately have their place. In his view, "the serious problems in life are never fully solved. If ever they should appear to be so it is a sure sign that something has been lost." Indeed, "the meaning and purpose of a problem seem to lie not in its solution but in our working at it incessantly." In short, the journey of life is not about its destination, ultimately, but about its being *en route*.

From a narrative perspective, the key here is that just as every story has conflict within it—*must* have it, in fact—so every life must have its conflict as well. Moroever, the conflict never ends. Just when we think we are settled and have everything under control, something invariably disrupts the equilibrium we have carefully put in place. For this reason, life is by definition a continuous challenge, to the point where some might conclude that if it is an adventure, it is a tragic one at best, insofar as, storywise, it traces a tragic trajectory. Once again, we are born, we suffer, we die. Whether or not we draw such a conclusion will depend on our particular experience within this overriding story line. However, that conflict is ultimately a necessity for growth is the point we want to stress—for growth of our character, we might say. "Character," writes Schiebe (1986, p. 134), "is built out of repeated exposures to trials, risks, and uncertainties of venturing forth." In short, "our life evokes our character" (Campbell & Moyers, 1988, p. 130).

As for the stages of crisis and completion, what relevance do they have with regards to the adventure of living? Again, in high adventure, crisis and completion come close to the end. Is the end of life—is death—the completion, then, of the adventure of living? If so, it may seem a rather depressing goal to spend a lifetime seeking, and would seem to settle the question of whether life is ultimately an adventure or a tragedy. Unless, that is, we subscribe to a longer view instead, in which case we see death not as the completion but as the crisis—or *one* of the crises—of a larger adventure still: the big adventure (Friedan, 1993). It is to such a longer view that Florida Scott-Maxwell would appear to allude when she writes: "All is uncharted and uncertain, we seem to lead the way into the unknown" (1968, p. 139).

The final stage of the adventure of living—that is, before death—is that of communication, of returning to tell the tale, of imparting to others whatever insight or experience we have acquired along the way. With respect to *le grand aventure* in which each of us is immersed, this pivotal stage coincides with yet another type of adventure, one that is intellectual, spiritual, and absolutely essential, and one that can be embarked on at any point. It is the autobiographical adventure. In our view, it represents the most critical stage of all since it provides us the opportunity—and presents us with the responsibility—to try to make explicit our ordinary wisdom. In Chapter 3, we saw that the meaning of a story is not actualized until we read the story. In Chapter 4, we argued that the storying moment is the necessary condition for discovering the wisdom in our journeys. In the same way, we would submit, the wisdom that pervades our lifestory is not fully actualized until we are able, first, to get it out and, second, to learn to *read* it. Before moving from the adventure of living to the autobiographical adventure, we need to look more closely, though, at what *reading* our story might mean.

READING OURSELVES

Reading is itself an adventure, part vicarious but part real, one that is inner, intellectual, aesthetic, and even spiritual all at once. By definition, all readers are adventurers. We are speaking primarily here, of course, of reading narrative, and of narrative fiction on top of that; what is more, of literary fiction as opposed to pulp—although, if we include biography and autobiography, of literary nonfiction as well.

It is integral to our narrative intelligence of course that we are reading all the time, not only written texts but spoken and enacted ones too, such as we encounter in events, in situations, or in the actions of others. The supposedly simple process of getting to know someone, for instance, involves not only hearing the story that they tell us with their words but intuiting and interpreting the one they express with their gestures and decisions, movements and behaviors—even their silences as well. If we took them at face value and never speculated on their motives or innermost thoughts, we would be naive in the extreme. The act of reading others deserves treatment of its own, for surely it, too, can be a source of wisdom (Kenyon & Randall, 1997). Here, however, our focus is on reading ourselves.

By reading we mean, basically, making sense, whether the text of which we are trying to make sense is a verbal one, as we find in a book, a verbal-visual one, as we encounter on a stage or screen, or a visual-enacted one, as we meet in a human life. For the reader, as adventurer, every new story—every novel worthy of the name—raises new questions to consider and new visions to ponder. It thus represents an undiscovered country, a fresh frontier, a new imaginative terrain. To read is to set out on a journey into the unfamiliar region of another imaginative world, following the trail that is laid by the plot, not knowing exactly where it will lead. And a good story is told in such a way that we want to be led, to read on and find out. Granted, our journey will take us through the known, insofar as the words and images the story employs are essentially familiar and adhere more or less to common conventions. However, their precise combination in a particular text will always be unique and, in that sense, unknown. As a journey from the known to the unknown, then, reading is, like any adventure, a metaphorical process.

It is also an active process, not a passive one. As we indicated in Chapter 3, theorists on reading (see Bogdan & Straw, 1990) are generally agreed that texts have no meaning that is somehow inherent within them. Instead, in the course of reading itself, the reader realizes such meaning as the text might otherwise be said to possess. In effect, no reader, no meaning; and no meaning no story. Reading is thus a creative process. It is a process of making something: meaning. Though the text provides countless clues as to what, from the author's perspective, the meaning of the story might be, and though it sets broad restrictions on which readings are reasonable or right, there is no final limit to the meaning the reader can make. Theoretically, the meaning of any text is indeterminate. Any story is infinitely meaning filled, endlessly meaningful. Both literally and literarily, there is no end to what we can extract from the complex web of its plot, its characters, and its themes. Moreover, each time we return to it, there is more meaning, and often different meaning, that still can be gleaned.

To read is always, then, to discover. It is to discover not just what is in the text, however, but what is in ourselves as well. This point is important to note since it has profound implications for how we read and reread the texts of our own lives and for how we expand and evolve, as persons, as a result. Again, reading is not passive but active. Like a story itself, the activity of reading a story is far from innocent. During the reading, indeed because of it, we reconstruct the story-world that the author has attempted to create. In effect, we fashion a virtual text (Iser, 1978) that, for all intents and purposes, becomes the text, as far as we are concerned. We do our reconstructing, though, in terms of the contents of our own memory and our own imagination as much as of the contents (the words, images, and allusions) of the text itself (Beach, 1990). For this reason, reading literature really means reading ourselves. As put by Sallie TeSelle (1975), every story is about us.

The process at work here is that of the hermeneutic circle. We interpret the literary text in terms of our life text: the vast range of story material, past, present, and future, by which we identify who we are. At the same time, we reinterpret our past, present, and future in light of the new literary experience, and the new ways of thinking and feeling, that are offered or prompted *by* the text (Rosenblatt, 1983). This means that reading is essentially exploration—exploration of the vast, sprawling, largely unread realms that lie within ourselves (Beach, 1990). Reading puts us in touch, explicitly or implicitly, with "the layers of our own history" (Birkerts, 1994, p. 21), providing us the images and words for memories and emotions, questions and dreams, that have hitherto defied articulation and to that degree experience. "I read books," says Sven Birkerts (1994), "to read myself" (p. 102).

But we have gotten ahead of ourselves. In Chapter 3, we suggested that each life is a bottomless text from which there is no end of meaning to be gleaned. In reality, many of us are, self wise, rather illiterate. Though much of our education involves learning to read the texts of the world—that is, to interpret events, to perceive and analyze trends in politics, history, and nature, even human nature—scant emphasis is placed on learning to read ourselves. Our training in reading stops short of self-reading. Perhaps it is because we have no idea that self-reading is a possibility, or because we are simply not an introspective culture. It seems ironic though, that, from grade school on, we are taught how to interpret every type of text except the one we are continually composing ourselves. The very text to which, psychologically, we are the most intimately tied, is the one we are the last to learn to read. What is needed, it could be argued then, is a degree of literary *self*-literacy. By this we mean a literacy with respect to the texts of our own lives, a probing, subtle sensitivity not just to the events of our lives but to the potential significance behind them, to the themes between the lines, and so on.

There is another way to put this point. Because the potential meanings within a given text vastly exceed those a given reader is able to extract from it, even when it is regularly reread or discussed with other readers, most texts go astoundingly underread (Kermode, 1980). If this is true of a literary story, then we would propose it is triply—and tragically—true of a lifestory. Most of us, we could say, vastly underread the texts of our own lives, which means that much meaning is unfortunately squandered and ultimately lost. For such reasons, we would submit that reading our lives represents the ultimate challenge, the ultimate responsibility, and the ultimate adventure.

As for what "reading ourselves" means, we need to return to the notion of the novelty of our lives. In relation to the true novel that each of us lives, we have numerous points of view. Just as a literary novel has an author, is mediated through a narrator, is about certain characters, and is realized by a reader in the act of reading it, so we may be said to be, at once, the author of our own life-novel (though this may ultimately be a metaphysical issue); its narrator, as in the one most able to talk about it; its central character, the person it is, at its core, about; and, finally, its principal reader, the one closest to it and (theoretically) best positioned to make sense of it. Of course, we must not underestimate the incredible complexity that is involved here, insofar as the text being authored, narrated, and read in this case is not out there, in a book, but in here, in us—indeed, *as* us. Nonetheless, all of these perspectives, all of these relationships to our own lifestory, are experienced by us daily. They are intrinsic to our "self"-consciousness (Randall, 1995), and we are constantly shifting between them.

There are times when we are busy concentrating on the task at hand, noses to the grindstone, no time to muse on the meaning of life. Other times, in the company of the right sort of listener, all we do is talk. Granted, in our talking may be mixed some measure of self-reading, but the aspect of performance *to* our audience may limit it. Reading per se, then, is something which, consciously or otherwise, we may reserve for a space and a time of its own. It is on this latter activity of reading the self, or of reading our lifestory, that we wish to focus now, for it is pivotal to the view of wisdom we are proposing in this book.

What is it, though, that reading ourselves involves? What is the focus of the literary self-literacy we should be seeking to acquire? What is it, specifically, we can read? What we read, we would venture, are the texts of our memories, dreams, actions, gestures, fashions, fantasies, decisions, and relationships, and, of course, our words, whether they be written, in a journal or a diary, or spoken, either casually in conversation or formally in therapy, and so on. And what is it we read these things for? For the same things for which we read any work of narrative literature: the plot (the connecting thread through time), the characterizations, the themes, and so on (Kenyon & Randall, 1997). However, as we began to see in Chapter 3, reading for such things in the texts that have been laid down inside us across the years is no small task. Certainly, any sort of complete self-reading is out of the question. As we saw earlier when we considered the adventure of living, there is a paradox involved, insofar as the stage of communication follows that of completion. To read ourselves completely, in other words, we would need to be dead. Technically, some might say, it is only in death that we are in possession of a complete life to examine (Charmé, 1984).

Another problem is that we would need to be able to read ourselves *as reader*, or to read ourselves reading. This seems an epistemological impossibility—although acquiring a sense of our storying style and of how we habitually interpret the events of our lives is possible indeed, once we become alert to the biographical dimensions of our own aging. Nonetheless, even as we are in the process of reading our own life text, we are laying more of it down. "Because life is unfinished," then, as Kerby (1991, p. 31) reminds us, "so is the meaning of the past." What this tells us, as we have elaborated in Chapters 3 and 4, is that we can have no access to some ultimate wisdom concerning our own lifestory in a once-and-for-all sense since, as long as we are living it, it is still unfolding. Could we imagine reading the latest work by our favorite novelist, let alone presuming to understand it, before it was even written? The story of my life is never closed or complete in the way that a novel is, in the end, confined between two covers.

So, the process of reading our own lives is scarcely straightforward, and it is made even harder because of the inscrutable complexity of the process of reading any text. Despite attention paid by literary scholars to the intricate interpretive interaction between author, text, and reader, and between language, imagination, and memory (see Bogdan & Straw, 1990), the very act of reading—what happens in it, what operations are entailed, how it is aided or impeded, and what goes on *within the reader* during it—is largely enshrouded in mist. Unfortunately, when such scholars write about reading per se, they are not always noted for their clarity. In a refreshingly accessible treatment of the mystery of reading, however, author Sven Birkerts (1994) claims that the type of deep reading required in reading great fiction changes us in fundamental ways, not only in terms of our ideas about life but with respect to our entire relationship to both our surroundings and ourselves. As a result of our exposure to such writing, he says, we come to have a "different orientation to . . . the project of [our own] life," acquire "a larger concepton of the meaningful," and become imbued with "the dangerous and exhilirating idea that a life is not a sequence of lived moments, but a destiny," that it has "a unitary pattern inscribed in it" (pp. 84ff).

In terms of the sophistication of the interpretive process entailed, deep reading is at the opposite end of the scale from what theorists call stock response (Bogdan & Straw, 1990). A stock reading of a text is one that remains on the surface, that reads for the plot (Brooks, 1985) and little else, that takes at face value the words on the page and the images they describe. As the word itself suggests, deep reading penetrates below the level of what meets the eye. It inquires more consciously into what this event or image might mean in relation to that one, what is behind the text, what themes are being alluded to between its lines, what issues and implications are being raised, and how the meaning of the text changes or develops from beginning to end. The deeper our reading of a given text goes, the more we are in the realm of literary criticism, which itself can be described as a process of discovery. The point is: There is reading and there is *reading*. Higher degrees or deeper levels of reading yield, in a sense, grander, fuller, more powerful experiences of the text in question, whether literary or lived. It could be argued, and certainly Birkerts would argue, that people who have been avid and deep readers all of their lives are, as a result of their reading, different individuals— cognitively, emotionally, and spiritually— than people who have not. That people who become avid and deep readers of the texts of their own lives are different from others in similar ways is a possibility we turn to now as we extend our discussion to what may be the most important adventure of all.

THE AUTOBIOGRAPHICAL ADVENTURE

We are adventurers by nature. The question is Which adventure will we choose? We have just been considering the adventure of living—that is, living our particular life. Insofar as we have had little to say in the matter of being born, however, this adventure is one that effectively chooses us, though we may choose whether to embrace it or ignore it. We now consider the additional adventure of reading our life. While living our lives is adventure enough, reading them—and trying to make sense of them—can be an adventure all its own. Furthermore, it is one over which we have decidedly more agency and choice.

This additional adventure reflects many of the dimensions we have been referring to throughout, insofar as it is intellectual and spiritual, interpersonal and individual, all at once. It is much more, therefore, than icing on the cake, more than a frill activity to be indulged in by the idle few. It is, we could say, the completion of the adventure of living. It is not in conflict with that adventure nor a safe substitute for it. It is its culmination. It is the stage in which we attempt to comprehend that adventure and to communicate what it is we comprehend. It is the stage of returning from our journey to tell our tale, of sharing such insights and wisdom as we have acquired along the way. Moreover, it is critical to the ripening (Manning, 1989) of age, to generativity. While it is certainly true that the unlived life may not be worth reading, so the unread life, and the *untold* life, may not be worth living.

We can look at the matter this way. Our journey is, for each of us, unique, or, as we said in Chapter 4, it is personal. No matter how dull or unadventurous it might strike us as being, no one could have made it but us. No one has gone where we have gone nor seen what we have seen. No one has had the same obstacles to contend with, the same genetic inheritance to work with, the same temperament or nature to cope with. No one has had the same demons with which to do battle, the same narrative environments by which to be shaped, the same life course and life events to try to understand, nor the same educational opportunities and sociocultural constraints. No one has had the same characters to interact with and be coauthored by, the same issues to tackle, the same challenges to surmount, the same conflicts and confusions to overcome, the same questions to ponder. In short, no other lifestory, and therefore no other lifestory-meaning, no other *wisdom*, is quite like ours.

Of course, when we compare ourselves with others, we may conclude that our story is not remarkable, not unique, not interesting at all. From the perspective we are proposing here, nothing could be further from the truth. Because we are novel, all comparisons are off. Regardless of its content, our story *is* remarkable, it *is* unique, and it *is* interesting, precisely because it is ours. No one else has lived it and therefore no one else can tell it. For this reason, it is incumbent on us to explore that story as deeply as we can, for no one can do so but us. If we fail to get our story out—*our* story, that is, and not someone else's version of it—then no one will ever know it, and the wisdom it mediates will, tragically, be lost. There is thus an urgency involved. Much is at stake. The words of Annie Dillard (1989, pp. 67ff), urging fellow writers to attend to their art, articulate how much: "Why do you never find anything written about that idiosyncratic thought you advert to, about your fascination with something no one else understands? Because it is up to you. . . . You were made and set here to give voice to this, your own astonishment."

We must stress here that the autobiographical adventure is truly an adventure, with its own stages of call, calculation, consolidation, and so forth. For instance, the call can come from outside of us: from the urging of a therapist or friend to search our soul and increase our awareness of who we are. Or it can come from some still, small voice within us. It can grow gradually in volume over time or sound suddenly in our ears. For example, leafing through a photo album, we may find ourselves forced to remember an entire period of our lives that we have, for all intents and purposes, forgotten. Yet it still lies puzzlingly there, demanding to be explored, its significance to be pondered and its lessons to be listed. The calculation stage, then, involves asking ourselves, more or less consciously, whether we want to go there, to visit a part of our story that may turn up issues that will require much time to examine and much courage to face.

The autobiographical adventure also has its own range of challenges. In other words, living our lives may turn out to be easy compared to trying to understand them. One challenge, for example, is simply to get our story out, to find a voice, a language, a set of images, a code, that is adequate to express it. This challenge never ends, for each day brings more events and thus more story to express. To meet it, we sooner or later require a good listener, a respectful, sensitive, compassionate, coauthoring audience to share our story with and from whom to receive company and encouragement, as we journey to places we may have assiduously avoided. Such places include those dark corners of our inner life that we have struggled for years to seal off, perhaps out of "certainty that [our] audience will not understand," as Lawrence Langer (1991, p. xiii) expresses it in his moving study of "the ruins of memory" among survivors of the Holocaust.

Another challenge is tied to the fact that we cannot recall our lives completely. All we have is a set of stories that we have edited for ourselves about our life—past, present, and future—and that, mysteriously, we have come to think of as true. In other words, we have no direct access to the events of our life in the raw. All we have are interpretations, which themselves are constantly shifting and changing, depending on our present concerns, present moods, and present agendas, audiences, and issues. The facts of our life, that is, do not determine the interpretations we place upon them so much as the other way around: Our interpretations determine what we count as the facts. Another challenge, as we have also seen, is that memory itself is not an archive so much as an art gallery, not an organized repository of the past so much as a collage of impressions about the past and future both. Our remembering self is not a photographer so much as a fiction writer, a spinner of tales, a dreamer of dreams—above all, of the dream we call our self.

Still another challenge lies in the fact that our lifestory is not a single narrative that we can trot out and be done with. Rather, it is like a library of stories, and not an especially organized one at that, more like a tangle of tales (Cupitt, 1990). Each of these tales reflects the influence of different larger stories in which our lives are set. And it reflects the interests of the different sides of our personality, or the different characters within us, of the different themes, the different points of view, and the different plot lines—determining the course of any one of which, of course, is like trying to hit a moving target. As Polkinghorne puts it, "We are constantly having to revise the plot as new events are added to our lives" (1988, p. 150). As it were, life never turns out the way we expect. It is like "a diary," one source says, "in which we mean to write one story but are forced to write another" (Allen, 1978, p. 79). To put it another way, the act of reading our lives is hampered by the fact that, while reading them, we are still living them, still authoring them, still acting within them. For several reasons, then, the autobiographical adventure is far from a straightforward affair. In the phrase that the author Graham Greene (1936) made the title of one of his books, it is a journey without maps.

We have considered how the process of reading is ultimately an adventure in reading ourselves. The adventure of reading ourselves in the course of reading great fiction is unavoidable, but it can be especially evident when we read nonfiction as well, in particular biography and autobiography. Reading the stories of others' lives, whether told by themselves or by someone else, is a veiled and vicarious way of reading our own lives. As TeSelle (1975) puts it, "We read autobiographies to find out about ourselves" (p. 146), to get "a form of practical wisdom" (p. 156). Our curiosity about how others managed the challenges facing them is directly connected to our curiosity about how we are managing the challenges facing us. The many connections between the writing and reading of biography, of autobiobraphy, and of *our own* autobiography, are intriguing to trace.

Biographer Stephen Oates describes writing biography as high adventure (1986)—high, however, not in the sense of canned, as we have just critiqued, but of intense, of filled with discovery and surprise. In *The Adventurer*, Paul Zweig (1974) speaks of autobiography in a comparable way, viewing the adventure story as "an odd permutation of autobiography." "Like Job's servant," he says, "the adventurer returns, crying: 'I only have escaped alone to tell this.' And he does tell us, as if the act of adventure and the act of literature were one" (p. 83). In an essay on "The Self as History," Alfred Kazin (1981) suggests that the writing of autobiography is a kind of holy quest, "an effort to find salvation, to make one's own experience come out right" (p. 35). It is also, he says, a kind of eyewitness account by a breathless journalist just back from the front: "I am the man, I got the story first, I was there" (p. 40). When we talk here, however, about the autobiographical adventure, we are not necessarily talking about written autobiography. As John Paul Eakin (1985, p. 9) reminds us, we are involved in "the autobiographical act" all the time, whether or not it results in a formal document. Formal or informal, public or private, autobiographical activity is integral to the exercise of our narrative intelligence. Everyone of us is busy narrating all of the time, if only to ourselves. Everyone, says Eakin, is driven by "the autobiographical imperative" (p. 277). Everyone, echoes Kazin (1981, p. 41), "is constantly making up the progress report of his life."

Again, this does not mean that there are no differences between written autobiography and unwritten autobiography. Putting our story into words changes it, even if the words we put it into are not for public consumption but for our eyes alone. Something significant happens when we move from our silent thoughts and secret fantasies to their expression in a line of words. Some refraction or slippage (Spence, 1982) inevitably occurs when we go from the complexity of our emotions, the fuzziness of our memories, and the maze of our ideas to the conventions of paragraphs and grammar. In short, our inside story and our inside-out story are not the same version.

What we have been arguing throughout this book is that the inner autobiography each of us is continually composing is essentially a work of literature (Charmé, 1984). It is a work in progress, however, whose shape we can never transcend and see as a whole, as we can, at least more easily, in the case of the novel in our hands. Rather, as its author, character, narrator, and reader all at once, we are ultimately inside of it. This is part of what is implied in the notion of the novelty of our lives. Each novel represents a more or less original, groundbreaking endeavor that ushers us, individually and collectively, to a new place of understanding and to a fresh vision of reality, or to a new angle from which to critique it. In the same way, we would urge, each of our lifestories, each of our inner autobiographies, concerns a one-off venture, a creative launching into the unknown terrain of our particular life. It thus has the potential to mediate a unique range of meanings, to embody a unique set of themes, to convey a unique message, and to pose to the world a unique set of questions about what it means to be not only us in particular but human in general. It opens us to a unique sense of the possibilities that humanness itself can hold. The lifestory of each of us, it could be said then, is a parable of the possible, an extended metaphor from the known to the unknown, a unique revelation of the mystery of being. This, in a nutshell, is ordinary wisdom, expressed sometimes in small things, sometimes in big things. Either way, our life is thus a "sacred text" (Charmé, 1984, p. 53).

In Chapter 3 we began to explore the possible parallels between the ways stories mean and the ways lives mean. There we got a sense of the fundamentally mysterious process whereby each additional event in a story effectively means more in relation to the story as a whole, and a greater and greater symbolic interconnectedness (Gardner, 1985) prevails between all of the events, details, and themes in the story. The same strange logic (Brooks, 1985)—narrative logic—is at work in lifestory, whose meaning also accumulates with time. As Edward Casey (1987) puts it in his analysis of remembering, undertaken from a phenomenological perspective, the past thickens. By this, as we have seen, he is referring to such features of memory as its ever increasing "historical depth" and "temporal density" (p. 265). Another way of capturing the idea of thickening is to say that our stock of biographically accrued capital (Mader, 1996), or our narrative capital, steadily increases. Accordingly, "the meaning of the past [is] something that *develops* throughout life" (Charmé, 1984, p. 40; emphasis ours).

This is a core insight concerning the biographical dimension to our lives. From a poetic perspective, our lives can be seen as growing more meaningful as we age—meaningful, that is, in the sense not of the meaning *of* life but of the meaning *in* life (see Reker & Chamberlain, 2000). Such a perspective is supremely ironic, however, insofar as our society can tend to see older persons in the opposite manner, as less meaningful, both to society and, in a sense, to ourselves. In any event, because the meaning of particular life events is never fixed, we have the opportunity to understand them progressively better and deeper by seeing them in dynamic interrelationship with the ever increasing number of other events that follow and precede them in time, as well as with present concerns, which themselves are continually changing, and with our ever revisable projections as to where our story is unfolding in the future.

Mezirow (1978) describes this same sort of process in relation to the concept of maturity, which he calls "a developmental process of movement . . . toward meaning perspectives that are progressively more inclusive, discriminating, and more integrative of experience" (p. 106). In his view, then, "becoming older may indeed mean becoming wiser, because wisdom can mean interpreting reality from a higher perspective." In light of such thinking, we could even say that certain events possess potentially limitless depth, requiring more reflection over a longer time to appreciate anything approaching the full range of meanings they may have. In the words of May Sarton again: "The deeper the experience, the more time is required to sort it out" (1986, p. 173). As Mark Freeman (1993, p. 184) observes, our lives are "like richly ambiguous texts to be interpreted and understood, whose meanings are inexhaustible, whose mysterious existence ceaselessly calls forth the desire to know, whose readings cannot ever yield a final answer." The call to the autobiographical adventure, we would echo, is thus issued anew each day because, once again, our past is never finished. It lives on and on. Accordingly, the invitation to ponder it and savor it is always open.

Another way of putting these points is the phrase of novelist L. P. Hartley (1953), which we referred to in Chapter 3: "The past is a foreign country." Picking up on such an image is Dag Hammarskjöld's (1957) confession that "the longest journey is the journey inward." Sooner or later that journey takes us down the proverbial memory lane. Insofar as we live by story time more than clock time, however, it also takes us not only back into our past but deep into our present and, in a sense, far into our future as well. Once more, memory lane is never about the past alone. As we can clearly see, therefore, story language and journey language beg, again and again, to be merged. Indeed, one writer speaks freely about "the story journey" (Stone, 1996, p. 191). In his view, however, memory lane leads not to a tidy garden of neatly remembered events but to a veritable "wilderness" (p. 2)—"the territory we call experience and memory"—where we can easily lose our way.

Patricia Hampl (1996) provides an intriguing illustration of just how easily this can happen, that is, how easily, as one of our colleagues once put it, you can get lost in your own story. At the same time, Hampl shows us how, when we *do* get lost, we can find ourselves becoming wonderfully aware of the mystery of our own life. In an article entitled "Memory and Imagination," where she describes memoir as a species of "travel-writing" (p. 211), she begins by recounting a simple enough incident from when she was seven: her first piano lesson. She expands the initial image into a full-blown recollection, replete with story line, sketched-in characters, and appropriate atmosphere and theme, all the while employing the vocabulary and artistry not of the child she was then, of course, but of the adult she is now.

Suddenly, she interrupts her narrative and launches into a fascinating but unsettling assessment of what she has just done. Besides heightening her sense of "the curious relation a fiction writer has to the material of her own life" (p. 205), Hampl's reflections lead her to the entertain the possibility that the actual event may bear little resemblance to her mature recollection of it. This in turn prompts for her the pivotal realization that our memories, so-called, have agendas of their own. Assessing the real trouble with her failed first draft of the event in question, she acknowledges that there is more in this memory than meets her eye, that it is by no means finished, that it is *active* par excellence, with, it would appear, a mind and a will of its own. Literarily speaking, her past is alive. In her words, "the piece hasn't yet found its subject; it isn't yet about what it wants to be about. Note: what *it* wants, not what I want" (p. 206). She concludes with the realization that what is essential is that "we learn not only to tell our stories but to listen to what our stories tell us" (p. 209). Such a haunting insight is reminiscent of what depth psychologists might insist about our dreams: that they say more about us than they do about the people or events to which they may refer.

Hampl's remarks also take us to the heart of autobiographical learning,a phrase that clearly belongs in the lexicon of ordinary wisdom. Autobiographical learning can be defined as learning both *about* ourselves and *from* ourselves. For educator Michael Brady (1990, p. 51), such learning is the most important in which we can possibly engage. "Is this not our destiny as human beings," he writes,"to learn, to grow, to come to know ourselves and the meanings of our life in the deepest, richest, most textured way possible? If we do not know the self, what can we know? If we cannot learn from reflection upon our own lived experience, from what can we learn?" Of course, viewed from the perspective of biographical aging, what Brady calls the self—or our own lived experience—has no existence independent of the set of stories by which the self tells itself who it is. In other words, autobiographical learning requires reading the self's *story*. Practices such as life review, reminiscence, and guided autobiography represent some of the strategies by which such reading, and thus such autobiographical learning, can be fostered, and our truth and our meaning can therefore be found.

Hampl has in fact just illustrated such a strategy for us, one that enables us to move from mere remembering to meaning. It involves reading one of the countless stories from our own library, in particular, one of what we call our signature stories. It involves, first, telling or writing that story out of ourselves, then stepping back from it the way a literary critic would examine and interrogate a particular text.

For instance, what is in it or what is it about? How accurate might it be? Why have we remembered it and continued to recount it? Why do we tell it in the way we tend to do? How does our telling of it vary with our audience, and why? What genre does it reflect? What is behind it? In what larger stories might it have its roots? What can it tell us about the pivotal themes and conflicts of our lives, about the central issues we face, about how we characterize ourselves in relation to others, about our philosophy of life and our guiding personal myth? What does it say to us that, of all the stories we might have composed about our life, of all the events we might have woven anecdotes around, this is one of the ones that has stuck? Where has the rest of our life gone, and why?

And what is the relationship between what we remember and what we forget, between the stories we tell and the countless others that we discover we have previously left untold? What might we learn about how we have storied our lives if we could explore the time and space between this story and any others we recall from the same period? Also, what does this story say about not only our past as we have chosen to interpret it but also our present as we experience it and our future as we anticipate it? What pattern does it point to in the ways we tend to tell our lives, in the spins we put on everyday events, and in the perspective, the genre, through which we make sense of our world? Moreover, what clues might this story hold for where we should venture from here, or in what direction we might need to *re*-genre-ate, to *re*-story?

The list of questions could, of course, be expanded. The point not to be missed, though, is that not only is our autobiography as a whole conceivably a kind of parable (TeSelle, 1975), but so, too, is each of the stories we include within it, whether short or long, solo or shared, of the future or of the past, and so on. We soon realize after questioning, after reading deeply only a few of these stories, in other words, that there is much more to us than has hitherto met our eyes. We realize that, as Freeman (1993) has argued, there is no end to the discoveries we can make and to the meanings we can find in the material of our own lives. Each time we return to any portion of it, we can see something new, something more, something we failed or refused to see before—perhaps particularly in what we would consider our adventures, whose cash value, as Schiebe (1986, p. 144) has proposed, only increases with age. As we have been stressing all along, therefore, there is no final, definitive reading of our lives, no official version that is valid once and for all. We can never know ourselves completely, never settle the question of who we are. We are, ourselves, the final frontier. There is always more to be explored, always more to be learned. We are bottomless reservoirs of potential meaning. We are infinitely deep. Appreciating this depth dimension to our own lifestory and seeing the inexhaustibility of that story as far as meaning is concerned is critical to making the shift from, for example, dwelling *on* the past to drawing *from* it, or from living *in* the past to living *off* it—off the interest, so to speak, of our narrative capital.

Like a historian or anthropologist (Berman, 1994), a journalist, detective, or novelist all rolled into one, we can find in the otherwise familiar terrain of our own lifestory fresh clues to the mystery in "my story." Indeed, exploring that mystery is "another instance of adventure" (Schiebe, 1986, p. 134). Moreover, peering through the glass of that mystery, we begin to glimpse the mystery of existence in general, as well as of countless ordinary things in the midst of everyday life that we otherwise scarcely consider. In short, we begin to wonder. It is thus that wisdom need not require our going anywhere else. It is here and it is now. It is seeing the same things differently, both *in* our story and *through* it.

So, if our lives are adventure stories, then they are mystery stories too. "Life as mystery" is a logical extension of "life as adventure." The mystery in my life, in my story, relates to the fact that my fundamental state is one of agnosticism, of *not knowing*. The words of Carl Jung, written in his eighties, capture this state quite poignantly. "The older I have become," he says, "the less I have understood or had insight into or known about myself" (1963, p. 358). The sense of mystery involves not knowing—exactly— where I have come from, where I am going, and why I am here. It involves not knowing the nature either of the ultimate larger story within which I live—the world story, the universe story—or of my own individual story: where it began, where it will end, and what, in the muddle (Atkinson, 1995), it might mean. It involves not even knowing what sort of story it is. Is it a fantasy, a legend, a dream? Is it a comedy that provides the rest of the world with a little relief or a tragedy that possesses the dignity and pathos pertaining thereto? Or is it ultimately "a tale told by an idiot, full of sound and fury, and signifying nothing"?

Final, definitive answers to these kinds of questions will always elude us. What we are calling the adventure of living, and, within it, the auto-biographical adventure, lies in becoming comfortable with such questions, even respectful of them, certainly in continuing to ask them. As the expression runs, the journey itself is home. In other words, life is not an adventure in the high sense of having a guaranteed, Hollywoodized ending in which all conflicts are resolved, all questions answered, all meanings made clear, all yearnings satisfied, and all longings met. A literary story with an ending of this sort we would instinctively suspect. It might be comforting in some superficial sense, but it would ultimately be boring as well. It would certainly be unsatisfactory as a work of art. Art, properly so-called, challenges us. It leaves us thinking. We go away questioning, pondering, wondering. Rather than opening up such wondering so that the story continues living inside us, a tidy conclusion, with every possibility accounted for, closes things down. The adventure of living, as we are proposing the phrase can be used, is not adventure therefore in this conventional, cliché sense. It is the lower and much deeper adventure, the uncertain reaching out, that all good stories are. While, technically, such stories must end, aesthetically, they never end at all. They go on and on, their meanings rippling in all directions through the hearts of us who read them, the vision they articulate forever affecting how we see our world. Our vision in this book is that lives are like that too. Viewing our own lives in a similar way is where the autobiographical adventure will lead.

CONSCIOUS AGING

"A long life makes me feel nearer truth," writes Florida Scott-Maxwell (1968, p. 142), "but it won't go into words, so how can I convey it? I can't, and I want to. I want to tell people approaching and perhaps fearing age that it is a time of discovery. If they say, 'Of what?,' I can only answer, 'We must each find out for ourselves, otherwise it won't be a discovery.' I want to say—'If at the end of your life, you have only yourself, it is much. Look, you will find.' "

Discovery, truth, look, find—such language is adventure language. It conjures up images of heroic quests to distant lands in search of holy grails. The logical conclusion of our exploration into story and journey, we believe, is to entertain this type of imagery, albeit cautiously, and to think of aging itself as an adventure. This means approaching the process of aging not passively but proactively, in a positive, eyes-open way. The upshot of our exploration, in other words, is to age *consciously*, to open ourselves acceptingly to our own aging, to take responsibility for creating our own experience of aging, and, ultimately, to prepare ourselves to age with dignity, integrity, and grace. Indeed, it is to see growing old as truly *growing*—growing *into* old age "as the self moves toward completion and wholeness" (Luke, 1987). Our reflections in this section will elaborate on this notion of aging as an adventure—indeed, an adventure within an adventure. Again, the main goal of this adventure is to express and explore, honor and share, the treasure of ordinary wisdom that has been steadily amassing within us during our journey through time, quietly accumulating amid the texts of our own ever thickening, infinitely meaning-filled stories.

One point to be made is a broad and, in a sense, an obvious one. It can be summed up in the idea that *seniors are pioneers*. They "seem to lead the way into the unknown," Scott-Maxwell would say (1968, p. 139). Though the unknown in question can be viewed in a theological sense, as the ultimate unknown of death, it is outside our scope to speculate here beyond what we said about death in Chapter 4. However, the unknown can also be viewed in an individual sense, not to mention in a demographic and sociocultural sense as well.

Individually, as we should now see clearly, the aging process is a unique experience for each of us. I have never seen this day before, never reached this age before, never lived this long before, never felt these feelings before, never asked these questions, nor known these thoughts. Nor, as the years have unfolded, have I had to cope with such challenges before: the deaths of partners and friends, the demise of my body and its faculties, the loss of my mobility, my freedom, my youth.

Demographically, our world has never witnessed so many of us reaching such ages before. Due largely to the advancements and interventions of medical science, the steady increase in average life expectancy forces a fundamental rethinking of what we mean by terms such as youth, middle age, old age, and, simply, old.

Socioculturally, this important demographic shift also forces fundamental restructuring within society. It affects everything from the stereotypes by which we understand and treat the elderly to the priorities we assign and the resources we allocate to health care, housing, and education. We are living longer; we naturally carry whatever curiosity we have about the world—we carry our hunger for learning—for a longer period of time. By virtue of these simple facts, then—that our population as a whole is aging and that we are each living longer and therefore, potentially, learning more—we are journeying into an ever brave new world in which the very notion of what it means to be human, and what possibilities humanness brings, is evolving before our eyes. In an important and basic sense, this is what the adventure of living involves. To have real meaning, however, this sense needs to be brought home to each one of us as an aging individual.

The second point takes this ever changing situation in society at large as inspiration and invitation to take greater authority for the one dimension of our aging over which we have the most choice and most control: the biographical dimension. Not that we have no control over the biological dimension (we can all eat better and exercise more) or no impact on the socioeconomic dimension that shapes how the aged are treated (we can all write letters to our leaders, can all combat ageism), but in the biographical realm we can all make a definite dent. Accordingly, we all need to become biographers of our own lives, to embark on the autobiographical adventure.

We have seen how the study of history, like that of theology, is a continual inquiry concerning the story within which we live, since so many stories can be spun from the same set of facts. In light of this, we can appreciate the anonymous observation that the way to change the course of history is to become a historian. The hunger many people experience to recover their roots—to learn about the history of their particular clan—originates, in part, in this sense that the past can be changed, that it is alive, that it is not a settled matter, that there is more than one way to story it, that we have a choice in how we remember it, most important, that if we fail to examine it at all, to view it in alternative ways, we are doomed to repeat it. The same might be said of ourselves, as historians and biographers of our own lives. The events are one thing and in a technical sense they are fixed. But the interpretations we place on them can be several and varied. This, of course, makes all the difference, insofar as events are never what they are in themselves. They are what they are *for us*. They are what we understand them to mean.

This means that, as Leon Edel (1986) puts it, "The biographer is as much of a storyteller as the novelist or historian." Granted, biographers—and autobiographers, for that matter—are constrained in ways that novelists are not. That is, "a biographer is a storyteller who may not invent his facts but who is allowed to imagine his form, . . . the form into which facts must be put" (p. 20). However, because there is theoretically no limit on the number of forms, a host of biographies—and therefore autobiographies— can be composed for every person. As Bruner and Weisser (1991) put it, "anyone can reel off multiple autobiographies of his own life, can include different materials, organize it around different themes (within limits), make it match different moods, slant it for different audiences, and so on" (p. 135). In effect, then, none of us ever quite knows "what's the story?" whether in relation to our own life or in relation to the world in which we live it. Indeed, asking the question is a lifelong endeavor. If we see such a situation not as an occasion for despair, however, but as an invitation to be in awe of the infinite and kaleidoscopic richness of who we are—more-over, as permission to story our life in a way that frees us from old, out-grown, no longer functional versions—then we can begin to view the autobiographical act, with Edel (1986), as "a noble and adventurous art" (p. 20).

It has been quipped by an anonymous psychoanalyst that "it's never too late to have a happy childhood." Turning this around, we may say that it is also never too soon to have a happy old age. Technically and intrinsically, the events of our life from infancy to senescence are neither positive nor negative, happy nor sad. Rather, thinking makes them so. The title of a se-ries of popular children's books, *Choose Your Own Adventure*, may thus be taken as a metaphor for the opportunity—and responsibility—that each of us has in relation to how we think about our lives. It is that of choosing the adventure of expressing, exploring, and celebrating our own story, an ad-venture that no one but us can ultimately undertake, an adventure that en-tails, moreover, some assessment as to what sort of story our story is.

Such an opportunity-responsibility is central to our successful manage-ment of what one senior in our acquaintance has called the late life crisis. It may also be the prelude to a radical restorying (Kenyon & Randall, 1997), a fundamental reframing, or, in the context of our discussion here, a basic re-genre-ation. By this we mean the reconstrual, on the one hand, of individ-ual memories. In other words, we always have options in how we remem-ber particular events. We have choices as to what official version we assign them over time (and it may take much time and much listening from others): whether a version that hobbles us in anger, guilt, or grief or one that enables us to forgive, to let go, and to move on; whether one that keeps us stuck in a tragic interpretation of a particular period as the worst thing that ever hap-pened or allows us to accept it as just part of our story, as a worthy and nec-essary chapter in our overall story, no matter how painful its contents, with its own lessons to teach us about the larger adventure of becoming our-selves. The same re-genre-ation, we would submit, is possible with respect to how we construe not just specific events but the shape of our life as a whole.

To reiterate, though, we are in no way suggesting that everyone's life should assume the shape of an adventure in the high sense of having a happy ending. Rather, the adventure of living lies in the search itself—the search for the sort of story our story is. It may well be that, when all is said and done (or told and read), the lives of many of us must be counted as tragedies, saturated as they can be with sadness and loss, laden with seem-ingly unredeemable failure or pain. And surely few of us get away with no regrets, no lingering sense that things have turned out differently than we had hoped or planned or that there are lives within us that we have not yet lived. But, for that very reason perhaps, our lives possess their own unique dignity and depth, their own integrity and truth, and deserve to be hon-ored and even celebrated as such—if only by others and not by ourselves. In any case, tragedy certainly has as much of a place in the world of litera-ture as has any other mode. Within that world, King Lear is as valued a citi-zen as Odysseus or anyone else. If it had all romances and no tragedies, it would be a dull, unilluminating world indeed.

In no way of course do we wish to downplay the harsh reality of human suffering. Nor do we wish to diminish the appalling waste involved as the adventures of countless lives get derailed by disorders of body and mind, cut off by uncontrollable addictions or untimely deaths, or overtaken by the larger, insidious adventures pursued by the company, economy, or country in which they are lived. Yet might it not be the case that, viewed from the broadest possible *aesthetic* perspective, the world of lifestories would be boring and bland in similar ways if, by some miracle, every indi-vidual story were essentially the same?

How we engage in the search for the story we are is by experimenting with the various forms into which the facts of our life can legitimately be placed and by accepting that there are numerous valid versions of "the story of my life." We engage in that search by exploring and celebrating the novelty of our lives. We may have been brought up, however, to dis-trust such self-reading and to dismiss it as so much self-indulgence, as ego-tistical and self-centred, as navel-gazing. *Who do we think we are?!* a critical voice may demand of us from somewhere deep inside: the very question that keeps so many of us self-deprecating where our own experience is concerned. Our belief in this book, however, is that it is not navel-gazing in which we are involved but "novel-grazing." It is tasting and savoring and being nourished by the fertile material of our own unique life, material whose meaning-potential increases, exponentially almost, with the sheer passage of time.

In effect, the past grows or develops (Charmé, 1984), not just in a linear, chronological way, obviously, but, more important, in a poetical way as well. This is why we have taken pains throughout to distinguish between clock time and story time. It is this growth to which it would seem May Sarton (1981, p. 231) is referring when she says that "as life goes on, it becomes more intense because there are tremendous numbers of associations and so many memories." We would argue that it is because of these associations that, with age, we are also increasingly capable of what could be called metaphorical learning, that is, of understanding, reading, and relating to our own experience the allusions and implications, the nuances and innuendoes, that we find not only in literature but also in ordinary events and in the comments and actions of others in everyday life. Unfortunately, the topic of such learning deserves a section of its own and is beyond our scope to examine in detail here.

In relation to fictional literature, the concept of symbolic interconnectedness that we discussed in Chapter 3 captures what, for author and reader alike, is the equivalent of the phenomenon that Sarton describes: that everyone and everything that has been part of our life, everything that has happened, somehow fits, that our life as it has unfolded and as we have interpreted it has a unity and coherence that parallels that of a deliberate work of art. Getting a greater and greater sense of that intrinsic coherence to the novelty of our own lives we see as a critical goal of the autobiographical adventure. The pursuit of it is no mere self-indulgence; it is self-understanding and self-acceptance. If we avoid it, we do so at tremendous cost. To put it another way, an unread novel, into whose composition some poor author had poured years of her life, would be a terrible waste, not only aesthetically but psychologically, philosophically, and even spiritually as well. A comparable waste, we believe, and equally tragic, is the underread or unread novels of our own lives. But a related tragedy, both practical and political in nature, is also at stake.

As we saw in Chapter 3 regarding the larger stories in which our personal stories are rooted, and as we shall be reminded in the Epilogue, we never compose our lifestories in an interpretive void. Rather, we are continually being nudged into narrative shape by the numerous persons and forces around us. In the words of philosopher Daniel Dennett (1991, p. 418), "Our stories are spun, but for the most part we don't spin them; they spin us." The ultimate tragedy, we would submit, is never to realize this, never therefore to take authority for our own lives. As David Carr (1986) insists, "The story which knits together and renders coherent and whole the loose strands of my life, whether it is new and original or has been told and lived many times before me, is ultimately my responsibility, whether I consciously choose it or assume it by default or inadvertence" (p. 94).

Unfortunately, if I do not choose it, and therefore do not assume authority for my own life, someone else inevitably will—parents, partners, peers, even (and perhaps especially) political powers. In Hampl's (1996) words, "If we refuse to do the work of creating [our own] personal version of the past, someone else will do it for us" (p. 208). Whether we are talking about a totalitarian regime or the warm context of family and home, someone else is only too ready to tell us who we are, what our story is and means, and what we can and cannot do and be. If we never question their stories of us, though, never critique the storyotypes in terms of which they interpret us and treat us, never interrogate the larger stories by which they have been shaped and which they believe to be true, if we never set out on our own adventure in search of our own truth, then—from the perspective of everything we have been advancing in this book—we are denying meaning, life, and *wisdom*, to both ourselves and our world.

In the Epilogue, we will return briefly to this tragedy whereby others can be continually coercing us into ways of self-storying that seriously limit our lives. In the meantime, we will conclude our admittedly tentative forays into life as adventure on an appropriately adventurous note—with a litany of "what ifs."

What if we could spend less time and energy, and less money, either denying or trying to postpone the aging process and, instead, start accepting it, trying to understand it, embracing and even steering it? What if we could learn to truly grow into old age and begin doing so far earlier in our lives? What if we could learn the art of befriending time and of trusting the process in which, as creatures of time, we are inevitably immersed? What if we could learn to be better *readers* of ourselves? What if we could be tutored in the art of storying our own lives? What if we could exercise more authority, more active control, over our own autobiographical development and greater aesthetic agency in the project that all of us face, that of composing a life?

What if, much sooner during the course of our life, perhaps even as children, we could embark on the autobiographical adventure and so learn to see through the same old stories in which we otherwise get stuck, the scripts and myths, the plots and genres that shape and misshape the interpretations by which we make sense of events and determine who we are? What restorying, what re-genre-ation might we then experience, and with that experience, what freedom might we enjoy and what originality and creativity might we express?

What if we could launch more consciously and confidently, and at a younger age, into the journey of discovering and becoming ourselves, a journey whose destiny is undetermined, whose ending is unknown, and whose future is open, a journey to be undertaken not with certainty but with positive *un*certainty, that is, with hope; not with foreknowledge so much as with courage, and not with proof so much as with trust? What a story would we have to tell, what interestingness and meaningfulness would we find that story to possess, and what wisdom would we see it to embody?

Epilogue

[T]here is little of greater importance to each of us than gaining a perspective on our own life story, to find, clarify, and deepen meaning in the accumulated experience of a lifetime.

—James Birren and Donna Deutchman (1991)

Everyone has their own wisdom, and when you let a person talk you allow this life wisdom to emerge.

—Sogyal Rinpoche (1994)

WHERE TO FROM HERE?

The list of "what ifs" with which we ended Chapter 5 dramatizes the prescriptive agenda that has been running through this book. Not content with speculation on the concept of wisdom from a theoretical perspective, we have been trying to talk about our topic in a way that will make a difference in people's lives, both our own and those of others. We have been wondering if, for example, wisdom can be taught, if all of us can in fact learn to be more wise. Overall, we have been nudging the discussion of wisdom out of the academy and into the arena of everyday life.

Given that we are gerontologists, this sort of practical agenda should come as no surprise. Gerontology is, among other things, an applied field. The line between theory and practice is seldom sharp. It is also not surprising given the moral-ethical dimension of wisdom that we have been stressing all along, plus the dynamic nature, the purposefulness in fact, of the three metaphors whose implications we have been endeavoring to explore. Ultimately, stories imply conclusions, journeys suggest destinations, and adventures presume goals. Using these metaphors, then, for rethinking wisdom inspires a creative restlessness. It makes us want to go somewhere. It drives us to move from mere reflection to transformative action, from thinking about wisdom to finding ways in which people's wisdom has opportunity to emerge. In these final pages, then, we want to peek past the horizon of the territory we have been investigating thus far and envision the environment that would best allow our wisdom to be discovered and articulated, honored and exchanged.

AREAS FOR FURTHER INQUIRY

In viewing wisdom through the lens of our three guiding metaphors, we have opened as many questions as we have closed and raised as many issues as we have resolved. Many may be the very questions and issues that will lure us to embark on further inquiries still, just as our previous venture, *Restorying Our Lives* (Kenyon & Randall, 1997), has led us to tackle this one. Before pondering the shape of a wisdom environment, then, and before considering the quality of coauthoring that we feel it must involve, let us briefly identify two broad areas in which our musings might be extended into the future.

First, in our effort to propose a different framework within which an inquiry into wisdom can be carried out, we have been focusing on, so to speak, the *form* of ordinary wisdom more than on its *content*. Both theoretically and actually, that content will vary, no doubt profoundly. It will vary not only from individual to individual but also, for better or worse, from one web of larger stories by which our lives are shaped to another, including the family, class, and culture, the gender and generation of which we have been part. In other words, once we open the door to the socially constructed nature of our identity, our memory, and our self, the social constructedness of our wisdom must be evaluated as well.

Second, insofar as the text analogy (White & Epston, 1990) leads us to explore the links between life and literature, then to appreciate fully the poetics of wisdom, we shall have to push past the, essentially, introductory level on which we have been operating in this book. Not only will we need to open ourselves to the countless entailments of the narrative root metaphor, which is inexhaustible to begin with, but we shall need to become more conversant with the conventions and varieties of literature, the intricacies of the process by which literature is composed, the mysteries of the literary experience, and the complexities of the concepts with which the analysis of literature is done, such as character, theme, and plot.

This will be no straightforward task. The realm of literary theory, as of narratology in general (see Bal, 1985), is one of great subtlety and complexity. The logical processes that we employ in the social sciences, with their underlying goals of explanation, prediction, and control, can seem unidimensional beside the ambiguous and circuitous analyses that literary theorists can bring to the strange logic of the material on which their inquiries are carried out. Similarly, the categories and distinctions in terms of which we think as social scientists can seem stolid in comparison with the richness and elusiveness of even the most elemental concepts associated with literature. The classic case is that of story itself. Wielding such concepts, then, we risk making a conceptual mess, like the proverbial bull in a china shop. Not only this, but of all academic fields, literary theory has been among those most obviously in a state of ferment. Taken together, such limitations might appear to bode badly for a narrative geronto-*logy*.

Clearly, the move toward a more soulful science of aging and a more humanized analysis of human development, which is what narrative gerontology has as a principal aim (Kenyon, Ruth, & Mader, 1999), involves us in a potentially awkward endeavor, that of trying to interface two traditionally distinctive domains: the sciences, on the one hand, and the humanities, on the other. Any researcher who has attempted to reconcile a quantitative paradigm with a qualitative one will be familiar with how awkward that endeavor can be. The respective vocabularies and visions, indeed the very definitions of "knowledge" that characterize these two domains, certainly the sense of what constitutes progress or advancement within such knowledge (Frye, 1963; Sarbin, 1994), can make them rather strange bedfellows indeed.

Psychology and poetics, for example: It can seem odd even to utter such words in the same breath, and in many academic circles, we may be enjoined against doing so. A bridge concept such as narrative intelligence, which we introduced in Chapter 3, is a case in point, as is narrative truth. So, certainly, is autobiographical memory and autobiographical learning, not to mention story-time, the novelty of lives, and indeed biographical aging itself. So, of course, is what has been for us a critical construct, all the way through, that of lifestory-meaning. What "meaning"— and indeed "reading"—mean in terms of lifestory, let alone what they mean in terms of literature, is an issue whose contours and relevance we are only beginning to discern. Nonetheless, while many conceptual-theoretical challenges undoubtedly lie ahead, the task of interweaving these two overriding frameworks invites us on an adventure that we believe it behooves us to undertake, one which, of all fields, gerontology is suited to pursue.

COAUTHORING OUR LIVES

Two aspects of wisdom that are central to the perspective we have been developing are its idiosyncratic expression and its interpersonal dimension. These dimensions find convenient convergence in a concept, or rather a process, to which we have been alluding in everything said so far. It is coauthoring.

By invoking a term such as *coauthoring*, we are, as a colleague of ours has put it, "operationalizing a postmodern epistemology" (Clews, 1999). The metaphor of coauthoring is directly related to, and is in our view an obvious entailment of, the narrative root metaphor. As we said in Chapter 3, when considering the socialization of autobiographical memory, we do not compose our lives in a vacuum. We do not generate the narratives by which we understand ourselves—and feel and believe and act—in some sort of intepretive void. Nor do we discover and assume authority over our lives in a way that is divorced from how others do the same. We do so only in terms of an interlocking network of larger stories that we live our lives within.

These larger stories represent narrative environments that mediate the narrative templates, the forms of self-telling, the recipes for structuring experience (Bruner, 1987) by which we construe our realities and fashion the stories we are. As we share our stories with others whom we encounter in those environments, their reactions shape (however slightly) both the content and the form of what it is we share. In turn, they shape how we understand ourselves thereafter, and thus how we feel, believe, and act.

Furthermore, as Sarbin (1994) sees it, "Any self-narrative is necessarily a collaborative, negotiated enterprise" (p. 9). If you will, our self-narratives are interknit with those of other people. One implication of this is that we do not experience other people directly but in terms of the likely stories we compose about them and the "storyotypes" we impose upon them. To me, "you" are not who you are *in* yourself or who you might be *to* yourself. You are "you" only as I experience you or internalize you. To put this a different way, "you" are a character, however open-ended and ever evolving, in *my* lifestory, as "I" am a character in *yours*. Where my lifestory (and thus my life) begins, then, and your lifestory (and thus your life) ends, is impossible to say. The inside-out story that I present to you is always partly constructed in terms of what I perceive to be the outside-in story (or impression) that you have of me. This means that these two levels of the story of my life are impossible to disentwine.

Storywise, we are intersubjectively connected in incredibly complicated ways. As we have been suggesting all along, every encounter is thus a biographical encounter from which each of us leaves influenced, changed, restoried. You tell me your story and I tell you mine, and no matter how ordinary our meeting might be, both of us emerge, to some degree, transformed. No narrative exchange between us, no storytelling-storylistening interaction, is ever innocent. Furthermore, the listening is as critical a component of that interaction as the telling. It is one-half of an indivisible whole. As the expression goes, "You can't tell who you are unless someone is listening" (Keen & Fox, 1974). Or as the psychotherapist, Susan Baur, words it, "There is no story without a listener" (1994). At bottom then, or descriptively, these are the things that *coauthoring* means. As we employ the term here, however, it has an evaluative or prescriptive component as well.

While coauthoring suggests a balanced exchange, where we exercise an equal influence on the story of each other's life, the fact is that, in many of our relationships, a less parallel process prevails. Rather than coauthoring, it is *coercion* that is commonly at work, where one person assumes—or usurps—a potentially undue authority over the other, for example, teachers over learners, clinicians over clients, employers over employees. Rather than assisting in the storying of that person's life, such a lopsided linkage tends instead to, as it were, mis-*under*-story it, even *de*-story it. Between certain people, to certain degrees, and for certain periods, such imbalances of poetical power surely have their place, for example, with parents over children. For a while, the latter need the former to tell them who they are and what the world is like, at least until they have acquired sufficient sense of their past and future to assume agency for their own autobiographical development (McAdams, 1996). What we have in mind here, however, as worthy of the label of coauthoring is a more equitable quality of biographical encountering, the kind that is conducive to exploring and celebrating our story and thus to evoking our ordinary wisdom, or to eliciting our wisdom story. Such encountering, we would say, is more therapoetic.

Our phrase for the context in which such coauthoring encounters might naturally happen is a wisdom environment. Sketching the characteristics of such an environment is how we will conclude the story-journey-adventure in which we have been engaging up to now.

TOWARD A WISDOM ENVIRONMENT

In our hectic and often dangerous world, it is becoming clearer all the time that what we need is wisdom. Although we are knee-deep in knowledge, overwhelmed by information, and all but drowning in data, only wisdom will help usher us safely through the coming years. But where shall wisdom be found? This is the question we have been pondering from the start. While we may have advanced no definitive answer, we feel we have at least proposed a perspective—a poetic one, as we call it—from which the question can profitably be asked. In the process, we have been hinting at the type of narrative environment in which mutual coauthoring can be a regular reality and thus the practice of wisdom has a chance to occur.

Ordinary or otherwise, of course, wisdom cannot be forced. As we have emphasized throughout, it arises at the intersection of the paradoxical processes of both creating and discovering, both doing and being, both making an effort and sitting still. Moreover, we do not know by what means it decides to show itself to a particular person at a particular time. In addition, wisdom is intensely personal. It resides in, and arises through, our inside stories, which are both unique and, to some extent, ineffable. When it comes to ordinary wisdom, then, "no one else knows what it takes for another person to open the door" (Chodron, 1994, p. 57). Having said this, the stories, journeys, and adventures that we *are*, are, at the same time, interpersonal. They are not lived in isolation; they are shared. Despite the many forms of separation and alienation that can characterize our lives, there is a fundamental relatedness about us. Even though for some, hell is indeed other people, other people hold a critical key to our ordinary wisdom, indispensable to the emergence of which are the ordinary activities of storytelling and storylistening.

Practically speaking, however, not everyone appears to possess the same capacity to learn from their own experience, the same capacity for autobiographical learning. This disparity may be partly a function of differences in narrative intelligence. In any case, it seems that not everyone has the same basic access to the stories of their life and, thus, to their wisdom. Among these are the dementing. Even if we grant that, theoretically, no such differences exist, there still seem to be three basic groups of people.

First, there are people who will become wise no matter what. They will grow in wisdom in spite of ageism, physical decline, or anything else that life may throw at them, and perhaps even *because* of these things. Such people exemplify the way of life that Ruth and Öberg (1996) call "the hurdle race," in that difficulties become challenges for them to overcome and then continue on their journey. Second, as we discussed in Chapter 4, some people may simply be too hardened by life to open themselves to their wisdom story. Their journey is effectively closed. Although, from a narrative perspective, we can never assume that a person is incapable of restorying, or that they are stuck in their facticity, the reality is that many people die without apparently finding or even seeking their own wisdom. According to Ruth and Öberg's typology, they lead "the bitter life." However, while the lives of such people may be said to trace tragic stories, they still possess an integrity and can still provide a measure of wisdom, if only to the rest of us and not to themselves. Third and finally, though, there are many, perhaps most of us in fact, who can benefit from a wisdom environment.

Apart from certain exceptional examples, then, it is our belief that more opportunity to tell and listen to each other's stories in an open, nonjudgmental manner can always be provided and in any number of domains. It can be provided in the domain of friendship, for instance, or of marriage or of an intimate relationship of any kind. It can be provided in the area of education and of professional caring, and in the realm of religion and of counseling—perhaps especially in models of counseling that employ a narrative approach (see White & Epston, 1990; Monk et al., 1997; Kropf & Tandy, 1998). And it can be provided in the context of activities such as life review, reminiscence, and guided autobiography. Most significant, though, from the perspective we have been elaborating here, it can be provided in the context of everyday conversation.

The detailed analysis of each of these modes of interaction, as occasions for coauthoring in the direction of wisdom, will have to be left to another book. In the meantime, we will confine ourselves here to sketching what we see to be a few of the broad characteristics of a wisdom environment. How we will do this is in terms of the six intertwining dimensions of wisdom to which we have been referring from the start.

In the service of setting these forth, we first offer the following as an illustration of the sort of mutually beneficial exchange that is always a possibility within ordinary conversation. It represents for us a bird's-eye view of the type of helpful, coauthoring relationship that can best evoke our ordinary wisdom. "Talk affects self-creation," insists the philosopher Jonathan Glover (1988, p. 153). "When we talk together," he says, "I learn from your way of seeing things, which will often be different from mine. And, when I tell you about my way of seeing things, I am not just describing responses that are already complete. They may only emerge clearly as I try express them, and as I compare them with yours. In this way, we can share in the telling of each other's inner story, and so share in creating ourselves and each other." Glover's words capture in a nutshell many of the characteristics that we see as central to a wisdom environment, wherever, whenever, for however long, and in whatever context it gets realized between us.

The Cognitive Dimension

You help me—as I help you—to investigate the events of my life for the patterns and themes that may be running through them. You help me to gather up my past and to re-member my life as a whole. You help me to appreciate its intricate unfolding over time. You help me to inquire concerning what insights have been accumulating within me across the years and what meanings might lie between the lines of my actions, gestures, and words. You help me to acknowledge how I habitually interpret the people and situations I encounter, in terms of what genres I am inclined to cast occurrences and what conclusions I tend to draw. You help me to gain an affectionate detachment from—so that I can creatively critique—how I characteristically construe my reality and, accordingly, how I believe and feel and act.

The Dimension of Idiosyncratic Expression

You help me to tell *my* story of my life, not society's story of my life nor my family's nor any one else's but my own, real, *inside* story, with its unique potential for discovery and adventure, for meaning and truth. You help me to identify my doubts, my confusions, and my fears, as well as my loves, my hopes, and my dreams—including my lost loves, shattered hopes, and broken dreams as well. You help me to celebrate my own individuality, warts and all, to honor the novelty of my particular life course, and to appreciate, even wonder at, the incomparable combination of life events, storying styles, and narrative environments that have contributed to fashioning who I am.

The Interpersonal Dimension

You help me to see how my way of seeing things has, throughout my life, been influenced by others' ways of seeing things too. You help me to appreciate how I have been continually coauthored. You also help me to notice the many ways in which, in the middle of each day, I coauthor others in turn. More to the point, you help me to see how I can influence for the good how they make sense of their lives and how I can invite them, as I have been invited by you, to discover their own wisdom and to view both themselves and their world in positive, more meaning-filled ways.

The Moral-Ethical Dimension

You help me to become more aware of the larger stories in which I have lived and by which, for better or worse, I have been shaped. You help me to identify the master narratives that are embedded in the ideologies and creeds that may surround me and that are mediated through the various institutions—educational, political, medical, and other—by which my life is bound. You encourage me to critique the authority these narratives have had over the dominant version by which I understand who I am. And, where these versions have assumed an unwarrantedly coercive and unduly de-storying power over me, you empower me to be and to behave *sub*-versively toward them. You also help me to see the value, the necessity even, of the conflicts, the struggles, and the mistakes that I have experienced in my life. You help me to appreciate the potential for learning that each of them carries. Through your patient listening to and, with me, your creative reframing of otherwise negative events, you help me to transform the pain and regret in my life into sources of openness and compassion in my relationships with others. You help me to experience these others, fundamentally, as interesting, as intricate, and as inexhaustible as I can experience myself.

The Spiritual-Mystical Dimension

You help me to restory a given event, or indeed my life as a whole, so as to produce more positive versions of what has happened. With respect to the loss of a job, for instance, you help me to re-genre-ate the experience in a more optimistic light, so that I can see it not as the ultimate tragedy it might seem at the time but as, conceivably, a necessary, if painful, first step in a much larger and more exciting adventure still, that of developing my deepest gifts and of exploring the mysteries of my own experience. Rather than allowing me to wallow in a story that says, essentially, "I'm incompetent," you help me to realize that in fact "I'm free," that "I finally have the impetus and opportunity to pursue what has always been my dream." With respect to my entire life, you help to coax forth and affirm a different and more liveable story of who I am. Rather than "I've been a failure," you help me to understand that in fact "I've been a survivor." Such a story puts a radically different spin on what might otherwise seem a life of inadequacy, incompetency, and loss. It increases my self-esteem and my sense of purpose on this planet, and it helps me acquire some sense of trust toward the larger and ultimately mysterious processes within which, along with your own, my existence is unfolding.

The Practical-Experiential Dimension

You help me to see that, within the context of my own particular life, I possess significant experience, insight, and wisdom. You help me to have respect for the details of my ordinary, everyday life, with its ever changing web of relationships and responsibilities, stresses and circumstances, pleasures and pains, and to acknowledge each of them as invitations to continually learn—about myself, about others, about the world, about life as a whole.

In all, these features of a wisdom environment are anything but exotic. They are common and everyday. They are under our noses, as ordinary as the wisdom that has been our focus in this book.

References

Abrahams, R. (1986). Ordinary and extraordinary experience. In V. Turner & E. Bruner (eds.), *The anthropology of experience*. Urbana, IL: University of Illinois Press. 45–72.

Aftel, M. (1996). *The story of your life: Becoming the author of your experience*. New York: Simon & Schuster.

Ågren, M. (1992). *Life at 85: A study of life experiences and adjustment of the oldest old*. Gothenberg, Sweden: University of Gothenberg.

Ågren, M. (1997). How do the oldest old experience and adjust to the increasing uncertainty of existence? A qualitative longitudinal study on life at the ages of 85, 93, and 95. Paper presented at the Annual Meeting of the Gerontological Society of America. Cincinnati, Ohio.

Albright, D. (1994). Literary and psychological models of the self. In U. Neisser & R. Fivush (eds.), *The remembering self: Construction and accuracy in the self-narrative*. New York: Cambridge University Press. 19–40.

Alheit, P. (1995). Biographical learning: Theoretical outline, challenges, and contradictions of a new approach in adult education. In P. Alheit, A. Born-Wojciechowska, E. Brugger, & P. Dominice (eds.), *The biographical approach in adult education*. Vienna: Verband Wiener Volksbildung. 57–74.

Allen, C. L. (1978). *All things are possible through prayer*. New York: Jove.

Allen, W. (1949). *Writers on writing*. London: E. P. Dutton.

Allport, G. (1955). *Becoming: Basic considerations for a psychology of personality*. New Haven, CT: Yale University Press.

Anderson, W. (1980). *Open secrets: A Western guide to Tibetan Buddhism*. New York: Penguin.

Ardelt, M. (1997). Wisdom and life satisfaction in old age. *Journal of Gerontology: Psychological Sciences*. 52B. 1:15–27.

Atkinson, R. (1995). *The gift of stories: Practical and spiritual applications of autobiography, life stories, and personal mythmaking*. Westport, CT: Bergin & Garvey.

Augros, R., & Stanciu, G. (1988). *The new biology: Discovering the wisdom in nature.* Boston: New Science Library.

Bal, M. (1985). *Narratology: Introduction to the theory of narrative.* Toronto: University of Toronto Press.

Baltes, P., & Smith, J. (1990). Toward a psychology of wisdom and its ontogenesis. In R. Sternberg (ed.), *Wisdom: Its nature, origins, and development.* New York: Cambridge University Press. 87–120.

Bateson, M. (1989). *Composing a life.* New York: Atlantic Monthly Press.

Bateson, M. (1993). Composing a life. In C. Simpkinson & A. Simpkinson (eds.), *Sacred stories: A celebration of the power of stories to transform and heal.* San Francisco: HarperCollins. 39–52.

Baur, S. (1994). *Confiding.* New York: HarperCollins.

Beach, R. (1990). The creative development of meaning: Using autobiographical experiences to interpret literature. In D. Bogdan & S. Straw (eds.), *Beyond communication: Reading comprehension and criticism.* Portsmouth, NH: Boynton/Cook Heinemann. 211–235.

Becker, B. (1999). Narratives of pain in later life and conventions of storytelling. *Journal of Aging Studies.* 13:1. 73–87.

Becker, C. (1959). What are historical facts? In H. Meyerhoff (ed.), *The philosophy of history in our time.* New York: Doubleday Anchor. 120–137.

Bengston, V., & Schaie, K. W. (eds.). (1999). *Handbook of theories of aging.* New York: Springer.

Benjamin, W. (1969). *Illuminations.* New York: Schocken.

Berman, H. (1994). *Interpreting the aging self: Personal journals of later life.* New York: Springer.

Bianchi, E. (1995). *Aging as a spiritual journey.* New York: Crossroad.

Birkerts, S. (1994). *The Gutenberg elegies: The fate of reading in an electronic age.* New York: Fawcett.

Birren, J. (1987, May). The best of all stories. *Psychology Today.* 74–75.

Birren, J. (1988). A contribution to the theory of the psychology of aging: As a counterpart of development. In J. Birren & V. Bengtson (eds.), *Emergent theories of aging.* New York: Springer. 153–176.

Birren, J., & Birren, B. (1996). Autobiography: Exploring the self and encouraging development. In J. Birren, G. Kenyon, J.-E. Ruth, J. Schroots, & T. Svensson (eds.), *Aging and biography: Explorations in adult development.* New York: Springer. 283–299.

Birren, J., & Deutchman, D. (1991). *Guiding autobiography groups for older adults: Exploring the fabric of life.* Baltimore, MD: The Johns Hopkins University Press.

Birren, J., & Feldman, L. (1997). *Where to go from here: Discovering your own life's wisdom in the second half of your life.* New York: Simon and Schuster.

Birren, J., & Fisher, L. (1990). The elements of wisdom: Overview and integration. In R. Sternberg (ed.), *Wisdom: Its nature, origins, and development.* New York: Cambridge University Press. 317–332.

Birren, J., Kenyon, G., Ruth, J.-E., Schroots, J., & Svensson, T. (eds.). (1996). *Aging and biography: Explorations in adult development.* New York: Springer.

Bogdan, D. (1990). Reading and "the fate of beauty": Reclaiming total form. In D. Bogdan & S. Straw (eds.), *Beyond communication: Reading comprehension and criticism.* Portsmouth, NH: Boynton/Cook Heinemann. 167–195.

Bogdan, D., & Straw, S. (eds.). (1990). *Beyond communication: Reading comprehension and criticism.* Portsmouth, NH: Boynton/Cook Heinemann.

Booth, W. (1988). *The company we keep: An ethics of fiction.* Berkeley: University of California Press.

Brady, M. (1990). Redeemed from time: Learning through autobiography. *Adult Education Quarterly.* 41:1. 43–52.

Brewer, W. R. (1996). What is recollective memory? In D. Rubin (ed.), *Remembering our past: Studies in autobiographical memory.* New York: Cambridge University Press. 19–66.

Bridges, W. (1980). *Transitions: Making sense of life's changes.* Toronto: Addison-Wesley.

Bridges, W. (1981). January. In J. R. Staude (ed.), *Wisdom and age: The adventure of later life.* Berkeley, CA: Ross Books. 73–83.

Brookfield, S. (1990). *Developing critical thinkers: Challenging adults to explore alternative ways of thinking and acting.* San Francisco: Jossey-Bass.

Brooks, P. (1985). *Reading for the plot: Design and intention in narrative.* New York: Vintage.

Brown-Shaw, M., Westwood, M., & de Vries, B. (1999). Integrating personal reflection and group-based enactments. *Journal of Aging Studies.* 13:1. 109–119.

Bruner, E. (1986). Ethnography as narrative. In V. Turner & E. Bruner (eds.), *The anthropology of experience.* Urbana, IL: University of Illinois Press. 135–155.

Bruner, J. (1986). *Actual minds, possible worlds.* Cambridge, MA: Harvard University Press.

Bruner, J. (1987). Life as narrative. *Social Research.* 54:1. 11–32.

Bruner, J. (1990). *Acts of meaning.* Cambridge, MA: Harvard University Press.

Bruner, J. (1994). The "remembered" self. In U. Neisser & R. Fivush (eds.), *The remembering self: Construction and accuracy in the self-narrative.* New York: Cambridge University Press. 41–54.

Bruner, J. (1996). *The culture of education.* Cambridge, MA: Harvard University Press.

Bruner, J. (1999). Narratives of aging. *Journal of Aging Studies.* 13:1. 7–9.

Bruner, J., & Weisser, S. (1991). The invention of self: Autobiography and its forms. In D. Olson & N. Torrance (eds.), *Literacy and orality.* Cambridge: Cambridge University Press. 129–148.

Butler, R. (1963). The life-review: An interpretation of reminiscence in the aged. *Psychiatry.* 26. 63–76.

Callahan, D. (1995). Terminating life-sustaining treatment of the demented. *Hastings Center Report.* 25:6. 25–31.

Campbell, Jeremy (1989). *Winston Churchill's afternoon nap: A wide-awake inquiry into the human nature of time.* London: Paladin.

Campbell, Joseph, & Moyers, B. (1988). *The power of myth.* New York: Doubleday.

Capra, F. (1989). *Uncommon wisdom: Conversations with remarkable people.* New York: Bantam New Age.

Carr, D. (1986). *Time, narrative, and history.* Bloomington, IN: Indiana University Press.

Casey, E. (1987). *Remembering: A phenomenological study.* Bloomington, IN: Indiana University Press.

Chandler, M., & Holliday, S. (1990). Wisdom in a postapocalyptic age. In R. Stern-berg (ed.), *Wisdom: Its nature, origins, and development.* New York: Cambridge University Press. 121–141.

Charmé, S. (1984). *Meaning and myth in the study of lives: A Sartrean perspective.* Phila-delphia: University of Pennsylvania Press.

Chatman, S. (1978). *Story and discourse.* Ithaca, NY: Cornell University Press.

Chethimattam, J. (1982). The place and role of the aged in the Hindu perspective. In F. Tiso (ed.), *Aging: Spiritual perspectives.* Lake Worth, FL: Sunday Publica-tions. 63–83.

Chodron, P. (1994). *Start where you are: A guide to compassionate living.* Boston, MA: Shambala Publications.

Clayton, V., & Birren, J. (1980). The development of wisdom across the lifespan: A reexamination of an ancient topic. In P. Baltes & O. Brim Jr. (eds.), *Life-span de-velopment and behavior.* Vol. 3. New York: Academic Press. 103–135.

Clews, R. (November 19, 1999). Personal communication.

Cole, T. (1992). *The journey of life: A cultural history of aging in America.* New York: Cambridge University Press.

Cole, T., Achenbaum, A., Jakobi, P., & Kastenbaum, R. (eds.). (1993). *Voices and vi-sions of aging: Toward a critical gerontology.* New York: Springer.

Cole, T., van Tassel, D., & Kastenbaum, R. (1992). *Handbook of the humanities and ag-ing.* New York: Springer.

Cole, T., & Winkler, M. (eds.). (1994). *The Oxford book of aging.* New York: Oxford University Press.

Coleman, P. (1986). *Aging and reminiscence processes.* New York: Wiley.

Conway, M. (1990). *Autobiographical memory: An introduction.* Philadelphia: Open University Press.

Cornford, F. (trans.). (1968). *The republic of Plato.* London: Oxford University Press.

Crisp, J. (1995). Making sense of the stories that people with Alzheimer's tell: A journey with my mother. *Nursing Inquiry,* 2. 133–140.

Crites, S. (1971). The narrative quality of experience. *Journal of the American Acad-emy of Religion.* 39:3. 291–311.

Crites, S. (1986). Storytime: Recollecting the past and projecting the future. In T. Sarbin (ed.), *Narrative psychology: The storied nature of human conduct.* Westport, CT: Praeger. 152–173.

Csikszentimihalyi, M. & Beattie, O. (1979). Life themes: A theoretical and empirical exploration of their origins and effects. *Journal of Humanistic Psychology,* 19:1. 45–63.

Csikszentimihalyi, M., & Rathunde, K. (1990). The psychology of wisdom: An evo-lutionary interpretation. In R. Sternberg (ed.), *Wisdom: Its nature, origins, and development.* New York: Cambridge University Press. 25–51.

Culler, J. (1975). *Structuralist poetics: Structuralism, linguistics, and the study of litera-ture.* Ithaca, NY: Cornell University Press.

Cupitt, D. (1991). *What is a story?* London: SCM.

Daloz, L. (1986). *Effective teaching and mentoring: Realizing the transformational power of adult learning experiences.* San Francisco: Jossey-Bass.

Danto, A. (1985). *Narration and knowledge.* New York: Columbia University Press.

de Beauvoir, S. (1973). *The coming of age.* New York: Warner.

Dennett, D. (1991). *Consciousness explained.* Boston: Little Brown.

Dillard, A. (1989). *The writing life*. San Francisco: HarperPerennial.

Doctrine Commission of the Church of England. (1976). *Christian believing: The nature of the Christian faith and its expression in holy scripture and creeds*. London: SPCK.

Eakin, J. (1985). *Fictions in autobiography: Studies in the art of self-invention*. Princeton, NJ: Princeton University Press.

Edel, L. (1986). The figure under the carpet. In S. Oates (ed.), *Biography as high adventure*. Amherst, MA: The University of Massachusetts Press. 18–31.

Eliot, T. S. (1940). *The waste land and other poems*. London: Faber and Faber.

Erikson, E. (1963). *Childhood and society*. New York: Norton.

Erikson, E. (1979). Reflections on Dr. Borg's life cycle. In D. van Tassel (ed.), *Aging, death, and the completion of being*. Philadelphia: University of Pennsylvania Press. 29–67.

Feinstein, D., Krippner, S., & Granger, D. (1988). Mythmaking and human development. *Journal of Humanistic Psychology*. 28:3. 23–50.

Ferguson, N. (1997). Virtual history: Towards a "chaotic" theory of the past. In. N. Ferguson (ed.), *Virtual history: Alternatives and counterfactuals*. London: Papermac. 1–90.

Flynn, D. (1991, Spring). Community as story: A comparative study of community in Canada, England, and the Netherlands. *The Rural Sociologist*. 24–35.

Forman, F. (1989). Feminizing time: An introduction. In F. Forman (ed.), *Taking our time: Feminist perspectives on temporality*. Toronto: Pergamon. 1–9.

Forster, E. M. (1962). *Aspects of the novel*. London: Penguin.

Fowler, G. (1995). *Dance of a fallen monk*. New York: Addison-Wesley.

Frankl, V. (1962). *Man's search for meaning*. New York: Simon and Schuster.

Frankl, V. (1997). *Man's search for ultimate meaning*. New York: Plenum Press.

Freeman, M. (1993). *Rewriting the self: History, memory, narrative*. London: Routledge.

Freidan, B. (1993). *The fountain of age*. New York: Simon & Schuster.

Friedman, M. (1981). Aging and the caring community. In J. R. Staude (ed.), *Wisdom and age: The adventure of later life*. Berkeley, CA: Ross Books. 135–155.

Frye, N. (1963). *The educated imagination: The Massey lectures—second series*. Toronto: CBC Enterprises.

Frye, N. (1966). Fictional modes and forms. In R. Scholes (ed.), *Approaches to the novel*. San Francisco: Chandler. 23–42.

Frye, N. (1988). *On education*. Toronto: Fitzhenry & Whiteside.

Fulford, R. (1999). *The triumph of narrative: Storytelling in an age of mass culture*. Toronto: Anansi.

Furlong, M. (1984). *Travelling in*. London: Cowley.

Gardner, H. (1982, March). The making of a storyteller. *Psychology Today*. 49–63.

Gardner, H. (1985). *The mind's new science: A history of the cognitive revolution*. New York: Basic Books.

Gardner, H. (1990). *Frames of mind: The theory of multiple intelligences*. San Francisco: Basic.

Gardner, H. (1993). *Multiple intelligences: The theory in practice*. New York: HarperCollins.

Gardner, J. (1978). *On moral fiction*. New York: Basic.

Gardner, J. (1985). *The art of fiction: Notes on craft for young writers.* New York: Vintage.

Gelatt, H. B. (1991). *Creative decision making using positive uncertainty.* Los Altos, CA: Crisp.

Gergen, K. (1992). *The saturated self: Dilemmas of identity in contemporary life.* New York: BasicBooks.

Gergen, K., & Gergen, M. (1983). Narratives of the self. In T. Sarbin & E. Schiebe (eds.), *Studies in social identity.* New York: Praeger. 254–273.

Gergen, K., & Gergen, M. (1986). Narrative form and the construction of psychological science. In T. Sarbin (ed.), *Narrative psychology: The storied nature of human conduct.* New York: Praeger. 22–43.

Gergen, M., & Gergen, K. (1984). The social construction of narrative accounts. In K. Gergen & M. Gergen (eds.), *Historical social psychology.* Hillsdale, NJ: Lawrence Erlbaum Associates. 173–189.

Glover, J. (1988). *I: The philosophy and psychology of personal identity.* London: Penguin.

Gold, J. (1990). *Read for your life: Literature as a life support system.* Markham, Ontario: Fitzhenry & Whiteside.

Goldberg, M. (1991). *Theology and narrative: A critical introduction.* Philadelphia: Trinity Press International.

Goleman, D. (1995). *Emotional intelligence.* New York: Bantam.

Greene, G. (1936). *Journey without maps.* London: Penguin.

Gubrium, J. (1993). *Speaking of life: Horizons of meaning for nursing home residents.* Hawthorne, NY: Aldine.

Gubrium, J. (in press). Narrative, experience, and aging. In G. Kenyon, P. Clark., & B. de Vries (eds.), *Narrative gerontology: Theory, research, and practice.* New York: Springer.

Gubrium, J., & Holstein, J. (1998). Narrative practice and the coherence of personal stories. *The Sociological Quarterly.* 39:1. 163–187.

Guse, L., Inglis, J., Chicoine, J., Leche, G., Stadnyk, L., & Whitbread, L. (in press). Life albums in long-term care: Resident, family, and staff perceptions. *Geriatric Nursing.*

Haight, B., & Webster, J. (eds.). (1995). *The art and science of reminiscing: Theory, research, methods, and applications.* Washington, DC: Taylor & Francis.

Hallberg, I. (in press). A narrative approach to nursing care of people in difficult life situations. In G. Kenyon, P. Clark, & B. de Vries (eds.), *Narrative gerontology: Theory, research, and practice.* New York: Springer.

Hammarskjöld, D. (1957). *Markings.* London: Beacon.

Hampl, P. (1996). Memory and imagination. In J. McConkey (ed.), *The anatomy of memory.* New York: Oxford University Press. 201–211.

Hanh, T. N. (1995). *Living Buddha, living Christ.* New York: Riverhead Books.

Hartley, L. P. (1953). *The go-between.* London: Hamilton.

Hauerwas, S., & Jones. L. G. (eds.). (1989). *Why narrative? Readings in narrative theology.* Grand Rapids, MI: Eerdmans.

Haught, J. (1984). *The cosmic adventure: Science, religion, and the quest for purpose.* New York: Paulist Press.

Haughton, R. (1976). *The drama of salvation.* London: SPCK.

Heidegger, M. (1962). *Being and time.* New York: Harper & Row.

Heilbrun, C. (1988). *Writing a woman's life.* New York: Ballantine.

Hillman, J. (1975). The fiction of case history: A round. In J. Wiggins (ed.), *Religion as story*. New York: Harper & Row. 123–173.

Hillman, J. (1989). *A blue fire*. New York: Harper & Row.

Holliday, S., & Chandler, M. (1986). *Wisdom: Explorations in adult competence*. Basel, Switzerland: Karger.

Holst, G., Edberg, A.-K., & Hallberg, I. (1999). Nurses' narrations and reflections about caring for patients with severe dementia as revealed in systematic clinical supervision sessions. *Journal of Aging Studies*. 13:1. 89–107.

Hook, S. (1943). *The hero in history: A study in limitation and possibility*. Boston: Beacon.

Hopkins, R. (1994). *Narrative schooling: Experiential learning and the transformation of American education*. New York: Teachers College Press.

Horner, J. (1982). *That time of year: A chronicle of life in a nursing home*. Amherst: University of Massachusetts Press.

Horney, K. (1945). *Our inner conflicts*. New York: W. W. Norton.

Howard, G. (1994). The stories we live by: Confessions by a member of the species *homo fabulans* (man, the storyteller). In J. Lee (ed.), *Life and story: Autobiographies for a narrative psychology*. Westport, CT: Praeger. 247–273.

Hume, D. (1955). *An inquiry concerning human understanding*. Indianapolis, IN: Bobbs-Merrill.

Huxley, A. (1962). *The perennial philosophy*. New York: Meridian Books.

Ignatieff, M. (1993). *Scar tissue*. Toronto: Viking.

Iser, W. (1978). *The act of reading*. Baltimore, MD: The Johns Hopkins University Press.

Jaspers, K. (1970). *Philosophy*. Vol. 2. Chicago: University of Chicago Press.

Josso, M.-C. (1998). Histoire de vie et sagesse: La formation comme quête d'un art de vivre. [Life-history and wisdom: Development as a quest for an art of living]. In R. Barbier (ed.), *Education et sagesse* [Education and wisdom]. Paris: Albin Michel.

Joyce, J. (1916). *A portrait of the artist as a young man*. London: Hammondsworth (reprint Penguin, 1976).

Jung, C. (1963). *Memories, dreams, and reflections*. New York: Vintage.

Jylha, M. (1997). Vitality 90+: Stories of completed lives. Paper presented at the Annual Meeting of the Gerontological Society of America, Cincinnati, Ohio.

Kaufman, S. (1986). *The ageless self: Sources of meaning in late life*. New York: New American Library.

Kaufman, S. (1988). Illness, biography, and the interpretation of self following a stroke. *Journal of Aging Studies*. 2:3. 217–227.

Kazin, A. (1981). The self as history: Reflections on autobiography. In A. Stone (ed.), *The American autobiography: A collection of critical essays*. Englewood Cliffs, NJ: Prentice-Hall. 31–43.

Keen, S. (1993). On mythic stories. In C. Simpkinson & A. Simpkinson (eds.), *Sacred stories: A celebration of the power of stories to transform and heal*. San Francisco: HarperCollins. 27–37.

Keen, S., & Fox, A. V. (1974). *Telling your story: A guide to who you are and who you can be*. Toronto: New American Library.

Kegan, R. (1982). *The evolving self*. Cambridge, MA: Harvard University Press.

Kekes, J. (1983). Wisdom. *American Philosophical Quarterly*. 20:3. 277–286.

Kelsey, M. (1980). *Adventure inward: Christian growth through personal journal writing*. Minneapolis, MN: Augsburg Publishing House.

Kenyon, G. (1980). The meaning of death in Gabriel Marcel's philosophy. *Gnosis*. 2:1. 27–40.

Kenyon, G. (1988). Basic assumptions in theories of human aging. In J. Birren & V. Bengston (eds.), *Emergent theories of aging*. New York: Springer. 3–18.

Kenyon, G. (1990). Dealing with death: The floating perspective. *Omega*. 22: 59–69.

Kenyon, G. (1991). *Homo viator*: Metaphors of aging, authenticity and meaning. In G. Kenyon, J. Birren, & J. Schroots (eds.), *Metaphors of aging in science and the humanities*. New York: Springer. 17–35.

Kenyon, G. (1996a). The meaning-value of personal storytelling. In J. Birren, G. Kenyon, J.-E. Ruth, J. Schroots, & T. Svensson (eds.), *Aging and biography: Explorations in adult development*. New York: Springer. 21–38.

Kenyon, G. (1996b). Ethical issues in aging and biography. *Ageing and Society*. 16:6. 659–675.

Kenyon, G. (2000). Philosophical foundations of existential meaning. In G. Reker & K. Chamberlain (eds.), *Exploring existential meaning: Optimizing human development across the lifespan*. Thousand Oaks, CA: Sage. 7–22.

Kenyon, G. (in press). Guided autobiography: In search of ordinary wisdom. In G. Rowles & N. Schoenberg (eds.), *Qualitative gerontology*. 2nd ed. New York: Springer.

Kenyon, G., Birren, J., & Schroots, J. (eds.). (1991). *Metaphors of aging in science and the humanities*. New York: Springer.

Kenyon, G., Clark, P., & de Vries, B. (in press). *Narrative gerontology: Theory, research, and practice*. New York: Springer.

Kenyon, G., & Randall, W. (1997). *Restorying our lives: Personal growth through autobiographical reflection*. Westport, CT: Praeger.

Kenyon, G., & Randall, W. (1999). Introduction: Narrative gerontology. *Journal of Aging Studies*. 13:1. 1–5.

Kenyon, G. M., Ruth, J.-E., & Mader, W. (1999). Elements of a narrative gerontology. In V. Bengston & W. Schaie (eds.), *Handbook of theories of aging*. New York: Springer. 40–58.

Kerby, A. (1991). *Narrative and the self*. Bloomington, IN: Indiana University Press.

Kermode, F. (1966). *The sense of an ending: Studies in the theory of fiction*. New York: Oxford University Press.

Kermode, F. (1980). Secrets and narrative sequence. In W. Mitchell (ed.), *On narrative*. Chicago: University of Chicago Press. 79–97.

Kimble, M., McFadden, S., Ellor, J., & Seeber, J. (eds.). (1995). *Aging, spirituality, and religion: A handbook*. Minneapolis, MN: Fortress Press.

Kirthisinghe, B. (1982). Buddhism and aging. In F. Tiso (ed.), *Aging: Spiritual perspectives*. Lake Worth, FL: Sunday Publications. 85–110.

Kliever, L. (1981). *The shattered spectrum: A survey of contemporary theology*. Atlanta: John Knox Press.

Kotre, J. (1990). *Outliving the self: Generativity and the interpretation of lives*. Baltimore, MD: The Johns Hopkins University Press.

Kramer, D. (1990). Conceptualizing wisdom: The primacy of affect-cognition relations. In R. Sternberg (ed.), *Wisdom: Its nature, origins, and development*. New York: Cambridge University Press. 279–313.

Kropf, N., & Tandy, C. (1998). Narrative therapy with older clients: The use of a meaning-making approach. *Clinical Gerontologist*. 18:4. 3–16.

Lakoff, G., & Johnson, M. (1980). *Metaphors we live by*. Chicago: University of Chicago Press.

Langer, L. (1991). *Holocaust testimonies: The ruins of memory*. New Haven, CT: Yale University Press.

Latimer, R. (1997). *You're not old until you're ninety*. Nevada City, CA: Blue Dolfin Publishing.

Le Guin, U. (1989). *Dancing at the edge of the world: Thoughts on words, women, places*. New York: Harper and Row.

Leitch, T. (1986). *What stories are: Narrative theory and interpretation*. University Park: Pennsylvania State University Press.

Lewis, C. S. (1966). On stories. In *Essays presented to Charles Williams*. Grand Rapids, MI: Eerdmans. 90–105.

Linde, C. (1993). *Life stories: The creation of coherence*. New York: Oxford University Press.

Lovelock, J. (1982). Gaia: A new look at life on earth. New York: Oxford University Press.

Luke, H. (1987). *Old age*. New York: Parabola Books.

MacIntyre, A. (1981). *After virtue: A study in moral theory*. London: Duckworth.

Maddi, S. (1988). On the problem of accepting facticity and pursuing possibility. In S. Messer, L. Sass, & R. Woolfolk (eds.), *Hermeneutics and pyschological theory*. New Brunswick, NJ: Rutgers University Press. 182–200.

Mader, W. (1991). Aging and the metaphor of narcissism. In G. Kenyon, J. Birren, & J. Schroots (eds.), *Metaphors of aging in science and the humanities*. New York: Springer. 131–153.

Mader, W. (1995). Thematically guided autobiographical reconstruction: On theory and method of "guided autobiography" in adult education. In P. Alheit, A. Born-Wojciechowska, E. Brugger, & P. Dominice (eds.), *The biographical approach in adult education*. Vienna: Verband Wiener Volksbildung. 244–257.

Mader, W. (1996). Emotionality and continuity in biographical contexts. In J. Birren, G. Kenyon, J.-E. Ruth, J. Schroots, & T. Svensson (eds.), *Aging and biography: Explorations in adult development*. New York: Springer. 39–60.

Mancusco, J. (1986). The acquisition and use of narrative grammar structure. In T. Sarbin (ed.), *Narrative psychology: The storied nature of human conduct*. Westport, CT: Praeger. 91–110.

Mancusco, J., & Sarbin, T. (1983). The self-narrative in the enactment of roles. In T. Sarbin & E. Schiebe (eds.), *Studies in social identity*. New York: Praeger. 233–253.

Mandel, B. (1980). Full of life now. In J. Olney (ed.), *Autobiography: Essays theoretical and critical*. Princeton, NJ: Princeton University Press. 49–72.

Manheimer, R. (1992). Wisdom and method: Philosophical contributions to gerontology. In T. Cole, D. van Tassel, & R. Kastenbaum (eds.), *Handbook of the humanities and aging*. New York: Springer. 426–440.

Manheimer, R. (1994). Sarah's laugh: Humor as wisdom and life stage. *Aging and the Human Spirit*. 4. 1.

Manning, G. (1989). Fiction and aging: "Ripeness is all." *Canadian Journal on Aging*. 8:2. 157–163.

Marcel, G. (1952). *Metaphysical journal*. Chicago: Henry Regnery Co.

Marcel, G. (1956). *The philosophy of existentialism*. Secaucus, NJ: Citadel Press.

Marcel, G. (1962). *Homo viator*. New York: Harper and Row.

Marcel, G. (1964). *Creative fidelity*. New York: Noonday Press.

Marcel, G. (1973). *Tragic wisdom and beyond*. Evanston, IL: Northwestern University Press.

Marchand, P. (1991, April 21). Telling stories. *Saturday Magazine: Toronto Star*. Toronto.

Maurois, A. (1986). Biography as a work of art. In S. B. Oates (ed.), *Biography as high adventure: Life-writers speak on their art*. Amherst, MA: University of Massachusetts Press. 3–17.

McAdams, D. (1988). *Power, intimacy, and the life story: Personological inquiries into identity*. New York: Guilford.

McAdams, D. (1994). *The stories we live by: Personal myths and the making of the self*. New York: William Morrow.

McAdams, D. (1996). Narrating the self in adulthood. In J. Birren, G. Kenyon, J.-E. Ruth, J. Schroots, & T. Svensson (eds.), *Aging and biography: Explorations in adult development*. New York: Springer. 131–148.

Meacham, J. (1990). The loss of wisdom. In R. Sternberg (ed.), *Wisdom: Its nature, origins, and development*. New York: Cambridge University Press. 181–211.

Mezirow, J. (1978). Perspective transformation. *Adult education*. 28:2. 100–110.

Monk, G., Winslade, J., Crocket, K., & Epston, D. (eds.). (1997). *Narrative therapy in practice: The archaelogy of hope*. San Francisco: Jossey-Bass.

Moody, H. (1991). The meaning of life in old age. In N. Jecker (ed.), *Aging and ethics: Philosophical problems in gerontology*. Clifton, NJ: Humana Press. 51–92.

Moody, H. (1994). Simplicity. *Aging and the Human Spirit*. 4:2.

Moore, T. (1992). *Care of the soul: A guide for cultivating depth and sacredness in everyday life*. New York: HarperCollins.

Morrison, M. (1998). *Let evening come: Reflections on aging*. New York: Doubleday.

Munnichs, J. (1966). *Old age and finitude*. Basel, Switzerland: Karger.

Munro, A. (1986). The progress of love. In *The progress of love: Stories by Alice Munro*. Toronto: Penguin. 1–38.

Neisser, U. (1986). Nested structure in autobiographical memory. In D. Rubin (ed.), *Autobiographical memory*. New York: Cambridge University Press. 71–81.

Neisser, U. (1994). Self-narratives: True and false. In U. Neisser & R. Fivush (eds.), *The remembering self: Construction and accuracy in the self-narrative*. New York: Cambridge University Press. 1–18.

Neisser, U., & Fivush, R. (1994). *The remembering self: Construction and accuracy in the self-narrative*. New York: Cambridge University Press.

Nin, A. (1981). The personal life deeply lived. In A. Stone (ed.), *The American autobiography: A collection of critical essays*. Englewood Cliffs, NJ: Prentice-Hall. 157–165.

Novak, M. (1971). *Ascent of the mountain, flight of the dove*. San Francisco: Harper & Row.

Nussbaum, M. (1989). Narrative emotions: Beckett's genealogy of love. In S. Hauerwas & L. Jones (eds.), *Why narrative? Readings in narrative theology*. Grand Rapids, MI: Eerdmans. 216–248.

Oates, S. (1986). Biography as high adventure. In S. Oates (ed.), *Biography as high adventure: Life-writers speak on their art*. Amherst, MA: The University of Massachusetts Press.

Ochberg, R. (1995). Life stories and storied lives. In A. Lieblich & R. Josselson (eds.), *Exploring identity and gender: The narrative study of lives*. Vol. 2. London: Sage. 113–144.

Olney, J. (1972). *Metaphors of self: The meaning of autobiography*. Princeton, NJ: Princeton University Press.

Ortony, A. (ed.). (1979). *Metaphor and thought*. Cambridge: Cambridge University Press.

Owen, H. (1987). *Spirit: Transformation and the development of organizations*. Potomac, MD: Abbott.

Page, P. K. (1997). *Exile. The hidden room*, Vol. 2. Erin, Ontario: The Porcupine's Quill. 231.

Parry, A., & R. Doan (1994). *Story re-visions: Narrative therapy in the postmodern world*. New York: Guilford.

Pascal, R. (1960). *Design and truth in autobiography*. London: Routledge & Kegan Paul.

Pearson, C. (1989). *The hero within: Six archetypes we live by*. San Francisco: Harper & Row.

Pennington, M. B. (1983). *Monastery: Prayer, work, community*. San Francisco: Harper & Row.

Phillips, A. (1994). *On flirtation: Psychoanalytic essays on the uncommitted life*. Cambridge, MA: Harvard University Press.

Plantinga, T. (1992). *How memory shapes narratives: A philosophical essay on redeeming the past*. Lewiston, NY: Edwin Mellen Press.

Polkinghorne, D. (1988). *Narrative knowing and the human sciences*. Albany, NY: SUNY Press.

Polkinghorne, D. (1996a). Narrative knowing and the study of lives. In J. Birren, G. Kenyon, J.-E. Ruth, J. Schroots, & T. Svensson (eds.), *Aging and biography: Explorations in adult development*. New York: Springer. 77–99.

Polkinghorne, D. (1996b). Use of biography in the development of applicable knowledge. *Ageing and Society*. 16:6. 721–745.

Polster, E. (1987). *Every person's life is worth a novel*. New York: Norton.

Porter, B. (1993). *Road to heaven: Encounters with Chinese hermits*. San Francisco: Mercury House.

Prado, C. (1986). *Rethinking how we age: A new view of the aging mind*. Westport, CT: Greenwood.

Progoff, I. (1975). *At a journal workshop: The basic text and guide for using the intensive journal*. New York: Dialogue House Library.

Randall, W. (1995). *The stories we are: An essay on self-creation*. Toronto: University of Toronto Press.

Randall, W. (1996). Restorying a life: Adult education and transformative learning. In J. Birren, G. Kenyon, J.-E. Ruth, J. Schroots, & T. Svensson (eds.), *Aging and biography: Explorations in adult development*. New York: Springer. 224–247.

Randall, W. (1999). Narrative intelligence and the novelty of our lives. *Journal of Aging Studies*. 13:1. 11–28.

Randall, W. (in press). Storied worlds: Acquiring a narrative perspective on aging, identity, and everyday life. In G. Kenyon, P. Clark, & B. de Vries (eds.), *Narrative gerontology: Theory, research, and practice.* New York: Springer.

Reker, G., & Chamberlain, K. (eds.). (2000). *Exploring existential meaning: Optimizing human development across the lifespan.* Thousand Oaks, CA: Sage.

Reker, G., & Wong, P. (1988). Aging as an individual process: Towards a theory of personal meaning. In J. Birren & V. Bengston (eds.), *Emergent theories of aging.* New York: Springer. 214–246.

Riegel, C. (1976). The dialectics of human development. *American Psychologist.* 31. 689–700.

Rinpoche, K. (1992). *Dharma paths.* Ithaca, NY: Snow Lion Publications.

Rinpoche, S. (1994). *The Tibetan book of living and dying.* San Francisco: Harper-SanFrancisco.

Robinson, J., & Hawpe, L. (1986). Narrative thinking as a heuristic process. In T. Sarbin (ed.), *Narrative psychology: The storied nature of human conduct.* Westport, CT: Praeger. 111–125.

Rosen, H. (1986). The importance of story. *Language Arts.* 63:3. 226–237.

Rosenau, P. (1992). *Postmodernism and the social sciences: Insights, inroads, and intrusions.* Princeton, NJ: Princeton University Press.

Rosenblatt, L. (1983). *Literature as exploration.* New York: The Modern Language Association of America.

Rosenmayr, L. (1996). Fragmented life and fulfillment. *Aging and the Human Spirit.* 6.

Ross, R. (1992). *Dancing with a ghost: Exploring Indian reality.* Markham, Ontario: Octopus Publishing.

Rowles, G., & Schoenberg, N. (eds.). (2000). *Qualitative gerontology.* 2nd ed. New York: Springer.

Rubin, D. (ed.). (1986). *Autobiographical memory.* New York: Cambridge University Press.

Rubin, D. (ed.). (1996). *Remembering our past: Studies in autobiographical memory.* New York: Cambridge University Press.

Runyan, W. (1984). *Life histories and psychobiography: Explorations in theory and method.* New York: Oxford University Press.

Ruth, J.-E., & Coleman, P. (1996). Personality and aging: Coping and management of the self in later life. In J. Birren & K. W. Schaie (eds.), *Handbook of the psychology of aging.* 4th ed. San Diego, CA: Academic Press. 308–322.

Ruth, J.-E., & Kenyon, G. (1996a). Biography in adult development and aging. In J. Birren, G. Kenyon, J.-E. Ruth, J. Schroots, & T. Svensson (eds.), *Aging and biography: Explorations in adult development.* New York: Springer. 1–20.

Ruth, J.-E., & Kenyon, G. (1996b). Introduction: Special issue on aging, biography, and practice. *Ageing and Society.* 16:6. 653–657.

Ruth, J.-E., & Öberg, P. (1996). Ways of life: Old age in a life history perspective. In J. Birren, G. Kenyon, J.-E. Ruth, J. Schroots, & T. Svensson (eds.), *Aging and biography: Explorations in adult development.* New York: Springer. 167–186.

Ruth, J.-E., & Vilkko, A. (1996). Emotion in the construction of autobiography. In C. Magai & S. McFadden (eds.), *Handbook of emotion, adult development, and aging.* San Diego, CA: Academic Press. 167–181.

Ryff, C. (1989). In the eye of the beholder: Views of psychological well-being among middle-aged and older adults. *Psychology and Aging.* 4. 195–210.

Sacks, O. (1985). *The man who mistook his wife for a hat, and other clinical tales*. New York: Summit.

Saint Augustine (1961). *Confessions*. London: Penguin.

Salaman, E. (1982). A collection of moments. In U. Neisser (ed.), *Memory observed: Remembering in natural contexts*. San Francisco: W. H. Freeman. 49–63.

Sarbin, T. (ed.). (1986a). *Narrative psychology: The storied nature of human conduct*. New York: Praeger.

Sarbin, T. (1986b). The narrative as a root metaphor for psychology. In T. Sarbin (ed.), *Narrative psychology: The storied nature of human conduct*. New York: Praeger. 3–21.

Sarbin, T. (1994). Steps to the narratory principle: An autobiographical essay. In J. Lee (ed.), *Life and story: Autobiographies for a narrative psychology*. Westport, CT: Praeger. 247–273.

Sarton, M. (1977). *Journal of a solitude*. New York: W. W. Norton.

Sarton, M. (1981). *The house by the sea*. New York: W. W. Norton.

Sarton, M. (1986). *Recovering: A journal*. New York: W. W. Norton.

Sartre, J.-P. (1955). *No exit and three other plays*. New York: Knopf.

Sartre, J.-P. (1956). *Being and nothingness*. New York: Simon and Schuster.

Sartre, J.-P. (1965). *Nausea*. R. Baldick, (trans.). London: Penguin.

Sartre, J.-P. (1969). *The wall*. New York: New Directions.

Schacter, D. (1996). *Searching for memory: The brain, the mind, and the past*. New York: BasicBooks.

Schafer, R. (1992). *Retelling a life: Narration and dialogue in psychoanalysis*. New York: BasicBooks.

Schank, R. (1990). *Tell me a story: A new look at real and artificial memory*. New York: Scribner's.

Schank, R., & Abelson, R. (1977). *Scripts, plans, goals, and understanding: An inquiry into human knowledge structures*. Hillsdale, NJ: Lawrence Erlbaum Associates.

Schiebe, K. (1986). Self-narratives and adventure. In T. Sarbin (ed.), *Narrative psychology: The storied nature of human conduct*. Westport, CT: Praeger. 129–151.

Schroots, J., & Birren, J. (1988). The nature of time: Implications for research on aging. *Comprehensive Gerontology*. C. 1–29.

Schroots, J., Birren, J., & Kenyon, G. (1991). Metaphors and aging: An overview. In G. Kenyon, J. Birren, & J. Schroots (eds.), *Metaphors of aging in science and the humanities*. New York: Springer. 1–16.

Scott-Maxwell, F. (1968). *The measure of my days*. New York: Penguin Books.

Selden, R. (1989). *A reader's guide to contemporary literary theory*. Lexington, KY: University Press of Kentucky.

Shea, J. (1978). *Stories of God: An unauthorized biography*. Chicago: Thomas More Press.

Sherman, E., & Webb, T. (1994). The self as process in late-life reminiscence: Spiritual attributes. *Ageing and Society*. 14. 255–267.

Silver, R., Boon, C., & Stones, M. (1983). Searching for meaning in misfortune: Making sense of incest. *Journal of Social Issues*. 39:2. 81–102.

Singer, J. (1996). The story of your life: A process perspective on narrative and emotion in adult development. In C. Magai & S. McFadden (eds.), *Handbook of emotion, adult development, and aging*. San Diego: Academic. 443–463.

Spence, D. (1982). *Narrative truth and historical truth*. New York: W. W. Norton.

Spretnak, C. (1991). *States of grace: The recovery of meaning in the postmodern age.* San Francisco: HarperSanFrancisco.

Steele, R. (1986). Deconstructing history: Toward a systematic criticism of psychological narratives. In T. Sarbin (ed.), *Narrative psychology: The storied nature of human conduct.* Westport, CT: Praeger. 256–275.

Sternberg, R. (ed.). (1990). *Wisdom: Its nature, origins, and development.* New York: Cambridge University Press.

Stone, R. (1996). *The healing art of storytelling: A sacred journey of personal discovery.* New York: Hyperion.

Stroup, G. (1981). *The promise of narrative theology.* Atlanta: John Knox Press.

Svensson, T. (1996). Competence and quality of life: Theoretical views of biography. In J. Birren, G. Kenyon, J.-E. Ruth, J. Schroots, & T. Svensson (eds.), *Aging and biography: Explorations in adult development.* New York: Springer. 100–116.

Swimme, B., & Berry, T. (1992). *The universe story: From the primordial flaring forth to the ecozoic era—a celebration of the unfolding of the cosmos.* San Francisco: HarperSanFrancisco.

Tappan, M., & Brown, L. (1989). Stories told and lessons learned: Toward a narrative approach to moral development and moral education. *Harvard Educational Review.* 59:2. 182–205.

Taylor, S., Wood, J., & Lichtman, R. (1983). It could be worse: Selective evaluation as a response to victimization. *Journal of Social Issues.* 39:2. 19–40.

TeSelle, S. (1975). *Speaking in parables: A study in metaphor and theology.* Philadelphia: Fortress.

Tilley, T. (1985). *Story theology.* Wilmington, DE: Michael Glazier.

Tillich, P. (1952). *The courage to be.* New Haven: Yale University Press.

Tornstam, L. (1989). Gero-transcendence: A meta-theoretical reformulation of the disengagement theory. *Aging: Clinical and Experimental Research.* 1. 55–63.

Tornstam, L. (1994). Gero-transcendence: A theoretical and empirical exploration. In L. Thomas & S. Eisenhandler (eds.), *Aging and the religious dimension.* Westport, CT: Greenwood. 203–225.

Tournier, P. (1965). *The adventure of living.* San Francisco: Harper & Row.

Treffert, D. (1989). *Extraordinary people: Understanding savant syndrome.* New York: Harper & Row.

Truitt, A. (1987). *Turn: The journal of an artist.* London: Penguin.

Turner, M. (1996). *The literary mind.* New York: Oxford University Press.

van den Hoonaard, D. (1997). Identity foreclosure: Women's experiences of widowhood in autobiographical accounts. *Ageing and Society, 17.* 533–551.

van den Hoonaard, D. (1999). No regrets: Widows' stories about the last days of their husbands' lives. *Journal of Aging Studies.* 13:1. 59–72.

Wakefield, D. (1989). *The story of your life: Writing a spiritual autobiography.* Boston: Beacon Press.

Webster, J. (1999). World views and narrative gerontology: Situating reminiscence behavior within a lifespan perspective. *Journal of Aging Studies.* 13:1. 29–42.

Wechsler, D. (1958). *The measurement and appraisal of adult intelligence.* 4th ed. Baltimore, MD: Williams and Wilkins.

White, H. (1980). The value of narrativity in the representation of reality. In W. Mitchell (ed.), *On narrative.* Chicago: University of Chicago Press. 1–23.

White, M., & Epston, D. (1990). *Narrative means to therapeutic ends*. New York: W. W. Norton.

Whitehead, A. N. (1957). *The aims of education and other essays*. New York: The Free Press.

Wiesel, E. (1988). Interview. In G. Plimpton (ed.), *Writers at work: The "Paris Review" interviews*. Eighth series. London: Penguin. 225–264.

Yeshe, L., & Rinpoche, Z. (1982). *Wisdom energy*. Boston: Wisdom Publications.

Zweig, P. (1974). *The adventurer*. New York: Basic Books.

Index

Acceptance, 13, 29–30, 91, 97. *See also* Receiving, of experience

Adventure: and addiction, 132–133; of aging, 158–164; autobiographical, 144–157; biography as, 151; cash value of, 156; choosing our own, 160; definition of, 122–123, 134; event as implicit, 121; hero's, 129, 136; high vs. low, 127, 138–139, 157; inner, 134; as kind of journey, 120; learning as, 125; of living, 117, 141–144, 157; and mystery, 157; necessity of, 120, 123; reading as, 144–146; and romance, 120; stages of, 129–133, 141–142; -thinking, 140; and turning-points, 120; types of, 122–129. *See also* Life as adventure

Aging: adventure of, 158–164; biographical, 36–37, 76; Buddhist view of, 30; conscious, 120, 158–164; and death, 105–106; and growing old, 98, 158, 163; inner vs. outer, 102–105; inside of, 5–6; and maturity, 153; and ripening, 149; spiritual, 116–117; theories of, 9–10; and wisdom; 18–20, 98. *See also* Gerontology

Ågren, Margareta, 105–106

Alheit, Peter, 18

Anxiety, 101

Ardelt, Monika, 23, 27

Atkinson, Robert, 87, 88, 95, 96, 119, 129

Augustine, St., 102

Autobiographical adventure, 144, 149–157; as reading our lives, 149. *See also* Adventure, of living

Autobiographical learning, 155, 170. *See also* Narrative, intelligence

Autobiographical memory, 48–55; as inside story, 54; as story memory, 53–56; story time and, 48–55; titles and, 60. *See also* Memory; Repisodic memory

Autobiography: and adventure, 152, 160; development of, 36; as metaphor of self, 82; and ordinary wisdom, 110–113; as parable, 153; multiple, 160; written vs. unwritten, 152. *See also* Autobiographical memory.

Baltes, Paul, 22, 31

Bateson, Mary Catharine, 37, 136

Battle of stories, 67

Baur, Susan, 169

Behavior, 113–115. *See also* Wisdom, faces of

Bianchi, Eugene, 26, 30, 87, 97, 100, 103; on guarantees, 116; on inwardness, 112

Biographer, as storyteller, 160
Biographical activity, 83
Biographical aging, 36–37, 76. *See also*
Aging
Biographical encounter, 95, 97, 115, 168
Biographicity, 36
Biographizers, 65
Birkerts, Sven, 54, 67, 146, 148
Birren, James, 14, 23, 114, 165
Booth, Wayne, 85
Brady, Michael, 155
Bridges, William, 93
Brooks, Peter, 54, 76
Bruner, Jerome, 36, 38, 40, 41, 51, 64, 72, 74, 120, 138
Buber, Martin, 92
Buddhism, 25, 29–30, 32, 85, 97, 100, 104, 117
Butler, Robert, 5

Campbell, Joseph, 129, 136, 142, 143
Carr, David, 9, 43, 55, 111, 162
Casey, Edward, 49, 50, 51, 59, 153
Chandler, Michael, 11, 17, 19, 20
Character, 143
Characterization, 44–45
Charmé, Stuart, 62–63, 78, 147, 152–153, 162
Chodron, Pema, vii, 170
Choose Your Own Adventure, 160
Christianity, 67–68, 85, 124, 134
Clock time, 49, 90, 102–103, 162. *See also* Journey, and time
Coauthoring, ix, 28, 89, 150, 168–169, 171. *See also* Social construction
Cognitive dimension, 12, 21–24, 32, 35–36, 88, 121–122, 171–173. *See also* Wisdom, dimensions of
Cole, Thomas, 8, 10, 26, 29, 89, 101
Coleman, Peter, 94, 105, 109
Composing a life, 37, 40, 43, 163
Computer metaphor, limits of, 34, 50, 53
Conflict, necessity of: in life, 82, 143; in literature, 82–83
Conscious aging, 113, 118, 119–164.
See also Life as adventure
Counterfactuals, 59
Creation-discovery paradox, 88, 96–100

Crisp, Jane, 115
Crites, Stephen, 56
Crovitz, Herbert, 58

de Beauvoir, Simone, 116, 121
de Maupassant, Guy, 85
Death, and time, 105–106, 136; meaning of, 107–108. *See also* Journey, and death
Deep reading, 148
Dementing people, 79, 115, 170
Dennett, Daniel, 162
Despair, 101, 107
De-storying, 169
Deutchman, Donna, 165
Dillard, Annie, 150
Diminishment, and meaning, 30. *See also* Acceptance
Directionality, 13, 95, 117

Eakin, John Paul, 152
Edel, Leon, 160
Eliot, Thomas Stearns, vii
Emotionality, 92
Emotions: and narrative, 40, 59; and memories, 50
Emplotment, 43–44
Enlightenment, 100
Erikson, Erik, 5, 26, 87, 102, 113
Ethical-moral dimension, 12, 27–28, 32, 35–36, 88, 121–122, 171–173. *See also* Wisdom, dimensions of
Event, 57; as implicit adventure, 121
Existentialism, 137
Extraordinary wisdom, dimensions of, 11–12, 31–32. *See also* Ordinary wisdom; Wisdom

Facticity, 51, 62, 91–94, 104, 112. *See also* Possibility
Faction, 35, 51, 85
Ferguson, Niall, 59
Fictive situations, 22, 28
Floating perspective, 107–108. *See also* Death
Foley, Joseph, 115
Forgetting, 51, 54
Forman, Freida, 136
Forster, E. M., 83
Fowler, George, 21, 96, 113, 114
Frankl, Victor, 90, 99, 101, 103, 108

Freeman, Mark, 36, 154, 156
Frye, Northrup, 47, 72, 74, 133, 137, 139
Fundamental project, 65, 141
Furlong, Monica, 124

Galton, Sir Francis, 58
Gardner, Howard, 11, 41
Gender, and adventure, 136
Generativity, 112, 149
Genre-ation, 45
Genres, life, 85
Gergen, Kenneth, 52, 64
Gergen, Mary, 52
Gerontology, viii; narrative, x, 10, 91, 129, 167; research directions in, 104–105, 109–110; wisdom and age in, 4–6. *See also* Aging
Gero-transcendence, 94
Glover, Jonathan, 171
Godard, Jean-Luc, 74
Goldberg, Michael, 67
Grand narratives, 6–9. *See also* Narratives, master
Greene, Graham, 151
Gubrium, Jaber, 64, 106
Guided autobiography, 93–95, 155, 171

Haley, Alex, 6, 58
Hall, G. Stanley, 101
Hampl, Patricia, 154–155, 163
Hartley, L. P., 154
Haught, John, 83–84, 135
Heaviness, 95
Heidegger, Martin, 103, 106, 141
Hermeneutic circle, 49, 103, 145
Hermeneutics of recovery, 64
Hillman, James, 77, 85
History, 159
Holliday, Steven, 11, 17, 19, 20
Holocaust, the, 150
Homo viator, 88
Horner, Joyce, 106
Horney, Karen, 143
Hume, David, 91
Humean beings, 82
Humor, 114

Identity, and narrative, 40
Idiosyncratic expression, 12, 28–29, 32, 35–36, 88, 121–122, 171–173. *See also* Wisdom, dimensions of

Ignatieff, Michael, 42
Individuation, 141
Inside story, 56, 58–62, 88, 110, 116. *See also* Autobiographical memory; Wisdom
Inside-out story, 56–57
Intelligence, 21–23; multiple, 41; and stories, 42; and wisdom, 41, 47–48. *See also* Narrative, intelligence
Interpersonal dimension, 12, 25–27, 32, 35–36, 88, 121–122, 171–173. *See also* Wisdom, dimensions of

James, Henry, 45
Job, Book of, 2
Johnson, Mark, 9, 15
Josso, Marie-Claire, 11, 13
Journey: and death, 105–110; and story, 111–112; and time, 103; within, 96, 100; Zen-like aspects of, 94–97. *See also* Journey metaphor, characteristics of
Journey metaphor, characteristics of, 14; as interpersonal, 89–90; as personal, 88–89; as opaque, 90; and story, 154; as transitory, 90; as wonder-ful, 90–91. *See also* Journey; Metaphor; Story, metaphor of
Joyce, James, 142
Jung, Carl, 83, 102, 143, 157
Jylha, Marja, 114

Karma, 55, 104
Kaufman, Sharon, 98
Kazin, Alfred, 152
Kekes, John, 28, 110
Kerby, Anthony, 147
Kierkegaard, Søren, 75
Knowledge, and stories, 77
Kohana, Boaz, 121
Kohana, Eva, 121

Lakoff, George, 9, 15
Langer, Lawrence, 150
Language: adventure, 158; as itself adventure, 126; and literature, 75; and memory, 52; narrative nature of, 40; slippage in, 52, 152; social construction of, 40
Larger stories, 65–69, 91–92, 168. *See also* Grand narratives; Narratives, master

Late life crisis, 160
Latimer, Rebecca, 114
Le Guin, Ursula, 38
Life as adventure, 119–164; critiques
    of, 133–141. *See also* Adventure;
    Life as mystery
Life as journey, 87–118; characteris-
    tics of, 88–91; and life as story, 87,
    119–120, 166. *See also* Journey; Life
    as adventure; Life as story
Life as mystery, 157
Life as story, 33–86
Lifestory, 2; vs. anthology, 112; co-
    herence of, 111–112; as faction, 85;
    and journey, 87–88; levels of, 58,
    168; from life to, 39–41; and wis-
    dom, 13–14, 31–32. *See also* Life as
    story; Lifestory-meaning; Stories
Lifestory-meaning: as conflictual,
    82–83; as consequential, 83; as cu-
    mulative, 83–84; as ending-related,
    84, 86; as generic, 85; as indetermi-
    nate, 79–80; as nonlocalized, 81; as
    parabolic, 81; as reader-related, 79;
    as retrospectively assigned, 84;
    and suspension of disbelief, 82; as
    unique, 149. *See also* Meaning; Sig-
    nature stories; Story-meaning;
    Wisdom
Literary competence, 46
Literary self-literacy, 122, 146
Literature: life as, 64; meaning in, 69.
    See also Story-meaning
Luke, Helen, 98, 158

Maddi, Salvatore, 92
Mader, Wilhelm, 27, 65, 101
Mair, Miller, 65
Malaise, spiritual, 8. *See also* Mean-
    ing, crisis of
Managed life, 7
Manheimer, Ronald, 19, 23, 112, 113
Marcel, Gabriel, 4, 73, 87–88, 95, 107,
    109
Master story, 68. *See also* Grand nar-
    rative; Narratives, master
Maturity, 153
Maurois, André, 51
McAdams, Dan, 30, 40, 61
Meacham, John, 24, 26, 27, 34
Meaning, crisis of, 6–8; and death,
    108–109; in life, 25–26; and master

narratives, 68; and spirituality,
    29–31. *See also* Story-meaning;
    Lifestory-meaning
Memory: mathematization of, 48;
    passivist vs. activist approaches to,
    49, 155; repisodic, 60; ruins of, 150;
    semantic, 49; as story, 58; story-,
    53. *See also* Autobiographical mem-
    ory
Metaphor, 9–10; as core of language,
    126; entailments of, 90; limits of
    any, 78; root, 37, 12; thinking
    through, 9–10. *See also* Life as jour-
    ney; Life as story
Metaphorical learning, 162
Mezirow, Jack, 153
Mid-life crisis, 103
Monomyth, 129
Moody, Harry, 7, 96, 113, 117
Morrison, Mary, 117
Moyers, Bill, 127, 129, 136, 142, 143
Munnichs, Joep, 109
Munro, Alice, 125

Narration, 45
Narrative: capital, 153, 156; construal
    of reality, 138; and counseling, 171;
    grammar, 46; imagining, 42; intelli-
    gence, 41–48, 167; knowing, 42;
    lust, 70, 133, 138; mind, 42; school-
    ing, 42; self-, 55; and story, 37; tem-
    plates, 52; theology, 67; thought,
    41–42; understanding, 28. *See also*
    Narrative environment; Stories
Narrative environment, 35, 52, 65, 95,
    169–171
Narrative intelligence. *See* Narrative,
    intelligence
Narratives, master, 6–8, 67, 172. *See
    also* Grand narratives; Larger sto-
    ries; Meaning, crisis of
Narratology, 167
Narratory principle, 37
Nausea, 137–138
Near-death experiences, 84–85, 100
Neisser, Ulric, 42, 50, 55, 59
Nietzsche, Friedrich, 125
Nin, Anais, 124
Novak, Michael, 83
Novel: life as, 62–65; and modern
    physics, 64. *See also* Novelty, of our
    lives

Novelty, of our lives, 35, 62–65, 146–147, 150–152, 161
Nuclear episodes, 61, 120

Oates, Stephen, 151
Öberg, Peter, 114, 170
Ordinary wisdom, 12–14; and aging, 98; dimensions of, 13–14, 32, 88; examples of, 99–100; vs. extraordinary, 10–12; and loss, 100; Zen of 94–97. See also Wisdom
Outside story, 56
Outside-in story, 56, 79

Page, P. K., 51
Parable: autobiography as, 156; lifestory as, 82, 153. See also Lifestory-meaning, as parabolic; Story-meaning, as parabolic
Past, as foreign country, 53
Pearson, Carol, 61, 85, 134, 136
Perennial philosophy, 21, 31, 88
Personality psychology, 94
Pioneers, seniors as, 158–159
Plantinga, Theodore, 125
Plato, 5, 24
Poetics, 34; and psychology, 167
Polkinghorne, Donald, 28, 56, 84, 151
Polster, Erving, 58, 63
Popper, Karl, 37
Porter, Bill, 21, 25
Positive uncertainty, 140, 163
Possibility, 62, 92–94. See also Facticity
Postmodern, era, 6; and metaphors, 9–10
Practical-experiential dimension, 12, 24–25, 32, 35–36, 88, 121–122, 171–173. See also Wisdom, dimensions of
Presence, 109
Privatism, 8
Progoff, Ira, 84

Quest, 136; question as, 125

Reading: as adventure, 144–146; deep, 148, 156; for meaning, 87; ourselves, 144–149. See also Self-reading
Receiving, of experience, 25, 29. See also Acceptance

Re-genre-ation, 93, 156, 160–161, 173
Reminiscence, 5, 171
Repisodic memory, 60
Reporting narrative, 18. See also Aging, theories of
Restorying: agents of, 89; conversion as, 68; forms of, 97; radical, 93, 99, 160. See also Re-genre-ation
Restorying Our Lives: background of, vii; descriptive vs. prescriptive dimensions of, vii–viii
Rinpoche, Sogyal, 1, 13, 17, 23, 92, 165
Root metaphor: adventure as, 121; narrative, 37
Rosenmayr, Leopold, 117
Roth, Philip, 49
Ruth, Jan-Erik, xi, 8, 94, 109, 114, 170

Sacks, Oliver, 33
Sacred text, life as, 153
Sarbin, Theodore, 36, 37, 168
Sarton, May, 81, 83, 154, 162
Sartre, Jean-Paul, 51, 63, 73, 89, 103, 106, 116, 137–138. See also Nausea; The Wall
Schacter, Daniel, 50, 51, 58
Schank, Roger, 42, 48, 58, 77
Schiebe, Karl, 123, 134, 136, 143, 156
Scott-Maxwell, Florida, 14, 117, 119, 143, 158
Self as author, 63
Self-creation, 141; and talk, 171
Self-reading, 146. See also Autobiographical learning
Self-telling, forms of, 168
Sense of an ending, 76
Seven Samurai, The, 113
Shakespeare, William, 45
Shea, John, 33
Sheehy, Gail, 134
Sherman, Edmund, 95, 116
Signature stories, 60–61, 155–156; and adventure, 120. See also Reading; Self-reading
Smith, Jacqui, 22, 31
Social construction, 51, 66, 68, 89; of autobiographical memory, 51–52; and coauthoring, 168–169; of wisdom, 166. See also Larger stories
Solitude, 117
Spence, Donald, 51

Spirituality, 29–31, 87, 91, 112, 116.
  See also Meaning
Spiritual-mystical dimension, 12,
  29–32, 35–36, 88, 121–122, 171–173.
  See also Wisdom, dimensions of
Spretnak, Charlotte, 17, 21, 25
Stock response, 148
Stories: particular vs. general, 59;
  past vs. future, 59; public vs. private, 60; solo vs. shared, 60;
  strange logic of, 153; as structures
  for meaning, 70; surface vs. deep,
  61; told vs. untold, 60. *See also*
  Larger stories; Lifestory; Story,
  metaphor of
Story, metaphor of, 14; and journey,
  111–112. *See also* Metaphor
Story-meaning, 69–77; as conflictual,
  74; as consequential, 74; as contextual, 71; as cumulative, 76; as culturally rooted, 74; as
  ending-related, 75; as function of
  aesthetics, 73; as generic, 74; as indeterminate, 72, 145; as individualized, 72; as intermittent, 72; as
  moral, 73–74; as not localized, 72;
  as parabolic, 73; as reader-related,
  71; and reading, 145; as retrospectively assigned, 76–77; and wisdom, 76–77. *See also*
  Lifestory-meaning; Meaning, crisis
  of; Stories; Story time
Story time, 48–55, 76, 90. *See also*
  Clock time; Journey, and time
Storying moment, 88, 95, 144
Storying style, 63
Storylistening, 115, 150, 169. *See also*
  Coauthoring
Storyotypes, 57, 168
Storytelling, 96
Symbolic interconnectedness, 72, 153,
  162. *See also* Lifestory-meaning

TeSelle, Sallie, 82, 145, 151
Text, life as, 40, 62, 78, 166

Textualization, 39–40
Thematizing, 45
Thickening: in lifestory, 83, 153; in
  memory, 51, 153; vs. narrowing,
  83; in story, 76
Thomas, Dylan, 108
Tragedy, life as, 134, 161, 162
Truitt, Anne, 50
Truth: historical vs. narrative, 51; of a
  life, 64, 77
Turner, Mark, 42
Turning-points, 120

Versions, 62
Virtual text, 145

The Wall, 106
Ways of life, 85
Webb, Theodore, 95, 116
Wechsler, D., 21, 22
Weisser, Susan, 40, 51, 160
Whitehead, Alfred North, 83, 125
Widowhood, 98–99
Wiesel, Elie, 134
Winkler, Mary, 26, 89, 101
Wisdom: and age, 18–20; age irrele-
  vance of, 6; autobiographical, 48;
  difficulty defining, 1–2; dimen-
  sions of, 12, 35–36, 88, 171–173;
  eclipse of, 10, 17–20; and fools,
  28–29, 110–115; faces of,
  28–29, 110–115; faces of,
  neric, 138; hidden, 114–116; and
  lifestory, 2–3; loss of, 27, 102;
  poetics of, 33–36; return of interest
  in, 3–4; and stories, 69–77; story,
  169; and vision, 62, 66. *See also* Extraordinary wisdom; Inside story;
  Intelligence; Lifestory-meaning;
  Ordinary wisdom; Wisdom
  environment
Wisdom environment, 34, 169–173.
  See also Coauthoring
Wonder, 90–91, 108

Zweig, Paul, 151–152

About the Authors

WILLIAM L. RANDALL is a former Protestant minister who has taught English at Seneca College, adult education for Brock University and the University of New Brunswick, and the philosophy of education for Saint Bonaventure University. He is currently Research Associate in Gerontology at St. Thomas University, where he is Project Director of the Fredericton 80+ Study. Dr. Randall is the author of two earlier books, *The Stories We Are: An Essay on Self-Creation* (1995) and, with Gary Kenyon, *Restorying Our Lives* (Praeger, 1997).

GARY M. KENYON is founder and Director of Gerontology at St. Thomas University. He is also Adjunct Professor, Centre on Aging, Faculty of Medicine at McGill University, Montreal, and Honorary Research Associate at the University of New Brunswick. Among his publications are *Narrative Gerontology: Theory, Research and Practice* with P. Clark and B. de Vries and *Restorying Our Lives* (Praeger, 1997).